Super~Quick
MEDITERRANEAN
DIET COOKBOOK
FOR BEGINNERS

Master the World's Healthiest Diet in Just 28 Days with Stress-Free and Mouthwatering Recipes for an Effortless Weight Loss and Lifelong Health

Cynthia De Luca

Disclaimer

The publisher and the author are providing this book and its contents on an "as is" basis and make no representations or warranties of any kind with respect to this book or its contents. The publisher and the author disclaim all such representations and warranties, including but not limited to warranties of healthcare for a particular purpose. In addition, the publisher and the author assume no responsibility for errors, inaccuracies, omissions, or any other inconsistencies herein.

The content of this book is for informational purposes only and is not intended to diagnose, treat, cure, or prevent any condition or disease. You understand that this book is not intended as a substitute for consultation with a licensed practitioner. Please consult with your own physician or healthcare specialist regarding the suggestions and recommendations made in this book. The use of this book implies your acceptance of this disclaimer.

The publisher and the author make no guarantees concerning the level of success you may experience by following the advice and strategies contained in this book, and you accept the risk that results will differ for each individual. The testimonials and examples provided in this book show exceptional results, which may not apply to the average reader, and are not intended to represent or guarantee that you will achieve the same or similar results.

Table of Contents

Introduction

I once lived far removed from my Mediterranean roots. It wasn't until I faced constant fatigue and multiple health scares that I paused to think about my grandmother's old Italian recipes, filled with the vibrant colors and soul-soothing flavors of the Mediterranean. I didn't always appreciate this lifestyle; in fact, for a long time, I was embroiled in a chaotic world of fast food, sugary snacks, and relentless health problems. My life felt like one long health scare, coupled with overwhelming fatigue that left me drained. It wasn't until I reached this low point that I started yearning for a change, and it was then that I rediscovered the healing power of my family's culinary traditions.

I say culinary traditions, because it never felt right to call the Mediterranean diet a diet; it's a lifestyle that has its roots in the sun-kissed lands of Italy, Spain, and Greece. Imagine this—azure seas, olive groves stretching beyond the horizon, and tables filled with vibrant, fresh foods that nourish both body and soul. This lifestyle choice captured global attention already in the 1960s. Researchers were stunned to find communities around the Mediterranean basin enjoying long, fulfilling lives with incredibly low rates of heart disease, diabetes, and other lifestyle-related illnesses. And so, the diet gained its well-deserved fame, offering a panacea to modern health issues with its emphasis on fresh fruits, vegetables, lean proteins, and heart-healthy fats.

It took me a lot of trial and error (and slipping back into old habits) to really master the Mediterranean diet lifestyle, so I wanted to make the journey a lot easier for you.
The first chapter of this book is designed as a gentle introduction, guiding you through the essential ingredients, spices, and cooking techniques that are the backbone of Mediterranean cooking. No jargon, no complications—just straightforward information that helps you get started on the right foot.

What makes this book stand out are the recipes. These aren't just any recipes; they are a curated collection of traditional yet easy-to-master dishes. From tapenade to tabbouleh, from grilled sardines to gazpacho, these recipes have been chosen for their authenticity, simplicity, and speed. And we understand life gets busy; that's why these dishes are not just delicious but also quick to make.

Finally, I only started getting serious about changing my habit when I made a plan for myself, it took me a few tries, but that was the only way I really started changing my lifestyle and never looked back. So, I designed a meticulously crafted 28-day meal plan designed to ease you into your new lifestyle. This isn't a rigid, stress-inducing plan, but a flexible guide that adapts to your life, not the other way around. By the end of these 28 days, you won't just be following a diet; you'll be living a new lifestyle. You'll learn the art of savoring your food, enjoying your meals, and making choices that are not just tasty but also incredibly beneficial for your long-term health.

So come along, dive into this book, and let's embark on a transformative journey together. A journey towards better health, greater joy, and a life filled with delicious, Mediterranean-inspired sustenance. Welcome to the start of your vibrant, healthier new life.

Understanding the Mediterranean Diet

I magine the azure waters of the Mediterranean Sea lapping against the shores of ancient Greece, southern Italy, and the island of Crete. It's here that the Mediterranean diet has its deepest roots, grounded in what's known as the Mediterranean triad: wheat for bread, grapevines for wine, and olive trees for that golden nectar, olive oil. This isn't a flash-in-the-pan trend; it's a diet with a history that goes back thousands of years.

The modern scientific exploration of this diet had an unexpected start. In 1948, the Rockefeller Foundation went to Crete to investigate post-war living standards. What they discovered was that Cretans, who ate sparingly of meat but abundantly of greens, vegetables, and legumes, were astonishingly healthy. Their diet was drenched in olive oil and often accompanied by homemade wine, yet it met—and even exceeded—U.S. nutritional standards of the time.

This revelation caught the eye of U.S. physiologist Ancel Keys in the 1950s. Compared to American businessmen eating their meat-and-potatoes fare, men in southern Europe, particularly those from Crete, had drastically lower rates of cardiovascular disease. His landmark Seven Countries Study cemented this, particularly highlighting the high life expectancy of men in Crete. By the early '90s, this diet was transformed into a food pyramid model, presented at a conference organized by the Harvard School of Public Health. Today, it is lauded as the gold standard of diets, supported by extensive scientific research.

This lifestyle choice was further popularized by the National Geographic Fellow and author Dan Buettner, who identified five regions worldwide where people live much longer than the global average and called them Blue Zones. Two of these Blue Zones—Sardinia in Italy and Ikaria in Greece—are in the Mediterranean region. Residents in these zones not only live longer but they also have lower instances of heart disease, diabetes, and other chronic ailments. What's their secret?

It's not just what's on the plate; it's a lifestyle. Originating and still practiced mainly in specific regions like Crete, most of Greece, and southern Italy, this way of living incorporates not only a rich variety of plant-based foods but also emphasizes physical activity, social connections, and overall life enjoyment. When you adopt the Mediterranean diet, you're not just hopping on a health trend; you're embracing a way of life that's stood the test of both time and scientific scrutiny. It's a lifestyle that promises not just longevity but also a higher quality of life. Whether you're looking to manage your weight, boost your heart health, or simply find a sustainable and delicious way to eat, the Mediterranean diet checks all those boxes, making it not just a diet but a time-honored tradition worth celebrating.

NUTRITIONAL SCIENCE AND THE MEDITERRANEAN DIET

"The Mediterranean diet is one of the best-studied diets, rich in anti-inflammatory foods that help to combat chronic disease."
~ Dr. Walter Willett of the Harvard T.H. Chan School of Public Health

So, what does science say about the Mediterranean diet? Groundbreaking research has linked the Mediterranean lifestyle to many benefits, from cardiovascular health and mental acuity to longevity and reduced inflammation. These aren't just speculative claims; extensive, well-designed studies and clinical trials back them.

Cardiovascular Health
One of the most well-studied aspects of the Mediterranean diet is its impact on cardiovascular health. One seminal study, reported in 2013 in the *New England Journal of Medicine*, involved 7,447 people at high risk for heart disease. Due to its dramatic findings, researchers concluded the study early: Participants who adopted the Mediterranean diet lowered their risk of heart attacks, strokes, and deaths from heart disease by 30%. The monounsaturated fatty acids (MUFAs) found in olive oil, a staple of the diet, have been shown to reduce low-density lipoprotein (LDL) cholesterol—the "bad" cholesterol. Olive oil is also rich in polyphenols, which have antioxidant properties that protect endothelial cells lining the blood vessels. This helps to reduce inflammation and improve blood flow, thereby reducing the risk of arterial plaque buildup, a leading cause of heart disease.

Anti-Inflammatory Effects
The anti-inflammatory properties of the Mediterranean diet extend beyond heart health. Many ingredients, like oily fish, nuts, and whole grains, are rich in omega-3 fatty acids. These fatty acids are converted into eicosanoids in the body, which are signaling molecules that modulate inflammation. This is particularly effective in combating chronic inflammation, a common factor in many illnesses ranging from autoimmune diseases to cancer. It's been so effective that *Dr. Norton Fishman, Medical Director of Optimal Health Physicians in Rockville*, MD, recommends it as a key strategy for patients with chronic conditions like Lyme disease.

Blood Sugar Regulation
When it comes to managing diabetes and insulin sensitivity, the fiber-rich foods such as whole grains and legumes in this

diet play a vital role. Dietary fiber slows down the absorption of sugar, thus controlling blood sugar levels. Additionally, the phenolic compounds found in olive oil help to modulate the genes involved in insulin signaling, improving insulin sensitivity.

In a Spanish study involving 3,541 subjects with high diabetes risk, 87% were able to prevent the onset of the disease by adhering to the Mediterranean diet for four years.

Neuroprotective Properties

The Mediterranean diet is also gaining attention for its neuroprotective benefits. Antioxidants like resveratrol found in red wine, and vitamin E found in nuts and seeds, are known to reduce oxidative stress in neural tissues. This mitigates the progression of neurodegenerative diseases like Alzheimer's. Furthermore, omega-3 fatty acids are essential components of cell membranes in the brain, improving cognitive function and potentially delaying the onset of dementia.

Gut Health

The fiber in fruits, vegetables, and whole grains doesn't just regulate blood sugar; it also serves as prebiotics, nourishing the beneficial bacteria in the gut. A healthy gut microbiome is linked to improved digestion, better immune function, and even mental well-being.

Cancer Prevention

Rich in antioxidants like vitamins C and E, selenium, and carotenoids, the Mediterranean diet can aid in reducing the risk of certain cancers. These antioxidants neutralize free radicals, unstable molecules that can damage cellular structures including DNA, thereby reducing mutations that may lead to cancer.

Weight Management

You might also be interested in how this diet aids weight management. The high fiber content, combined with protein from lean sources like fish and legumes, promotes a feeling of fullness and reduces overall caloric intake. Moreover, the diet emphasizes the quality of food, focusing on nutrient-dense options that provide a range of vitamins and minerals, allowing for sustainable weight loss without nutrient deficiencies.

Longevity

As you now know two of the Blue Zones are in the Mediterranean area and that's not a coincidence. In fact, scientist have studied the diet's impact on telomeres, the protective ends of chromosomes. Shorter telomeres are associated with aging and age-related diseases, and some studies have suggested that the antioxidants in the Mediterranean diet can help maintain telomere length, thus potentially extending lifespan. Notably, a study published in the *Annals of Internal Medicine* followed the diets and lives of over 10,000 women in their fifties for fifteen years. The findings showed that those who followed a Mediterranean diet had a 40% higher chance of living past 70 without developing chronic illnesses or physical disabilities.

KEY PRINCIPLES

Now that we have established the health benefits of your new diet, nay lifestyle, let's find out how to implement this traditional, yet groundbreaking diet. In truth, there are very few principles, you should follow, there is no complicated calorie counting, improbable restrictions, or any complex servings or portion measurements that so often are required by fad diets. After all, the Mediterranean Diet is simply the lifestyle that has worked and that has been seamlessly applied by millions of people who have traditionally thrived in those regions.

PLANT-BASED FOUNDATION

Any traditional cuisine relies heavily on plants, since eating meat as often as we do in our modern society would have been enormously expensive and as we have discovered terribly unhealthy. This is particularly true of the Mediterranean diet where the bulk of the diets consist of whole grains and non-starchy vegetables and proteins and fats come from plant-based sources, such as legumes, nuts and seeds, and the ever-important olive oil.

Vegetables: More Than Just Sides

Vegetables are the mainstay of the Mediterranean diet, frequently taking up the largest portion of the plate. Vegetables are packed with essential vitamins, minerals, and fiber, as well as potent antioxidants like beta-carotene and vitamin C. These nutrients help reduce inflammation and protect against chronic diseases.

Legumes: Carbs and Proteins All in One

Often called the "meat of the poor," legumes like lentils, chickpeas, and various beans are crucial sources of plant-based protein in the Mediterranean diet. They offer not only proteins, but also low glycemic carbs. Legumes are rich in protein, fiber, and essential nutrients like iron, potassium, and folate. They have a low glycemic index, which makes them beneficial for regulating blood sugar levels.

Whole Grains: The Wholesome Carbs

In the Mediterranean diet, whole grains are preferred over refined grains, providing sustained energy throughout the day. Whole-grain bread, brown rice, and whole-grain pasta are commonly consumed, as well as lesser-known grains like farro and bulgur. Whole grains are rich in fiber, which aids digestion and promotes satiety. They also contain essential nutrients like B vitamins and magnesium, and their consumption has been linked to lower rates of heart disease and type 2 diabetes.

Nuts and Seeds: The Compact Nutrient Bombs

Nuts and seeds might be small, but they're integral to the Mediterranean diet. They are rich in healthy fats, primarily monounsaturated and polyunsaturated fats, as well as omega-3 fatty acids. These fats help reduce bad cholesterol and lower the risk of heart disease and stroke.

THE POWER OF MINIMALLY PROCESSED FOODS

Choosing fresh and minimally processed foods, will be a choice that reverberates positively through every aspect of your health and well-being. Processed foods often contain additives, preservatives, and high levels of salt and sugar, which can contribute to various health issues, from high blood pressure to diabetes. On the other hand, minimally processed foods retain most of their inherent nutrients and are generally free from added sugars and artificial ingredients.

Whole foods are nutritionally rich, providing an array of vitamins, minerals, fiber, and antioxidants that your body needs for optimal function. The Mediterranean diet capitalizes on this by focusing on foods that are as close to their natural state as possible. For instance, a whole apple offers more fiber and fewer sugars than apple juice. Whole foods contain complex forms of carbohydrates, proteins, and fats that your body needs to function optimally. The fiber content aids in digestion and can help regulate blood sugar levels, reducing the risk of type 2 diabetes.

While they may be convenient, highly processed foods are often stripped of essential nutrients during their manufacturing process and often contain unhealthy trans fats, high levels of sodium, and artificial additives, which can contribute to a range of health problems, from obesity to heart disease. Several studies have linked processed foods to an increased risk of obesity, heart disease, and high blood pressure.

Depending on where you live finding fresh vegetables and fruits may not always be easy, thankfully minimally processed foods like frozen vegetables, canned legumes, and whole-grain bread can still be part of a healthy Mediterranean diet. The key is to read labels carefully to ensure that these foods don't contain added sugars, sodium, or preservatives.

BUY LOCAL AND SEASONAL

If eating whole or minimally processed food is one of the key principles of the Mediterranean Diet, so is striving to consume local and seasonal produce. Consuming local and seasonal foods means you are eating fruits and vegetables at their peak nutritional value. These foods haven't been transported over long distances, which can lead to nutrient degradation. Moreover, seasonal foods are often grown in a more natural environment, free from artificial means to speed up or extend their growing season, resulting in better flavor and nutritional content. Some studies suggest that seasonal produce can have up to three times the nutrients compared to out-of-season, stored counterparts. As for implementing this principle in your daily life, start by visiting your local farmers' markets or consider subscribing to a community-supported agriculture (CSA) program, which can often be more convenient. These avenues not only keep costs low but also put money directly back into local agriculture. Check out the appendix at the end of the book for a seasonal fruits and vegetables guide.

SIMPLE, STRAIGHTFORWARD COOKING METHODS

In the Mediterranean culinary tradition, simplicity is key, and it serves a purpose beyond mere convenience or taste—it's about preserving the intrinsic flavors and, importantly, the nutrients in the food. The cooking methods commonly employed emphasize low-temperature, slow cooking techniques, such as stewing, braising, and grilling.

Sofrito
Sofrito, meaning basically stir-fried, is a technique that serves as the foundational element for many Mediterranean dishes. Generally, it involves sautéing onions, garlic, and tomatoes in extra virgin olive oil over low heat. Scientifically, this method is a nutrition powerhouse: olive oil is rich in monounsaturated fats, which can improve your cholesterol profile and provide vitamin E. Tomatoes provide lycopene, a potent antioxidant. Onions offer a type of flavonoid that acts as an antioxidant and anti-inflammatory agent. The combination also often includes garlic, which has been shown to have cardiovascular benefits. The act of sautéing these ingredients in olive oil allows the fat to draw out the fat-soluble nutrients, making them more available for your body to absorb.

Grilling
Grilling is a culinary favorite, especially in the summer months along the Mediterranean coast. It's more than just an outdoor gathering activity; it has health benefits too. Grilling vegetables enhances their natural sweetness and keeps their nutrient profile intact. While grilling fish and meat allows excess fats to drip away, reducing the overall caloric and saturated fat content. Importantly, grilling at a moderate temperature can prevent the formation of harmful substances like polycyclic aromatic hydrocarbons (PAHs) that can occur with high-heat methods.

Olive Oil-Based Marinades
Marinading meats and vegetables in a concoction of olive oil, lemon juice, and herbs isn't just a flavor enhancer. From a health perspective, the olive oil's monounsaturated fats are heart-healthy, while the citric acid from lemon has been shown to improve iron absorption from plant foods. Furthermore, marinating, particularly with herbs like rosemary, can mitigate the formation of harmful compounds like heterocyclic amines (HCAs) during the cooking process, especially in grilled meats. HCAs are compounds that have been linked to certain types of cancers.

Slow Cooking
Slow cooking, often seen in the form of hearty stews or "casseroles," allows for a mingling of flavors and nutrients. Slowly simmering meats with vegetables and herbs over an extended period makes the meat fibers tender and easier on digestion. The technique also lends itself to lesser cuts of meat, which are often more affordable. Importantly, low and slow cooking better preserves the vitamins and minerals in your foods, as many nutrients can be destroyed or reduced under

high heat. This is particularly relevant for water-soluble vitamins like vitamin C and some B vitamins.

Vegetable Stewing

Stewing is a popular cooking method in the Mediterranean diet, often done on the stovetop. Start by heating olive oil in a pan and sautéing onions until they're translucent but not brown. This sets the flavor base. Next, add your other ingredients like vegetables or proteins. Instead of pouring in a lot of water at once, add hot water gradually. This helps create a thick, flavorful sauce rather than a watery broth. Keep the heat low so the stew simmers gently, with just a few bubbles breaking the surface. This low simmer helps the flavors meld without making the ingredients mushy.

Lathera

If you want to cook like the Greeks, try making a Lathera dish. Start with a good amount of quality olive oil in a pot; it's the main flavor here. Add vegetables, beans, or rice, followed by tomatoes and herbs like oregano or basil. Simmer it all until the liquid turns into a rich sauce. The key is to end up with a dish where all you have is this flavorful sauce and olive oil, no water. So use low heat and let it simmer. When done right, what you're left with is a dish "with its oil," as the Greeks say— a testament to the role olive oil plays in Mediterranean cooking, not just as a 'good fat' but as a flavor catalyst.

Pan Roasting

Pan-roasting is the go-to method for special meals and it allows meat to retain all it's juiciness and flavor. Whether you're cooking chicken, lamb, beans, or even vegetables, the key ingredients are olive oil and careful water management. Start by placing your main ingredients in a pan, drizzling them generously with olive oil, and then roasting them in the oven, these cooks the first layer of proteins and sears in all the juices of the meat. If you're working with beans, consider boiling them first before roasting. Always add water cautiously and pour it into the corner of the pan, not directly over the food. This ensures you don't wash away the olive oil and seasonings, and helps you avoid a watery or undercooked dish.

Braising

Braising is a slow-cooking method that melds flavors and textures. Whether you're working with chicken, beef, or pork, start by browning the meat in olive oil over medium-high heat. This initial searing locks in flavor and helps the meat develop a rich, caramelized crust. Once browned, set aside the meat as you add a variety of vegetables to the pan, such as onions, garlic, carrots, or bell peppers. Sautée until softened. At this point, return the meat to the pan and a liquid—often a combination of broth, wine, or tomatoes—is added. Make sure that the liquid you add is hot, otherwise you risk toughening up the meat and again add to the corner of the pan not on top of the meat. The entire mixture is then left to simmer on low heat or in the oven for an extended period. This slow, moist cooking process tenderizes the meat and allows the flavors from the sauce and vegetables to thoroughly penetrate it, resulting in a flavorful, cohesive dish.

Savory pies

Savory pies are a staple in Mediterranean cuisine, with each region offering its own unique twist. In Greek cooking, phyllo dough serves as the crust. These paper-thin, unleavened sheets are stacked in layers, separated by a light brushing of olive oil to enhance crispiness and flavor. Between these layers, you'll find a variety of fillings such as spinach, feta, or minced meat. If you're working with phyllo, remember to defrost it fully in the refrigerator before use, and keep it covered with a damp towel to prevent drying out while assembling your pie.

In Italy, you'll encounter more robust crusts made from a basic dough of flour, water, and olive oil. Italian savory pies, like torta pasqualina, often feature richer fillings, including cheeses, meats, and vegetables, all encased in this more substantial crust.

In Spain, you'll discover "empanada," which has Galician origins. Unlike the smaller, half-moon-shaped empanadas of Latin America, the Galician empanada is usually a large, double-crusted pie filled with ingredients like tuna, pork, or chicken, often combined with bell peppers, onions, and tomatoes. The crust is typically made from wheat flour, water, and olive oil, and sometimes includes yeast for a slightly puffy texture. The filling is pre-cooked and seasoned, often with a dash of paprika or saffron for color and flavor.

Another popular Spanish dish resembling a pie is the "tortilla Española" or Spanish omelet. While not a pie in the traditional sense, this thick, hearty omelet filled with potatoes and onions serves a similar purpose, acting as a nutritious, filling meal that can be enjoyed hot or cold, much like a savory pie. It embodies the essence of Spanish and Mediterranean cuisine by making simple ingredients extraordinary through careful preparation.

THE LIQUID GOLD OF COOKING: OLIVE OIL

If you ask anyone what is their first association with the Mediterranean Diet, chances are they'll answer olive oil, and for good reasons: Extra virgin olive oil is more than just a cooking medium; it's a nutritional powerhouse that brings a myriad of health benefits to the table. Rich in monounsaturated fatty acids, specifically oleic acid, extra virgin olive oil has been shown to improve heart health by reducing levels of bad cholesterol and increasing good cholesterol. It's also abundant in polyphenols, antioxidants that combat oxidative stress and inflammation, offering protective effects against various chronic diseases like cardiovascular disease and even some cancers. Moreover, olive oil has been linked to better cognitive function and lower risks of neurodegenerative diseases like Alzheimer's, thanks to oleocanthal, a unique compound with anti-inflammatory properties. From a culinary standpoint, it offers a full-bodied, fruity flavor profile that enhances the natural taste of foods without overpowering them. Because it can withstand relatively high heat, it's incredibly versatile—ideal for everything from sautéing and roasting to drizzling over salads or using as a dip for crusty bread. Importantly, the fat content in olive oil increases the bioavailability of fat-soluble vitamins like A, D, E, and K, ensuring you get the most nutrition out of your vegetables and other foods. So, when you choose extra virgin olive oil as your primary fat source, you're not just adhering to culinary tradition; you're making a scientifically backed decision to optimize your health.

MAKE IT CHEESY

If vegetables are the main dish, then cheeses are the accompaniment of the Mediterranean Diet.

The sheer diversity of cheeses, ranging from the feta of Greece and Halloumi of Crete to the Pecorino and Parmigiano of Italy, is a testament to the rich culinary heritage and artisanal practices that have been passed down through generations. Cheeses in the Mediterranean are derived from an array of milk sources, including goat, sheep, cow, buffalo, and even camel in some Middle Eastern areas. The cheeses fall into three primary categories based on their water and sodium content: fresh and soft (lower sodium content and 45 to 70% of water), semi-hard (between 40 and 45% water content), and hard and aged (water content lower than 40% and higher sodium content, but also higher in calcium and vitamin D). This variety allows for broad culinary applications, from being a part of small plate tapas or meze in Spain and Greece to featuring in traditional cheese courses in France and Italy. In North Africa and the Middle East, cheese is predominantly consumed at breakfast or as snacks, often in its most unadulterated form.

In Western diets, dairy often finds itself sidelined, primarily due to overconsumption of milk causing digestive issues or the high-fat, high-cholesterol content of processed cheeses and butter. However, in the Mediterranean, the daily dairy intake is quite different, focusing on fresh, nutrient-rich cheeses like ricotta and feta that are lower in fat and cholesterol. For example, a Spanish study found that consuming two to three servings of low-fat dairy per day could halve the risk of high blood pressure. Similarly, a study from the University of Tennessee, Knoxville, showed that including calcium-rich yogurt in a calorie-restricted diet facilitated weight loss for participants.

Dairy products offer a beneficial dose of animal protein—around 9 grams in a 6-ounce (170 g) serving—along with other essential nutrients like calcium, vitamins B2 and B12, potassium, and magnesium. Calcium is recognized for its positive effects on bone health across all age groups. It's advisable to check nutritional labels to opt for brands that offer at least 20% of the daily recommended intake of both calcium and vitamin D, the latter of which is often added in Western countries to enhance calcium absorption.

The nutritional profile of traditional Mediterranean yogurt varies, depending on whether it is derived from goat, sheep, or cow's milk, or a blend. Yogurts containing live active cultures, or probiotics, are known to balance the gut's microbial community. Research from Tufts University suggests that such yogurts may enhance the immune system, modify gut microflora, and even influence how quickly food passes through the digestive system. Probiotics have shown promise in alleviating various digestive issues, including lactose intolerance, constipation, diarrhea, colon cancer, and inflammatory bowel disease.

Especially rich in protein and vitamin B12, locally produced yogurts, like Greek yogurt, are excellent options for vegetarians and athletes looking for a post-workout snack. These yogurts help in muscle recovery and hydration. A single 8-ounce (225 g) serving provides about 60% of the recommended daily B12 intake for adult women, along with substantial amounts of other nutrients like phosphorus, potassium, riboflavin, iodine, zinc, and vitamin B5.

Cheese also packs in protein and calcium, acting as an appetite suppressant. It's believed to slow down carbohydrate absorption when eaten in the same meal, thereby stabilizing blood sugar levels and improving mood. Like milk and yogurt, cheese offers calcium benefits and additionally contains zinc, which is thought to support skin, hair, and nail health, along with aiding tissue growth and repair.

LET'S GET FISHY

In Mediterranean countries, fish is not just a food; it's a celebration. Contrary to Western attitudes, where fish is often seen as a dietary sacrifice, the cultures surrounding the Mediterranean Sea have long revered fish and seafood as both culinary delights and symbols of their deep relationship with the sea. With numerous holidays featuring fish as a central part of the feast, from Christmas Eve in Italy to Eid al Fitr in Egypt, it's clear that these coastal societies value their sea's bounty in ways that transcend mere nutrition.

The Mediterranean diet advocates for the frequent consumption of fish and seafood, suggesting a minimum of two servings per week. High in protein yet low in calories, fish serves as an ideal food choice for muscle gain, weight loss, and cognitive enhancement. One of the key nutritional aspects of fish is its rich content of omega-3 fatty acids, essential for human health but not naturally produced by the body. These fatty acids are proven to reduce blood pressure, lower triglycerides, and decrease the risks of stroke and heart failure. Eating fish even just once a week has been shown to offer significant health benefits. A 2011 study revealed that just an additional serving of fish per week could cut the risk of heart disease in half. Moreover, women who didn't regularly include fish in their diet faced a 50% higher likelihood of heart issues, a threefold increase in disease risk, and elevated levels of blood fats compared to those who did.

Besides omega-3s, fish and seafood are packed with vital nutrients such as zinc for immune support, potassium for cardiovascular health, selenium with anti-cancer properties, and iodine for thyroid function. They are also sources of vitamins A and D, which benefit vision and bone health, respectively. Additional advantages of omega-3 and fish intake have been linked to:

- A potential reduction in the risk of Alzheimer's, dementia, and cognitive decline
- Alleviation of ADHD symptoms, including poor concentration and reading skills

- Prevention and relief of asthma symptoms
- Nourished skin and healthy hair
- Reversal of UV damage from sun exposure
- Improved mood, combating depression and Seasonal Affective Disorder
- Protection against Age-Related Macular Degeneration
- Anti-inflammatory benefits helpful for rheumatoid arthritis

Despite these compelling health reasons, some people still avoid fish due to concerns about mercury levels and water pollution. When buying fish, it's crucial to consider its mercury content, health advantages, and source. While there is no single guide that encompasses all these factors, organizations like the Environmental Defense Fund and the Monterey Bay Aquarium offer resources like the Seafood Selector and Seafood Watch program, respectively, to guide informed choices. My recommendation is to opt for the freshest local seafood, or imports from trusted sources, and to educate yourself thoroughly to maximize the health benefits. For serving, aim for 3.5 ounces (100g) of fish. I've designed quick and nutritious recipes that are sure to satisfy even the most skeptical palates. With these easy and delicious options, seafood will soon become your go-to choose for a hectic weeknight meal. To ensure safety, cook seafood to an internal temperature of 145°F (63°C) for 15 seconds, or until it becomes flaky, opaque, and loses its translucency.

THE CHICKEN AND THE EGG

Historically, chicken was a luxury item in the Mediterranean region, affordable only to royalty and the upper echelons of society, making the recipes that evolved truly lavish and flavorful.

Chicken is a source of high-quality protein with relatively low fat content. Moreover, the fat it does contain is largely unsaturated, which is heart-healthy. A 3-ounce (85 g) serving has only 1 gram of saturated fat and less than 4 grams of total fat but boasts 31 grams of protein—over half the daily recommended intake for adult women. Chicken is also rich in B vitamins, which play a critical role in metabolism, immune system support, and cell growth, among other functions. Additionally, it offers essential minerals like iron and zinc.

Eggs are another cornerstone in the Mediterranean diet. In southern Europe, eggs are typically consumed for dinner and occasionally for lunch, while in North Africa and the Middle East, they also make an appearance at breakfast. Rich in omega-3 fats and protein, eggs were traditionally viewed as an economical alternative to meat.

Eggs, particularly their yolks, have been stigmatized for years due to supposed links to cholesterol levels and cardiovascular diseases. However, more recent research, including a study from the American Journal of Clinical Nutrition, has found no strong correlation between egg consumption and the risk of heart attacks or strokes among healthy individuals. On the flip side, egg yolks contain choline, a nutrient that may help lower

cancer risk. They also have antioxidants that can prevent macular degeneration. High in protein, eggs can keep you full for longer, aiding in weight loss and muscle recovery post-workout. With each large egg containing just 72 calories and being versatile in cooking, eggs are a practical and healthy choice for both budget-conscious, health-aware foodies.

MEAT IN MODERATION

In the Mediterranean culinary tradition, red meats such as lamb, goat, veal, and beef hold a special place, though they are not consumed daily or in large quantities. These meats are deeply rooted in the culture and history of the Mediterranean, offering not only robust flavors but also various nutritional benefits.

For instance, lamb has been a popular choice of meat in the Mediterranean for centuries, bolstered by its symbolic significance in Judaism, Christianity, and Islam. With its easy preparation and health benefits, it's often featured during significant events such as Passover, Easter, weddings, and other springtime celebrations. Similarly, goat meat is prized for its digestibility, leanness, and environmental sustainability due to eco-friendly grazing patterns. Nutritionally, it boasts low cholesterol levels while providing a significant source of protein, iron, and other nutrients.

While red meat offers a range of B vitamins, zinc, and healthy fatty acids, the Mediterranean diet recommends moderation in consumption. Specifically, it advises less than 1 pound (about 455 grams) of red meat per month, roughly translating to one 4-ounce (115-gram) serving per week. This echoes the historic notion of meat as a 'special occasion' food, aligning with ancient practices where slaughtering an animal for its meat was often reserved for honoring guests or celebrating holidays and weddings.

This limited yet qualitative approach to red meat also extends to its use as a "seasoning" for vegetable dishes. Rather than being the primary focus of a meal, small amounts of red meat can enhance the flavors of a vegetable-centric dish.

This moderate intake of meat also allows the modern consumer, such as yourself, to focus on quality, rather than quantity. Opt for grass-fed animals and local supplier for a health-conscious and eco-conscious choice.

WATER AND WINE (AND TEAS AND COFFEE)

In the Mediterranean lifestyle, beverages play more than a mere supporting role; they are imbued with cultural, social, and even medicinal significance.

Water is, of course, the mainstay—consumed liberally and considered the elixir of life. Often, it's enjoyed with a splash of lemon or a handful of fresh mint leaves, not only enhancing its flavor but also introducing additional health benefits.

Tea and coffee are more than just beverages; they are rituals. Whether it's a meticulously brewed Turkish coffee enjoyed in hushed reverence or an afternoon Greek herbal tea sipped among friends, the act is always more than just quenching thirst—it's about community, dialogue, and sometimes even philosophy. These drinks often come infused with regional herbs and spices, not just for flavor but also for their purported health benefits. From antioxidant-rich green teas to anise-flavored brews, the choices are both delightful and diverse.

Wine, particularly red, holds a special place in the Mediterranean diet, consumed not for the purpose of intoxication but rather appreciated for its ability to enhance the flavors of a meal and promote cardiovascular health when consumed in moderation. The art of winemaking in the region dates back thousands of years, and the cultural respect for wine is evident in its mindful consumption. It's common to see a small glass of red wine accompanying dinner, sipped slowly to complement the food and extend the pleasure of the mealtime experience.

From a nutritional standpoint, the beverages of the Mediterranean region align with its food philosophy—minimal processing, high nutritional value, and maximum enjoyment.

FOR YOUR SWEET TOOTH

In traditional Mediterranean cuisine, the allure of sweets is tempered by a philosophy of moderation. While sugary delights are ubiquitous across marketplaces and shops, their consumption is generally reserved for special occasions and family gatherings. This cultural approach traces its roots back to ancient times, particularly in Egypt, where the high cost of sugar and refined flour made sweets a luxury beyond the reach of common folk. As a result, fruits, honey, and nuts became the go-to options for post-meal desserts.

Even today, when dining in homes across Southern Europe or the Mediterranean, you'll more likely find trays of seasonal fruits offered post-meal than elaborate sugary confections. Cakes and sweets primarily held ceremonial importance. The culinary arts evolved substantially during the Italian Renaissance, inspiring both the English and French to hire Italian pastry chefs. The shift in the baking culture led to more refined techniques and introduced new shapes, like the circular pans symbolic of life cycles. Even today, artisan bakers in the region prioritize quality ingredients and time-honored methods to create sweets that differ markedly from the overly sweet, mass-produced desserts common today.

While modern health advice seldom advocates for frequent sweet consumption, the general consensus holds that occasional indulgence can make it easier to stick to a healthy eating plan over the long term. Complete deprivation often leads to sliding back into harmful habits in the long run. So, indulge in a lovely baklava or a moist Moroccan Orange cake every once in a while, and taste all the history and tradition that comes with it, rather than munching on a much less healthy Snicker and breaking your new healthy habits.

KEY COMPONENTS

Now that you have a basic understanding of the principles of the Mediterranean Diet, let's translate that in a workable plan for your diet following the Mediterranean Diet Food Pyramid.

Base Layer: Physical Activity & Mindfulness
Daily Practice
In the Mediterranean lifestyle, physical activity and mindfulness are considered the foundation of good health. People are encouraged to engage daily in some form of exercise—be it walking, swimming, or even gardening. It's not just about breaking a sweat; it's about integrating physical activity into daily life as a natural habit.

First Layer: Fruits & Vegetables
Daily Servings: 5–10
Fruits and vegetables are the cornerstone of the Mediterranean diet. Consumed in abundance, they provide essential nutrients, fiber, and a variety of flavors and colors that make meals visually appealing. The aim is to consume between 5 to 10 servings daily, leaning toward fresh, seasonal, and locally sourced produce whenever possible.

Second Layer: Whole Grains & Legumes
Daily Servings: 6–8 for grains, 1–2 for legumes
Whole grains and legumes provide a steady source of energy and are consumed in moderate portions daily. Unlike processed grains, whole grains like brown rice, quinoa, and whole wheat bread are rich in nutrients and fiber. Legumes, such as lentils, chickpeas, and white beans, offer protein and fiber as well. They are essential in the Mediterranean diet not just as fillers, but as substantive elements that add both texture and nutrition to meals.

Third Layer: Healthy Fats
Daily Servings: 2–4
Healthy fats in the Mediterranean diet primarily come from sources like olive oil, nuts, and avocados. Unlike saturated fats, these fats are known for their heart-healthy properties. Olive oil is often used for cooking and as a dressing for salads, while nuts and seeds like almonds, flaxseed, and sunflower seeds are consumed in moderation. The aim is to include 2 to 4 servings of healthy fats daily, choosing options that also provide other nutrients.

Fourth Layer: Dairy & Poultry
Daily/Weekly Servings: Dairy (1–2 daily), Poultry (2–3 weekly)
In the Mediterranean diet, dairy is typically consumed in the form of yogurt or cheese rather than milk. Greek yogurt and various types of cheeses like feta are popular choices, rich in protein and calcium. Poultry is consumed in moderation, often just 2 to 3 times a week, and is usually grilled or baked rather than fried. Both dairy and poultry serve as additional sources of protein and are incorporated into meals in a way that complements the abundance of fruits, vegetables, and grains.

Fifth Layer: Fish & Seafood
Weekly Servings: 2–3

Fish and seafood hold a special place in Mediterranean cuisine. Rich in essential fatty acids and protein, these options are a staple, especially in coastal areas. Salmon, sardines, and mackerel are common choices that offer omega-3 fatty acids, known for their heart-healthy attributes. The aim is to include 2 to 3 servings of fish or seafood in your weekly diet, preferably opting for wild-caught or sustainably sourced options.

Apex: Sweets and Red Meat
Weekly Servings: Red meat once a week, sweets occasionally

Red meat, including lamb, beef, and pork, is enjoyed but in moderation. Reflecting a tradition where meat was often a luxury, the Mediterranean diet recommends limiting red meat to 1 serving per week. When consumed, the focus is on high-quality, lean cuts. In some dishes, small amounts of meat may also be used to "season" vegetable or grain dishes, adding flavor without making meat the focus of the meal.

In the Mediterranean lifestyle, sweets are not an everyday indulgence but are saved for special occasions and family gatherings. Desserts, often rich in natural sweeteners like honey and accentuated by nuts and fruits, are considered luxuries. The rarity with which they are consumed only adds to their allure and the pleasure of savoring them. This apex of the pyramid serves as a reminder that while life should be sweet, the keys to health are moderation and balance.

Essential Ingredients

If there is only one thing that you take from the previous chapter, it should be that the Mediterranean Diet is not a diet, it's a holistic lifestyle rooted in the traditions and daily practices of communities along the Mediterranean Sea. This lifestyle emphasizes the consumption of fresh vegetables, fruits, legumes, whole grains, and olive oil, often accompanied by fish. These simple yet diverse ingredients are not just staples in a dietary regimen; they are part of a broader tapestry that includes skills, knowledge, and cultural practices. From planting and harvesting to fishing, from food preservation to preparation, every element is thoughtfully integrated.

When you decide to adopt the Mediterranean lifestyle, your kitchen will transform. You'll want to stock up on the following essential items that make adhering to this lifestyle both convenient and delightful. These staples make it easy to whip up meals that are as nutritious as they are delicious, helping you stay committed to your health goals. For a complete pantry and refrigerator regulars list, check out the appendixes at the end of the book.

OLIVE OIL

At the heart of Mediterranean culinary tradition is extra virgin olive oil (EVOO), a veritable elixir bursting with monounsaturated fats. Filled with over 400 micro components, including powerful antioxidants and anti-inflammatory agents, extra virgin olive oil is a nutritional powerhouse that offers protection against an array of chronic diseases, including heart conditions, cancer, and cognitive disorders.

Though it may seem counterintuitive, incorporating 3 to 4 tablespoons (roughly 40-50 grams) of extra virgin olive oil into your daily diet can yield significant health benefits without contributing to weight gain. The reason lies in the oil's dual function: it not only enriches your body with antioxidants but also encourages the consumption of vegetables by making them tastier. Far from being a calorie bomb, the typical Mediterranean dish is vegetable-centric and relatively moderate in calories, even with a generous olive oil drizzle.

Moreover, extra virgin olive oil serves as the go-to fat for almost all cooking methods, from sautéing and frying to roasting. Beyond hot dishes, it's a staple in salads, bread spreads, dressings, and even baking. Contrary to the popular myth that its low smoke point makes it unsuitable for frying, extra virgin olive oil actually has a higher smoke point than many other oils, ranging from 365°F to 410°F (185°C to 210°C).

Not only does extra virgin olive oil have a relatively high smoke point, but it also contains antioxidants that inhibit food oxidation and during the cooking process these antioxidants are absorbed by the food cooked in olive oil

PICK THE RIGHT OLIVE OIL

If there is one downside to olive oil is that it's expensive. However, since all other components of the Mediterranean are cheap, easily available whole foods, make sure to keep room in your budget for a good olive oil.
So, what kind of olive oils should you choose?

Opt for Extra Virgin: The antioxidants that contribute to olive oil's celebrated health benefits are most abundant in extra virgin olive oil. Don't settle for oils labeled as "pure," "regular," "refined," or even "virgin," as these are of lower quality and have undergone physical and chemical refinement or may be mixed with other oils.

Prioritize Freshness: Remember that olive oil is, in essence, fruit juice. As such, its freshness matters greatly. Always check for an expiration date and, if available, a harvest date. Aim to consume olive oil within a year of its harvest and opt for bottles that have an expiration date at least two years from the day you purchase it. The fresher the oil, the richer it is in antioxidants.

Verify Origin: A high-quality olive oil will often specify the geographical origin of its olives. Single-origin oils, those sourced from one country, are generally preferable.

Taste Test: Quality olive oil has a distinctive flavor profile—it should be fruity, possess a hint of bitterness indicative of freshness, and carry a peppery undertone signaling the presence of antioxidants. Avoid oils that taste musty, vinegary, rancid, or excessively buttery.

HOW TO STORE OLIVE OIL

Preserving the integrity of olive oil is essential, not just for its flavor but also for retaining its myriad health benefits. The four principal foes of olive oil are light, oxygen, heat, and metal. To combat these, olive oil should be stored in a cool, dark environment and kept in a container that is both dark and airtight.

Container Choices: Glass bottles tinted green or brown are the most commonly recommended, as they can block out more light than clear bottles. Ceramic containers with a spout or a sealable top are also excellent options, as are stainless steel containers that are lined to prevent any metallic taste transferring to the oil. Avoid plastic containers, as they can interact with the oil over time.

Seal it Tight: Oxygen is another enemy of olive oil, so opt for containers that can be tightly sealed. Some even come with special pouring spouts that minimize exposure to air.

Timely Consumption: Once a bottle is opened, aim to use it within six months to ensure that it retains its optimal flavor and health properties. This is why purchasing in sensible quantities is advised. If you're not going to consume it quickly, steer clear of very large bottles.

Climate Considerations: The ideal storage temperature for olive oil is between 57-70°F (14-21°C). If you live in a warmer climate, you may consider storing your olive oil in the refrigerator. While this can cause it to solidify, its quality will not be compromised; it will return to liquid form when left at room temperature. A wine cooler is also a great option if you happen to own one. In colder climates, simply keeping it in a cool, dark cupboard away from any heat source like ovens or stovetops is generally sufficient.

Don't reuse: While some may be tempted to reuse olive oil since it's so damn expensive, doing so is not advisable. Reheating olive oil can diminish its antioxidant content and compromise its flavor. Fresh is best when it comes to this liquid gold.

FRUITS AND VEGETABLES

The Mediterranean diet is a celebration of the earth's bounty, and fruits and vegetables are a big part of it. These are your go-to foods for vitamins, minerals, fiber, and all-important antioxidants.

Non-starchy veggies like spinach, bell peppers, and tomatoes are low in calories and carbohydrates but high in nutrients. They should be the bulk of your vegetable intake. Feel free to eat these generously. You can grill, steam, or eat them raw; you can't go wrong.
Aim for at least five servings a day.

Starchy vegetables, on the other hand, include foods like potatoes, corn, and peas. They are higher in carbohydrates and calories, but they're not off-limits. They offer essential nutrients like Vitamin C, potassium, and fiber. The key is balance. If you're having a starchy vegetable, maybe go easy on other carb sources like bread or pasta.

When it comes to fruits and veggies, timing is everything. Seasonal produce not only tastes better but also has a higher nutrient profile. Strawberries in summer and oranges in winter—each season brings its delicious gifts. Be sure to consult the appendix for a comprehensive guide on what's best to eat and when.

WHOLE GRAINS

Whole grains are the backbone of a balanced diet, and when it comes to the Mediterranean way of eating, they play a starring role. Whole grains are grains that contain all three parts of the kernel—the bran, germ, and endosperm. Refined grains, on the other hand, have had these nutritious components stripped away, leaving you with fewer nutrients and less fiber. The result? Whole grains keep you fuller for longer, help manage blood sugar levels, and reduce the risk of heart disease. In contrast, refined grains can lead to quick spikes and crashes in blood sugar, which increase the risk of developing insuline-resistance and obesity.

BARLEY

Tracing its origins back to the Fertile Crescent, the cradle of civilization, barley is far more than just an ancient grain; it's a powerhouse of nutrients that has sustained humans for thousands of years. The high fiber content in barley aids in digestion and can help to regulate blood sugar levels, making it an excellent choice for those monitoring their glucose. It also promotes a feeling of fullness, which can be helpful for weight management. Moreover, it's an excellent and rich source of essential minerals like manganese, which plays a crucial role in bone formation and blood clotting, and selenium, an antioxidant that supports metabolic function and immunity.

Preparing and Cooking: Barley comes in various forms—hulled, pearled, and quick-cooking—to suit different culinary needs. Hulled barley retains more of its whole grain nutritional goodness but takes longer to cook, while pearled barley has been processed to remove some of the outer layers, cutting down cooking time at the cost of some nutrients. Quick-cooking barley is convenient and best for recipes that require a shorter cooking time.

Why don't you try a barley salad with roasted vegetables? Cook one cup of pearled barley according to package instructions and let it cool. In the meantime, roast an assortment of vegetables like bell peppers, zucchini, and cherry tomatoes with olive oil, salt, and herbs like rosemary or thyme. Once roasted, mix the vegetables with the cooled barley. Add a handful of chopped fresh basil or parsley, crumbled feta cheese, and a drizzle of extra-virgin olive oil. Toss everything together with the juice of one lemon, salt, and pepper to taste. A tasty and nutritious lunch in less than 30 minutes!

BULGUR

Hailing from the Middle Eastern region, bulgur is essentially whole wheat that's been parboiled and cracked.
High in fiber and proteins well as rich in minerals like iron, magnesium, and manganese, which contribute to various bodily functions, from oxygen transport to bone health.

Preparing and Cooking: Bulgur comes in different grinds, from very fine to coarse, to suit a variety of cooking methods and recipes. Fine bulgur often requires only soaking and is used traditionally in dishes like kibbeh, while medium and coarse grinds may need to be boiled or simmered but offer a chewier texture suitable for pilafs or casseroles. Regardless of the grind, bulgur generally cooks more quickly than other whole grains, making it a convenient choice for busy weeknight dinners.

How about a recipe where you don't need to turn on the stove? Soak a cup of bulgur in boiling water until it softens but remains chewy, then drain excess water. Toss the bulgur with whatever chopped veggies you have on hand—cucumbers, tomatoes, bell peppers work well. Add in some olives, perhaps Kalamata, and fresh herbs like mint or parsley if you've got them. Squeeze in the juice of a lemon, pour a generous glug of extra virgin olive oil, and season with salt and pepper. If you're a cheese fan, crumble some feta on top. Mix everything together, adjust seasoning to taste, and you've got yourself a quick, no-fuss Mediterranean bulgur salad.

FARRO

Tracing its roots back to the Fertile Crescent and popularized in Italy already during the Roman Empire, farro is a rich source of protein, fiber, and essential nutrients like iron, zinc, and B vitamins. Similar to barley, farro's fiber content aids in digestion and helps regulate blood sugar levels, making it an excellent choice for those concerned with glycemic control.

Preparing and Cooking: Farro is available in different forms: whole, semi-pearled, and pearled, each offering varying cooking times and nutrient levels. Whole farro retains all its nutrients but takes the longest to cook, while pearled farro is the quickest to cook but lacks some of the grain's nutritional benefits. Semi-pearled is a happy medium, offering a balance of nutrition and convenience. To prepare farro, simply boil it in water or broth until it reaches your desired level of tenderness, then drain any excess liquid before using.

How about a hearty farro mushroom risotto? Start by boiling a pot of salted water and tossing in a cup of semi-pearled farro. While it cooks, sauté some chopped garlic and shallots in olive oil until fragrant. Throw in some sliced mushrooms, or any other veggies you have on hand, and cook until tender. Once the farro is done (it should be chewy but not too hard), drain it and add it to your veggie mixture. Stir in a generous splash of white wine or chicken broth for added flavor, let it absorb, and finish off with a sprinkle of Parmesan cheese and a dash of your favorite herbs, such as thyme or rosemary. Dinner's served!

WHOLE WHEAT

Whole wheat, a grain that has been cultivated and consumed globally for centuries, offers a high fiber content and essential nutrients such as manganese and folate, a crucial nutrient for cellular function and tissue growth.
Whole wheat pasta is an excellent alternative to traditional white pasta, as it retains more of its natural nutrients and fibers.

Preparing and Cooking: Whole wheat pasta may require a slightly longer cooking time than its white counterpart, but the process is just as straightforward. Simply boil a pot of salted water, add the pasta, and cook until al dente. The firm texture of whole wheat pasta stands up well to a variety of sauces, from a hearty Bolognese to a zesty tomato basil.

BROWN RICE

Unlike white rice, brown rice retains its bran and germ layers, which means it's richer in nutrients and fiber. In addition to its benefits for digestive health and blood sugar regulation, brown rice is also high in antioxidants like ferulic acid, lignans, and phytic acid, which can combat oxidative stress and inflammation. Moreover, brown rice contains small amounts of zinc, which is vital for immune system function, and selenium, an antioxidant that may reduce the risk of certain cancers.

Preparing and Cooking: Brown rice is available in various forms, including short-grain, long-grain, and quick-cooking. The traditional versions require a longer cooking time compared to white rice due to the intact bran layer. However, quick-cooking brown rice offers a faster alternative, though some nutrients may be sacrificed. To cook, simply combine the rice with water (or broth for added flavor), bring to a boil, and then simmer until the rice is tender and the water is absorbed. If you are making a classic risotto, I would still opt for Arborio or Carnaroli rice, less healthy but it respects the flavor of the tradition.

Why don't you test (and taste) it with a quick risotto? Heat a glug of olive oil in a large pan and sauté minced garlic and diced onions until translucent. Toss in a cup of uncooked brown rice and stir until it's well-coated with the oil. Pour in a splash of white wine and let it evaporate. Add a ladleful of vegetable broth to the rice and stir until it's mostly absorbed. Keep adding broth, one ladle at a time, stirring frequently until the rice is cooked but still has a bite. Mix in some chopped sun-dried tomatoes, artichoke hearts, and a handful of spinach. Season with salt, pepper, and a sprinkle of oregano. Finish with a generous drizzle of extra virgin olive oil and a handful of grated Parmesan cheese.

OATS

Originating in Europe and Asia Minor, oats are especially high in fiber, which as you know by now, aids in digestion and can help regulate blood sugar levels. Oats also contain unique antioxidants known as avenanthramides, which are not found in most other grains. Avenanthramides have been shown to have anti-inflammatory and heart-protective effects, making oats an excellent choice for cardiovascular health.

Preparing and Cooking: Oats come in various forms, such as steel-cut, rolled, and quick oats, to cater to different cooking needs and preferences. Steel-cut oats are the least processed and take the longest to cook, but they offer a chewy texture and nutty flavor. Rolled oats, which have been steamed and rolled flat, cook faster and have a softer texture, making them ideal for quick morning meals or for use in recipes like cookies and bread. Quick oats are the most processed and cook the fastest, but they retain less of their texture. Whichever form you choose, oats can serve as a nutritious and hearty base for many delicious dishes.

How about waking up to find your breakfast waiting for you in the fridge? For a Mediterranean-inspired overnight oats, grab a jar and layer in half a cup of rolled oats, a teaspoon of chia seeds, and a handful of chopped dried figs or dates. Add a sprinkle of cinnamon and a dash of vanilla extract for flavor. Pour in enough almond milk to cover the mixture, give it a good stir, and then seal the jar tightly. Place it in the fridge overnight. In the morning, give it a good stir, top with a dollop of Greek yogurt, a drizzle of honey, and some slivered almonds or walnuts. Enjoy cold, or warm it up for a few seconds in the microwave if you prefer.

WHOLE WHEAT COUSCOUS

Native to North Africa, whole wheat couscous is a versatile grain made from coarsely-ground whole wheat semolina. Unlike its refined counterpart, whole wheat couscous retains more fiber and nutrients, making it a healthier alternative. Furthermore, the whole wheat version is an excellent source of protein and provides a variety of B vitamins, which play a crucial role in energy metabolism.

Preparing and Cooking: Whole wheat couscous is incredibly easy to prepare. Simply bring water or broth to a boil, stir in the couscous, remove from heat, and let it sit covered for about 5 minutes. Fluff it up with a fork, and it's ready to be used in a myriad of recipes. Because it's so quick to cook, whole wheat couscous is an excellent choice for incorporating whole grains into your meals without spending a lot of time in the kitchen.

Here is a quick recipe that really makes whole wheat couscous really shine! Heat your pan and dry-toast some pine nuts until golden; set aside. Then, in the same pan, sauté diced red bell peppers and zucchini with a bit of olive oil until they're just soft. Make your whole wheat couscous by boiling it in vegetable broth, as per package instructions. Once it's done, stir in a spoonful of harissa paste for some kick. Combine the couscous with the sautéed vegetables, add the toasted pine nuts, and finish it off with some chopped fresh mint and a dollop of Greek yogurt on top. For a burst of freshness, add some pomegranate seeds. A quick drizzle of olive oil and you're ready to serve.

MILLET

Originating from Africa, millet has been a staple food for thousands of years and is a gluten-free alternative that is gaining global popularity. It's especially high in magnesium, a mineral that's essential for maintaining heart health and regulating blood pressure. Additionally, millet is a good source of fiber and protein, making it beneficial both for digestive health and muscle repair.

Preparing and Cooking: Millet is generally available in whole grain form and is relatively quick and easy to prepare. To cook, rinse the grains and then simmer in water or broth until tender, which usually takes about 15–20 minutes. For added flavor, you can toast the millet in a dry skillet before boiling. Whether you're aiming for a creamy texture or a fluffier outcome, adjusting the water-to-grain ratio can help you

achieve your desired consistency. Once cooked, millet can be seasoned with herbs, spices, or a drizzle of olive oil, making it a nutritious and versatile ingredient for a wide range of meals. *Quick tip: Toast it before cooking to bring out a nutty flavor. Moreover, millet can be prepared as a creamy porridge or even popped like popcorn for a crunchy snack.*

FREEKEH

Freekeh is young green wheat that's harvested while still tender, then roasted to give it its distinct smoky flavor. Its nutritional profile is a selling point, with a particularly high content of protein and fiber.

Preparing and Cooking: Freekeh comes in both whole-grain and cracked forms. The whole-grain variety will take a bit longer to cook but will provide a chewier texture, while the cracked version cooks more quickly. To prepare, rinse the grains and simmer in water or broth until tender. The cooking time may vary from 20 to 45 minutes, depending on the form you're using. Once cooked, it can be fluffed with a fork and seasoned to taste, ready to be incorporated into a myriad of recipes.

QUINOA

Quinoa has found its place in many modern adaptations of the Mediterranean diet, even though it's not traditionally a part of it. Native to the Andean region of South America, quinoa is a grain-like seed that is also a complete protein source, meaning it provides all nine essential amino acids that our bodies cannot produce on their own. This makes quinoa particularly beneficial for vegetarians or those looking to reduce their meat intake.
Quinoa also contains significant amounts of antioxidants like quercetin and kaempferol, which have been shown to have anti-inflammatory, antiviral, and anticancer properties.

Preparing and Cooking: Quinoa comes in multiple colors—white, red, and black—each offering a slightly different texture and flavor profile. Before cooking, it's essential to rinse quinoa thoroughly to remove its natural coating of saponins, which can be bitter. To cook, the general ratio is two parts liquid to one part quinoa. Bring it to a boil, then cover and simmer until the quinoa is tender and the liquid is absorbed. Fluff it with a fork, and it's ready to be incorporated into your favorite Mediterranean-inspired dishes.

Pasta alternatives:
Whole wheat pasta is a star in the world of healthier noodles. Made from whole grains that keep the bran, germ, and endosperm, it offers a substantial boost in fiber and nutrients. The benefit? You'll feel fuller longer and experience a gentler rise in blood sugar. But whole wheat isn't the only nutritious pasta player on the field.

Chickpea and **lentil** pasta are gluten-free powerhouses, rich in protein and fiber. **Quinoa** pasta gives you all nine essential amino acids, while spelled and brown rice pasta provides a decent fiber punch along with essential nutrients like manganese and magnesium. **Soba** noodles, made from buckwheat, are another gluten-free alternative loaded with essential nutrients.

FISH AND SEAFOOD

When you're following a Mediterranean Diet, seafood, especially fish rich in omega-3 fatty acids, should make a regular appearance on your plate—aim for at least two servings per week. Omega-3s are essential fats your body needs but can't produce, and they're a boon for heart health, reducing inflammation, and even boosting brain function.

To source your fish, always look for those labeled as wild-caught or sustainably farmed. Your best bet is to get to know your local fishmonger or find a reputable online supplier that offers fresh, sustainably-sourced options.

SARDINES

A staple in Mediterranean diets, sardines are a treasure trove of omega-3 fatty acids packed into a small size.

In addition to their omega-3 benefits, sardines are a rich source of vitamin D. This vitamin plays a crucial role in bone health, as it aids in the absorption of calcium. Vitamin D also supports immune system functionality and can help regulate mood and ward off depression.

Fresh sardines can be grilled, broiled, or even pan-fried, while canned versions are perfect for toss-ins in salads, on toast, or as a pizza topping. Their unique, robust flavor profile—slightly salty, with a rich, oily texture—makes them stand out in dishes.

Moreover, sardines are a lower trophic level species, meaning their environmental impact when fished is typically less than larger fish. So, not only are they good for your health, but they're also a more eco-friendly seafood choice.

Quick recipe tips: Try grilling sardines and serving them with a lemon-herb sauce. Or put a canned sardine on an avocado toast for a savory breakfast!

ANCHOVIES

Anchovies are small, oily fish that are a staple in Mediterranean cuisine. Nutrient-dense, they are particularly high in omega-3 fatty acids, and a good source of vitamin B12, essential for nerve function and the formation of red blood cells. In the kitchen, anchovies are versatile; they can be used in sauces like puttanesca, spread on toast, or added to salads and pizzas. Like sardines, anchovies are considered a sustainable seafood choice.

MACKEREL

Mackerel is a fatty, cold-water fish that's highly regarded for its nutritional profile, especially its rich content of omega-3 fatty acids. Mackerel is also a good source of protein, vitamins like B12 and D, and essential minerals such as selenium. It can be grilled, smoked, or even enjoyed raw in dishes like sushi. Given its sustainability, particularly when caught in the wild, mackerel is not only a nutritious but also an environmentally responsible seafood choice.

Gourmet tip: Smoked mackerel can be flaked over salads for a quick and nutritious meal.

SALMON

Although not traditionally part of the Mediterranean diet, salmon has found its way into modern interpretations due to its robust nutrient profile. Rich in high-quality protein, this oily fish is a nutritional powerhouse, loaded with omega-3 fatty acids as well as a good source of essential vitamins like B12 and D, and minerals like selenium and potassium.

How about this quick recipe with an easy clean-up? Place a salmon fillet skin-side down on a sheet of foil or parchment paper. Drizzle it with olive oil and squeeze half a lemon over the top. Sprinkle with salt, pepper, and a pinch of oregano. Layer on some thinly sliced tomatoes, red onions, and a handful of kalamata olives. Close up the foil or parchment into a packet and bake in a preheated 400°F oven for 12-15 minutes, or until the salmon flakes easily with a fork. Open the packet, sprinkle with some freshly chopped parsley, and serve immediately. That's what I call flavor-packed!

TUNA

Unlike many other types of fish, tuna is incredibly rich in lean protein, providing about 25 grams per 3.5-ounce serving. This makes it a popular option for those looking to build muscle, lose weight, or simply incorporate more protein into their diet. It is also replete with essential Omega-3 fatty acids, specifically EPA and DHA, which have been linked to improved cognitive function, reduced inflammation, and better cardiovascular health.

It's also an excellent source of vitamin B12, phosphorus, important for bone health, and potassium, which helps regulate blood pressure.

Fresh tuna steaks can be grilled, seared, or even served raw in dishes like sashimi and poke bowls. The texture of fresh tuna is often compared to that of beef steak, making it a satisfying alternative for red meat. Canned tuna, meanwhile, is a pantry staple that can be turned into quick salads, sandwiches, and pasta dishes.

Note: It's worth noting that different types of tuna have varying levels of mercury, a heavy metal that can be toxic in large amounts. While light tuna is generally lower in mercury, albacore and yellowfin varieties tend to have higher levels. For this reason, it's recommended to limit consumption, especially for vulnerable groups like pregnant women and children.

SEA BASS

Nutritionally, sea bass is a good source of protein, supplying about 20 grams in a 3.5-ounce serving. Although not as rich in omega-3 fatty acids as some other fish like salmon or mackerel, sea bass still offers a respectable amount, contributing to cardiovascular health and anti-inflammatory benefits. Sea bass also contains iodine, a trace element necessary for proper thyroid function.

While sea bass is a delicious and nutritious option, it's worth noting that some varieties, like the Chilean sea bass, have been overfished. Consumers interested in sustainability should look for certified options or consider substituting with other sustainable white fish.

HERRING

Hailing from the cold waters of the North Atlantic and the Baltic Sea, herring is a small, oily fish that is a nutritional powerhouse. It's not only exceptionally high in omega-3 fatty acids, but also a single serving of herring can provide more than 100% of the recommended daily intake for vitamin D, which is crucial for bone health and immune function.

Culinarily, herring is quite versatile. It's commonly enjoyed in its smoked or pickled forms, but it can also be grilled, baked, or fried.

SQUID

Squid, a staple of the Greek and Italian Mediterranean diet, is a good source of protein, offering all the essential amino acids required for optimal body function. Furthermore, squid is rich in essential vitamins and minerals like vitamin B12 and selenium. Squid also contains a decent amount of zinc and copper, necessary for energy production and iron metabolism. Get it for seafood stews, salads, or as a simple grilled dish seasoned with herbs, lemon, and olive oil.

OCTOPUS

Octopus is a popular culinary ingredient in various Mediterranean cuisines. Not only is it a source of high-quality protein, but octopus also contains essential nutrients like vitamin B12 and selenium.

Its texture can be either tender or chewy, depending on how it's prepared. Traditional Mediterranean preparations often involve boiling the octopus with a cork or a bay leaf to tenderize it, then grilling or roasting it to perfection. Marinating it in olive oil, lemon, and herbs like oregano or thyme can enhance its flavor. Octopus can also be used in stews, salads, and pasta dishes.

How to get a tender octopus the traditional way: boil the octopus in a large pot of salted water, with added aromatics like bay leaves, onion, or a cork from a wine bottle to aid in tenderization. Boiling time varies depending on the size but is usually around 45-60 minutes for a medium-sized octopus. Then let it cool down in the water. When you'll get it out the meat wil tender and ready for any preparation you set out to do.

LEGUMES

Legumes are a cornerstone of the Mediterranean diet, recognized for their rich protein content, fiber, and variety of essential nutrients like iron and potassium. They are particularly beneficial for heart health, blood sugar control, and even weight management. You should include legumes in your meals at least two to three times a week. Whenever possible, opt for dry beans rather than canned ones to avoid added sodium and preservatives. If you must go canned, look for options with no added salt.

To cook dry beans, soak them in water overnight, rinse, and then simmer low and slow in fresh water (not the soaking water) until tender. The cooking time will vary depending on the type of bean, but generally, it ranges from 1 to 3 hours. *Quick tip: don't add salt as it will toughen the beans, wait to add it after they are cooked and ready to be used in recipes.* Cooked beans will keep in the fridge for a week, making it an excellent choice for meal prepping!

Chickpeas (Garbanzo Beans):
High in protein and fiber, chickpeas also offer manganese and folate. For a quick snack, roast chickpeas with olive oil and spices for a crunchy snack.

Lentils:
Rich in iron and folate, lentils don't require soaking and cook quickly. Lentil soup with veggies makes a hearty, nutritious meal.

Fava Beans (Broad Beans):
Faba Veans are high in fiber and protein, as well as B vitamins. Try them sautéed with garlic and olive oil as a simple side dish.

White Beans (including Cannellini and Navy Beans):
White beans are rich in fiber and a good source of magnesium. White bean hummus is a delicious alternative to chickpea hummus.

Kidney Beans:
Packed with protein and fiber, Kidney beans also contain iron and potassium. You can use them in a classic chili recipe for a protein-packed meal.

Black-Eyed Peas:
Black-eyes Peas legumes are a good source of fiber and protein. Try them in a Southern-style salad with corn and bell peppers.

Green Peas:
While often considered a vegetable, green peas are rich in protein and offer vitamins like A, K, and C. They're excellent in casseroles or as a simple side dish with a dab of mint butter.

Lima Beans:
Lima Brans are rich in fiber and protein, as well as micronutrients like manganese. People tend to enjoy in a succotash recipe, mixed with corn and peppers.

Butter Beans:
Butter Beans are a variant of lima beans but offer a buttery texture. They are a good source of iron and magnesium. You can try mashed beans as a healthier alternative to mashed potatoes.

NUTS AND SEEDS

Nuts and seeds are small but mighty components of the Mediterranean diet, providing a rich source of healthy fats, protein, and various essential micronutrients like antioxidants, vitamins, and minerals. The healthy fats (Monounsaturated and polyunsaturated fats) lower cholesterol levels, helping to keep the heart healthy. Nuts and seeds also contain quality protein, which is crucial for muscle repair and overall cellular function. They're rich in micronutrients like vitamin E, an antioxidant, and minerals like magnesium, which plays a role in over 300 enzymatic reactions in the body.

In recipes, nuts and seeds are versatile. You can add slivers of almonds to your yogurt, sprinkle chia seeds into your morning smoothie, or include crushed walnuts in your salad. You can also use nut butter like almond or tahini as bases for sauces and dressings. Now, let's go through some of the most important nuts and seeds commonly used in the Mediterranean diet:

Almonds:
High in vitamin E and magnesium, almonds are great for snacking or as a crunchy addition to salads. You can also use almond flour as a gluten-free baking option.

Walnuts:
Walnuts are excellent for heart health since they are high omega-3 fatty acid content, specifically ALA, They're also a delicious component in both savory dishes like pasta and sweet treats like walnut baklava rolls.

Hazelnuts:
Hazelnuts contain healthy fats and are a good source of vitamin E. They are often used in desserts but can also be incorporated into a homemade granola mix.

Pine Nuts:
High in vitamin K and manganese, pine nuts are commonly used in pesto recipes and can be sprinkled over salads or vegetable dishes for added crunch.

Pistachios:
Pistachios are rich in antioxidants, including vitamin E and selenium. They're perfect as a stand-alone snack or chopped as a topping for yogurt, smoothies, and desserts.

Flaxseeds:
Flaxseeds are high in fiber and a good plant-based source of omega-3 fatty acids. They can be ground and added to smoothies or used as an egg substitute in vegan recipes.

Chia Seeds:
Rich in omega-3s and fiber, chia seeds can be used to make chia pudding or as a thickener for smoothies and sauces.

Sesame Seeds:
Sesame is commonly used in the form of tahini, a key ingredient in hummus and various dressings. They are a good source of calcium and magnesium.

Sunflower Seeds:
High in vitamin E and selenium, these seeds can be eaten on their own or added to salads, yogurt, or homemade bread.

Pumpkin Seeds:
Also known as pepitas, the Pumpkin seeds are rich in magnesium and can be eaten as a snack or added to salads and grain bowls for crunch.

Incorporating nuts and seeds in your dishes can enhance satiety, making you feel fuller for longer, which can be helpful for weight management. Remember, nuts and seeds are calorie-dense, so moderation is key. A small handful per day is generally a good guideline.

HOW TO TOAST NUTS

Toasting nuts elevates their flavor, bringing out a richer, more complex taste, as well as making them crunchy!
Here are the best techniques for toasting nuts:

Stovetop Method:
Place the nuts in a dry skillet over medium heat. Stir or shake the pan occasionally for even toasting. This usually takes 5-10 minutes, and you'll know they're done when they become fragrant and turn a golden brown. This method is quick and allows for good control over the toasting process.

Oven Method:
Preheat your oven to 350°F (175°C). Spread the nuts in a single layer on a baking sheet. Toast for 5-10 minutes, shaking the pan halfway through for even toasting. The oven method is great for toasting a larger quantity of nuts at once.

Microwave Method:
Spread out nuts in the dish in a single layer. Microwave them on high for one minute, stir, and then continue microwaving in 30-second intervals until they're toasted to your liking. This method is speedy but offers less control over the toasting level.

Air Fryer Method:
If you have an air fryer, you can toast nuts at 300°F (150°C) for about 5 minutes. Shake the basket halfway through for even toasting.

DAIRY

When following a Mediterranean diet, both meat and dairy products should be consumed in moderation. This restrained approach has dual benefits: it promotes individual health by limiting the consumption of saturated fatty acids and it reduces greenhouse gas emissions, thereby mitigating the impact on the environment.

Dairy products in the Mediterranean diet primarily consist of yogurt and fresh cheeses, such as feta and ricotta, as opposed to hard cheeses, which are consumed less frequently.

Moderate consumption, which can mean a cup of yogurt or a small slice of cheese per day, is the key to enjoying these products while maintaining a balanced diet.

Yogurt:

Yogurt is great for gut health since it's rich in probiotics. Opt for plain, unsweetened Greek yogurt and flavor it yourself with fruit or a drizzle of honey to control sugar content.

Feta:

Tangy and rich in calcium and protein, feta cheese adds a burst of flavor to dishes. People often crumble it over salads, incorporate it into omelets, or serve it as a table cheese. Compared to many other cheeses, feta has a lower fat content.

Parmesan:

Rich in protein, calcium, phosphorus, and vitamin B12, Parmesan is a hard, aged cheese that elevates pasta dishes, risotto, and salads when grated over them. Though nutrient-dense, it's also high in sodium, so a little can go a long way in adding flavor.

Pecorino Romano:

Similar to Parmesan but made from sheep's milk, Pecorino Romano is rich in protein and calcium. It's often used in Italian cuisine in pasta dishes like cacio e pepe.

Gruyère:

Gruyère smooth-melting cheese is often used in dishes like fondue or quiches. It's a good source of protein, calcium, and vitamin A.

Goat Cheese:

High in protein and calcium, goat cheese is easier to digest and lower in fat compared to many cow's milk cheeses. People commonly use it in salads, spreads, and as a topping for cooked vegetables.

Blue Cheese:

Rich in calcium and protein, blue cheese has a strong flavor but is also high in sodium and fat. Use it sparingly to enhance salads or as a flavorful finish for steaks and vegetable quiches.

POULTRY AND EGGS

When it comes to the Mediterranean diet, poultry and eggs are preferred over red meat and are still consumed in moderation. The idea is to aim for balance; you don't need a chicken breast at every meal, but incorporating it a couple of times a week can be a healthy choice. Eggs are incredibly versatile and can fit easily into different meals, whether it's a vegetable omelet for breakfast or a hard-boiled egg as a snack.

Poultry:

Opt for skinless options, when possible, as the skin is high in saturated fat. Grilling, baking, roasting, and poaching are your best bets. These methods don't require added fats and help retain the meat's moisture and flavor. Steer clear of frying or cooking with a lot of added butter or cream-based sauces.

Egg:

Boiling, poaching, and scrambling with minimal butter or oil are healthy cooking methods. If you're making an omelet, fill it with plenty of veggies for added nutrients.

Sourcing:

Choosing your poultry and eggs carefully can significantly enhance both the nutritional value and flavor of your meals. When buying poultry, terms like "free-range," "organic," or "no antibiotics" indicate that the meat comes from animals raised in healthier conditions. Specifically, "free-range" suggests that the chickens had more room to roam and likely lived less stressful lives. "Organic" implies that the chickens were raised without synthetic hormones or antibiotics, making the meat a purer product. "No antibiotics" means the birds were not given antibiotics, reducing your exposure to antibiotic-resistant bacteria.

Similarly, for eggs, the labels "pasture-raised" and "organic" are good indicators of quality. "Pasture-raised" suggests that hens had more space and a varied diet, often resulting in eggs richer in nutrients like omega-3s and vitamin D. "Organic" indicates the absence of synthetic hormones and pesticides in the hens' diets, which also impacts the quality of the eggs

HERBS AND SPICES

Herbs and spices are the unsung heroes of the Mediterranean diet, turning simple ingredients into vibrant, flavorful dishes without the need for excess salt, sugar, or fat. Not only do they elevate the taste of your meals, but many herbs and spices are rich in antioxidants, vitamins, and anti-inflammatory compounds that offer a plethora of health benefits. They can aid in digestion, improve heart health, and even possess antibacterial properties.

Basil:

A cornerstone in Italian cooking, basil is used fresh in dishes like Caprese salad or as a primary ingredient in pesto. It's rich in antioxidants and vitamin K, which supports bone health.

Oregano:

This herb is commonly used in Greek and Italian cuisines and pairs well with tomato-based dishes and grilled meats. Oregano contains antioxidants and has antibacterial properties.

Rosemary:

Often used in roasting and grilling, rosemary has a strong, piney flavor. It's rich in antioxidants and has been shown to improve digestion and boost memory.

Thyme:

Thyme is versatile herb that is used in a variety of dishes, from soups to roasted vegetables and meats. It is a good source of vitamin C and has antimicrobial properties.

Mint:
Commonly used in both sweet and savory dishes, as well as beverages like teas, mint is rich in antioxidants and can aid in digestion.

Saffron:
Though expensive, a little goes a long way in imparting a unique flavor and color to dishes like paella, saffron rice, and risotto. Saffron has been found to have antidepressant and anti-inflammatory properties.

Paprika:
Made from ground peppers, paprika adds heat and flavor to dishes, especially in Spanish and Middle Eastern cuisines. It also enriches your meals with vitamin A and antioxidants.

Cumin:
Commonly used in Middle Eastern, North African, and Indian cuisines, cumin has a warm, earthy flavor. It's a good source of iron and has been linked to improving digestion.

Cinnamon:
Often used in both sweet and savory dishes, cinnamon is loaded with antioxidants and has been shown to have anti-inflammatory properties.

Turmeric:
While not native to the Mediterranean, this spice has been adopted into modern Mediterranean cooking. Known for its bright yellow color, turmeric is rich in curcumin, a powerful antioxidant with anti-inflammatory effects.

Coriander:
Coriander seeds are often used in spice mixes and offer a citrusy, nutty flavor. They are rich in antioxidants and have been shown to support heart health.

HOW TO ROAST AND BLEND SPICES

Roasting and blending your spices can significantly elevate your cooking. It's not just about fragrance and flavor; freshly roasted spices also pack more nutrients compared to their pre-ground counterparts. Let's dig into how you can master the art of roasting and blending spices at home.

Roasting Spices

- **Select Your Spices:** Always go for whole spices over ground ones. Whole spices maintain their flavor longer and allow for a fresher, more vibrant outcome.
- **Heat a Pan:** Place a dry skillet over low to medium heat. Ensure the pan is completely dry; even a small amount of moisture can disrupt the roasting process.
- **Add Spices:** Add your whole spices to the pan. Shake the pan occasionally to ensure even roasting and to prevent burning.
- **Watch and Smell:** The spices are done when they darken slightly and release a rich aroma. This usually takes just a few minutes, so keep an eye on the pan.
- **Cool Down:** Once roasted, remove the spices from the pan and let them cool completely. Roasting not only heightens flavor but also makes spices easier to grind.
- **Blending Spices**

- **Grinding:** Use a spice grinder or a mortar and pestle to grind the cooled, roasted spices into a fine powder.
- **Mixing:** If you're making a spice blend, this is when you mix the freshly ground spices. Make sure to do this in a bowl large enough to allow for thorough blending.
- **Taste Test:** After blending, give your spices a taste. If you feel a particular spice is not prominent enough, you can always roast and grind a bit more to add to the mix.
- **Storing Tips**
- **Air-Tight Containers:** Store your freshly roasted and blended spices in air-tight containers to maintain their flavor.
- **Label and Date:** Always label your spices and blends with the date they were made so you can keep track of their freshness.
- **Cool, Dark Place:** Store your containers in a cool, dark place away from direct sunlight. This helps to maintain their potency for a longer period.
- While it's great to make your blends, if you're short on time, go ahead and use store-bought spice mixes—but look for ones without added salt or other fillers.

BEVERAGES

When it comes to beverages in the Mediterranean diet, the focus is less on sugary drinks or high-fat lattes and more on simplicity and natural goodness. Water is the mainstay for hydration, while a little red wine adds not just flavor but also heart-friendly perks.

Water:
Water is the mainstay beverage in the Mediterranean diet, and for good reason. It keeps you hydrated, aids in digestion, and helps in nutrient absorption. Often, you'll find water infused with a slice of lemon or a sprig of mint for added flavor and nutritional benefits. Make water your go-to drink throughout the day for optimal hydration and overall well-being.

Wine:
Moderate wine consumption, particularly red wine, is a characteristic feature of the Mediterranean lifestyle. Why red? It's rich in polyphenols, naturally occurring compounds that have antioxidant properties. Polyphenols, such as resveratrol, have been shown to improve heart health by increasing 'good' HDL cholesterol and reducing 'bad' LDL cholesterol. But moderation is key. Consume one glass with dinner. Overindulgence can negate any health benefits and add unnecessary calories.

Tea:
Moroccan Mint Tea is a blend of green tea leaves and mint. It is rich in antioxidants, including a type of polyphenol called catechins. These compounds have been associated with lower risks of certain types of cancer and heart disease. Mint adds not just flavor but also a good dose of antioxidants and a soothing quality that can aid digestion.

Breakfast

SPANISH BREAKFAST TORTILLA

Start your day the Spanish way with a slice of this delicious potato and onion tortilla.

GLUTEN-FREE

Preparation Time: 10 minutes
Cooking Time: 20 minutes
Total Time: 30 minutes
Serves: 4-6

INGREDIENTS:
- 4 medium potatoes, thinly sliced
- 1 large onion, thinly sliced
- 6 large eggs
- 1/4 cup olive oil
- Salt and pepper to taste

INSTRUCTIONS:
1. Heat olive oil in a non-stick skillet over medium heat.
2. Add sliced potatoes and onions, and cook until tender but not browned.
3. In a separate bowl, whisk eggs and season with salt and pepper.
4. Pour the eggs over the cooked potatoes and onions, ensuring an even distribution.
5. Cover and cook on low heat until the eggs are set.
6. Flip the tortilla and cook for another 2-3 minutes.
7. Remove from heat, let it cool for a few minutes, and serve.

NUTRITIONAL INFORMATION (PER SERVING):
Calories: 250 kcal
Total Fat: 15 g
Total Carbohydrates: 20 g
Dietary Fiber: 2 g
Protein: 10 g
Sodium: 180 mg

MEDITERRANEAN SPINACH AND FETA OMELETTE

Kickstart your day with this protein-packed omelette, filled with the goodness of spinach and the rich flavors of feta and Mediterranean herbs.

SO QUICK!

Preparation Time: 10 minutes
Cooking Time: 5 minutes
Total Time: 15 minutes
Serves: 1

INGREDIENTS:
- 2 large eggs
- 1/4 cup milk or almond milk
- Salt and pepper, to taste
- 1 tablespoon olive oil
- 1/4 cup chopped onion
- 1/2 cup baby spinach leaves, washed
- 1/4 cup crumbled feta cheese
- Optional: A pinch of dried oregano or fresh herbs like basil or parsley for garnish

INSTRUCTIONS:
1. In a bowl, whisk together the eggs, milk, salt, and pepper until well combined.
2. Heat olive oil in a non-stick skillet over medium heat.
3. Add the chopped onion to the skillet and sauté for 2 minutes or until they begin to soften.
4. Add the baby spinach leaves to the skillet and sauté until wilted, which should take about 1-2 minutes.
5. Spread the sautéed onions and spinach evenly across the skillet and pour the whisked egg mixture over them.
6. Cook the egg mixture for 1-2 minutes or until it begins to set around the edges but is still slightly runny in the middle.
7. Sprinkle the crumbled feta cheese over one half of the omelette.
8. Carefully fold the omelette in half, covering the cheese.
9. Cook for an additional 1-2 minutes or until the omelette is fully cooked through but still moist.
10. Optionally, garnish with a pinch of dried oregano or fresh herbs before serving.

Chef's Note:
Feel free to add other Mediterranean veggies like bell peppers or sun-dried tomatoes to the omelette for more flavor and nutrition. This omelette pairs beautifully with whole-grain toast or a side of fruit.

NUTRITIONAL INFORMATION (PER SERVING):
Calories: 300 kcal
Total Fat: 23 g
    Monounsaturated Fat: 10 g
Total Carbohydrates: 6 g
    Dietary Fiber: 1 g
Protein: 16 g
Sodium: 540 mg

MEDITERRANEAN SCRAMBLED TOFU WITH SPINACH AND MUSHROOMS

Experience the Mediterranean flair in this vegan-friendly scrambled tofu dish, rich in protein and packed with nutritious spinach and mushrooms.

VEGAN

Preparation Time: 10 minutes
Cooking Time: 10 minutes
Total Time: 20 minutes
Serves: 4

INGREDIENTS:

- 1 block (14 oz) firm tofu, drained and crumbled
- 2 tablespoons olive oil
- 1 small onion, finely chopped
- 2 cloves garlic, minced
- 1 cup mushrooms, sliced
- 2 cups fresh spinach
- 1/4 cup nutritional yeast (optional)
- 1 teaspoon turmeric
- Salt and pepper, to taste
- Fresh herbs like oregano or basil for garnish (optional)

INSTRUCTIONS:

1. Heat olive oil in a large skillet over medium heat. Add chopped onion and sauté until translucent, about 2-3 minutes.
2. Add minced garlic and sliced mushrooms to the skillet and cook until the mushrooms are soft, approximately 5 minutes.
3. While the mushrooms are cooking, crumble the tofu into a separate bowl. Add turmeric, nutritional yeast if using, salt, and pepper. Mix well.
4. Add the crumbled tofu to the skillet and stir to combine with the mushroom mixture. Cook for about 3-4 minutes, stirring occasionally.
5. Fold in the fresh spinach and continue cooking until wilted, about 1-2 minutes.
6. Taste and adjust the seasoning with additional salt and pepper if needed. Garnish with fresh herbs like oregano or basil if desired.

Chef's Note:

This scrambled tofu dish can be easily customized. Feel free to add olives, sun-dried tomatoes, or even some vegan feta for different flavors. Great as a breakfast option or as a protein-packed addition to a Mediterranean-inspired lunch bowl.

NUTRITIONAL INFORMATION (PER SERVING):

Calories: 200 kcal
Total Fat: 12 g
    Monounsaturated Fat: 7 g
Total Carbohydrates: 10 g
    Dietary Fiber: 3 g
Protein: 16 g
Sodium: 220 mg

TOMATO AND BASIL FRITTATA

Make ahead and store in the fridge for up to three days for an easy savoury breakfast.

MEAL-PREP FRIENDLY

Preparation Time: 10 minutes
Cooking Time: 15 minutes
Total Time: 25 minutes
Serves: 4

INGREDIENTS:

- 8 large eggs
- 1/4 cup milk
- 1/2 teaspoon salt
- 1/4 teaspoon black pepper
- 2 tablespoons olive oil
- 1 small onion, finely chopped
- 1 garlic clove, minced
- 1 cup cherry tomatoes, halved
- 1/4 cup fresh basil leaves, chopped
- 1/2 cup grated Parmesan cheese

INSTRUCTIONS:

1. Preheat your oven to 400°F (200°C).
2. In a bowl, whisk together the eggs, milk, salt, and pepper. Set aside.
3. Heat olive oil in a 10-inch oven-safe skillet over medium heat. Add the chopped onion and garlic and sauté until translucent.
4. Add the halved cherry tomatoes to the skillet and cook for 2-3 minutes.
5. Pour the egg mixture over the vegetables in the skillet. Sprinkle with chopped basil and grated Parmesan cheese.
6. Let the frittata cook on the stovetop for 4-5 minutes, or until the edges begin to set.
7. Transfer the skillet to the preheated oven and bake for 8-10 minutes, or until the frittata is set in the center.
8. Remove the frittata from the oven and let it sit for a few minutes before slicing and serving.

Chef's Note:

Frittatas are wonderfully versatile. Here are some variations you can try:
1. Add sautéed spinach or kale for extra greens.
2. Substitute feta cheese for Parmesan for a tangier flavor.
3. Include diced bell peppers for added color and sweetness.
4. Incorporate cooked sausage or bacon for a meaty twist.
5. Serve with a side of mixed greens or a dollop of sour cream.

NUTRITIONAL INFORMATION (PER SERVING):

Calories: 290 kcal
Total Fat: 20 g
    Monounsaturated Fat: 10 g
Total Carbohydrates: 6 g
    Dietary Fiber: 1 g
Protein: 18 g

Sodium: 670 mg

GREEK YOGURT PARFAIT WITH HONEY AND WALNUTS

A healthy and quick Greek-inspired parfait layered with creamy yogurt, sweet honey, and crunchy walnuts.
MIX-AND-MATCH

Preparation Time: 5 minutes
Cooking Time: 0 minutes
Total Time: 5 minutes
Serves: 1-2

INGREDIENTS:
- 1 cup Greek yogurt
- 2 tablespoons honey
- 1/4 cup walnuts, chopped
- Fresh fruits (optional)

INSTRUCTIONS:
1. Layer a serving glass with Greek yogurt.
2. Drizzle honey over the yogurt layer.
3. Add a layer of chopped walnuts.
4. Repeat layers until the glass is full.
5. Optional: Top with fresh fruits of your choice.
6. Serve immediately or chill before serving.

Chef's note:
1) **Granola and Berries**: Layer Greek yogurt with granola and an assortment of fresh berries like strawberries, blueberries, and raspberries.
2) **Tropical Twist**: Add layers of chopped pineapple, mango, and a sprinkle of shredded coconut for a tropical flavor.
3) **Apple Cinnamon**: Mix in cooked apple slices with a dash of cinnamon and a drizzle of honey. Optionally, you can add some chopped walnuts for crunch.
4) **Chocolate and Banana**: Add layers of sliced bananas and chocolate chips or cacao nibs. Drizzle a small amount of chocolate syrup for added decadence.
5) **Nut and Seed Crunch**: Layer Greek yogurt with mixed nuts like almonds, walnuts, and cashews along with chia seeds and a drizzle of maple syrup.

NUTRITIONAL INFORMATION (PER SERVING):
Calories: 300 kcal
Total Fat: 20 g
Total Carbohydrates: 25 g
Dietary Fiber: 2 g
Protein: 15 g
Sodium: 50 mg

MEDITERRANEAN OVERNIGHT OATS

Elevate your toast game with this hearty, nutrient-packed combination of avocado and chickpeas, featuring Mediterranean flavors.
MIX-AND-MATCH

Preparation Time: 10 minutes
Cooking Time: 0 minutes
Total Time: 10 minutes (plus overnight chilling)
Serves: 2

INGREDIENTS:
- 1 cup rolled oats
- 1 cup almond milk
- 1/2 cup Greek yogurt
- 1/2 cup diced apple
- 1/4 cup almonds, chopped
- 1 tablespoon honey
- 1 teaspoon cinnamon

INSTRUCTIONS:
1. In a jar or bowl, mix together the rolled oats, almond milk, and Greek yogurt.
2. Add diced apple, almonds, honey, and cinnamon.
3. Stir well to combine.
4. Cover and refrigerate overnight.
5. Serve cold, or warm up in the microwave if preferred.

Chef's Note:
Try the combination pistachio and figs, peaches and almonds, or walnuts and apricots, depending on what's in season!

NUTRITIONAL INFORMATION (PER SERVING):
Calories: 320 kcal
Total Fat: 9 g
Monounsaturated Fat: 5 g
Total Carbohydrates: 45 g
Dietary Fiber: 7 g
Protein: 15 g
Sodium: 150 mg

MEDITERRANEAN AVOCADO AND CHICKPEA TOAST

Elevate your toast game with this hearty, nutrient-packed combination of avocado and chickpeas, featuring Mediterranean flavors.
VEGAN

Preparation Time: 10 minutes
Cooking Time: 5 minutes
Total Time: 15 minutes
Serves: 2

INGREDIENTS:
- 2 slices whole-grain bread
- 1 ripe avocado
- 1 cup canned chickpeas, drained and rinsed
- 1 small garlic clove, minced
- Juice of half a lemon
- Salt and pepper, to taste
- 1 tablespoon extra-virgin olive oil

- Optional toppings: cherry tomatoes, olives, red onion, herbs (parsley, basil, or cilantro)

INSTRUCTIONS:
1. Toast the whole-grain bread slices until they are crisp and golden.
2. In a small bowl, mash the ripe avocado using a fork until mostly smooth.
3. In another bowl, mix the chickpeas with minced garlic, lemon juice, salt, and pepper.
4. Heat the olive oil in a small skillet over medium heat. Add the chickpea mixture and sauté for 3-4 minutes until slightly golden. Remove from heat.
5. Spread the mashed avocado evenly over the toasted bread slices.
6. Spoon the sautéed chickpea mixture on top of the avocado layer.
7. Add optional toppings such as sliced cherry tomatoes, olives, red onion, or herbs, if desired.
8. Serve immediately, optionally drizzled with a little more extra-virgin olive oil or a sprinkle of sea salt.

Chef's Note:
This toast makes a great breakfast or snack. You can also double or triple the recipe for a simple yet satisfying lunch. The toast pairs wonderfully with a side salad or a bowl of vegetable soup.

NUTRITIONAL INFORMATION (PER SERVING):
Calories: 300 kcal
Total Fat: 16 g
    Monounsaturated Fat: 9 g
Total Carbohydrates: 32 g
    Dietary Fiber: 9 g
Protein: 9 g
Sodium: 250 mg

LEBANESE MANAKISH ZA'ATAR

Savor a Lebanese morning with this flatbread topped with a mix of za'atar and olive oil.
SPECIAL OCCASION

Preparation Time: 1 hour (includes dough rising)
Cooking Time: 10 minutes
Total Time: 1 hour 10 minutes
Serves: 4

INGREDIENTS:
1. 1 1/2 cups all-purpose flour
2. 1 teaspoon instant yeast
3. 1/2 teaspoon salt
4. 3/4 cup warm water
5. 1/4 cup olive oil
6. 3 tablespoons za'atar spice mix

INSTRUCTIONS:
1) In a bowl, combine flour, yeast, and salt.

2) Gradually add warm water and knead until a smooth dough forms.
3) Cover and let the dough rise for 1 hour or until doubled in size.
4) Preheat the oven to 425°F (220°C).
5) Divide the dough into 4 equal portions and roll into flat discs.
6) Mix olive oil with za'atar spice in a bowl.
7) Spread the za'atar mixture over each flatbread.
8) Bake in the preheated oven for 10 minutes or until edges are slightly golden.
9) Serve warm.

NUTRITIONAL INFORMATION (PER SERVING):
Calories: 290 kcal
Total Fat: 14 g
Total Carbohydrates: 36 g
Dietary Fiber: 2 g
Protein: 6 g
Sodium: 300 mg

CHIA SEED PUDDING WITH ALMOND MILK AND BERRIES

A simple yet decadent chia seed pudding that's rich in fiber and antioxidants, perfect for a guilt-free treat or breakfast.
LOW-CALORIES

Preparation Time: 5 minutes
Refrigeration Time: 4 hours or overnight
Total Time: 4 hours 5 minutes
Serves: 2

INGREDIENTS:
- 1/4 cup chia seeds
- 1 cup unsweetened almond milk
- 1 tablespoon maple syrup or honey
- 1 teaspoon vanilla extract
- 1/2 cup mixed berries (e.g., strawberries, blueberries, raspberries)
- A pinch of salt

INSTRUCTIONS:
1. In a mixing bowl, combine the chia seeds, unsweetened almond milk, maple syrup, and vanilla extract. Add a pinch of salt.
2. Whisk the mixture thoroughly to avoid clumping of chia seeds.
3. Cover the mixing bowl with a lid or plastic wrap and place it in the refrigerator.
4. Allow the chia seed mixture to set for at least 4 hours, or overnight for best results.
5. Once the chia pudding has set and achieved a gel-like consistency, give it a good stir.
6. Divide the chia pudding into serving bowls or jars.
7. Top each serving with an assortment of mixed berries before enjoying.

Chef's Note:

For a varied texture and additional nutrients, you can also add toppings like sliced almonds, coconut flakes, or a dollop of almond butter.

NUTRITIONAL INFORMATION (PER SERVING):

Calories: 160 kcal
Total Fat: 8 g
    Monounsaturated Fat: 1 g
Total Carbohydrates: 18 g
    Dietary Fiber: 9 g
Protein: 4 g
Sodium: 95 mg

SHAKSHUKA

Experience the Middle Eastern delight of poached eggs in a rich, spicy tomato sauce.

MIX-AND-MATCH

Preparation Time: 10 minutes
Cooking Time: 25 minutes
Total Time: 35 minutes
Serves: 4

INGREDIENTS:

- 4 large eggs
- 1 can (14.5 oz) diced tomatoes
- 1 onion, finely chopped
- 1 red bell pepper, diced
- 2 cloves garlic, minced
- 2 tablespoons olive oil
- 1 teaspoon cumin
- 1 teaspoon paprika
- Salt and pepper to taste
- Fresh parsley for garnish

INSTRUCTIONS:

1) In a large skillet, heat the olive oil over medium heat.
2) Add the chopped onion and cook until translucent.
3) Stir in the minced garlic and diced red bell pepper, cook for another 2-3 minutes.
4) Add the cumin, paprika, and diced tomatoes (with juice). Bring to a simmer.
5) Create small wells in the tomato mixture and gently crack the eggs into each well.
6) Cover the skillet and cook for 7-10 minutes, or until the egg whites are set.
7) Season with salt and pepper, and garnish with fresh parsley before serving.

Chef's Note:

Cheesy Shakshuka: Sprinkle some feta or mozzarella cheese on top of the eggs about 2 minutes before they're done

cooking. The cheese adds a creamy texture and a slightly tangy flavor.

Green Shakshuka: Swap out the red bell pepper for diced zucchini and spinach. Add the spinach last so it just wilts into the sauce. This gives a green, veggie-packed twist to the classic recipe.

Chorizo Shakshuka: Add diced chorizo to the skillet when cooking the onions. The spicy sausage adds a rich depth of flavor and some extra protein to the dish.

NUTRITIONAL INFORMATION (PER SERVING):

Calories: 220 kcal
Total Fat: 15 g
Monounsaturated Fat: 10 g
Total Carbohydrates: 14 g
Dietary Fiber: 4 g
Protein: 10 g
Sodium: 300 mg

TIROPITA

Enjoy a taste of Greece with these fluffy, cheesy phyllo pastries.

SPECIAL OCCASION

Preparation Time: 20 minutes
Cooking Time: 25 minutes
Total Time: 45 minutes
Serves: 12 pieces

INGREDIENTS:

- 1 package (16 oz) phyllo dough, thawed
- 2 cups feta cheese, crumbled
- 1 cup ricotta cheese
- 2 large eggs, beaten
- 1/2 cup unsalted butter, melted
- 1/2 teaspoon nutmeg
- Salt and pepper to taste

INSTRUCTIONS:

1. Preheat the oven to 375°F (190°C). Grease a baking sheet or line it with parchment paper.
2. In a mixing bowl, combine the crumbled feta, ricotta cheese, beaten eggs, nutmeg, salt, and pepper.
3. Lay out one sheet of phyllo dough on a clean surface and brush with melted butter.
4. Place a spoonful of the cheese mixture at one end of the phyllo sheet. Fold the sheet over the mixture, forming a triangle.
5. Place the filled triangle on the prepared baking sheet. Repeat with the remaining phyllo sheets and cheese mixture.
6. Brush the tops of the tiropitas with more melted butter.
7. Bake in the preheated oven for 20-25 minutes or until golden brown.
8. Serve warm.

NUTRITIONAL INFORMATION (PER SERVING):

Calories: 320 kcal

Total Fat: 23 g
Monounsaturated Fat: 10 g
Total Carbohydrates: 20 g
Dietary Fiber: 1 g
Protein: 11 g
Sodium: 600 mg

TURKISH MENEMEN

Explore the flavors of Turkey with this easy scrambled eggs and vegetable dish.
ONE-POT MEAL

Preparation Time: 10 minutes
Cooking Time: 15 minutes
Total Time: 25 minutes
Serves: 4

INGREDIENTS:

- 4 large eggs
- 1 onion, finely chopped
- 1 green bell pepper, diced
- 2 tomatoes, diced
- 2 tablespoons olive oil
- Salt and pepper to taste
- Fresh parsley for garnish

INSTRUCTIONS:

1. In a skillet, heat olive oil over medium heat.
2. Add the chopped onion and green bell pepper, sautéing until soft.
3. Add the diced tomatoes and cook for another 5 minutes.
4. Crack the eggs into the skillet, gently scrambling them into the mixture.
5. Cook until the eggs are done to your liking.
6. Season with salt and pepper.
7. Garnish with fresh parsley before serving.

NUTRITIONAL INFORMATION (PER SERVING):
Calories: 190 kcal
Total Fat: 14 g
Monounsaturated Fat: 8 g
Total Carbohydrates: 10 g
Dietary Fiber: 2 g
Protein: 9 g
Sodium: 220 mg

SPANAKOPITA ~ GREEK SPINACH AND FETA PIE

This savory blend of spinach and feta wrapped in flaky filo pastry is the perfect choice for a family weekend brunch or a sunny picnic.
KID FRIENDLY

Preparation Time: 20 minutes
Cooking Time: 45 minutes
Total Time: 65 minutes
Serves: 6

INGREDIENTS:

- 1 lb fresh spinach, washed and chopped
- 1 cup crumbled feta cheese
- 1 medium onion, finely chopped
- 2 cloves garlic, minced
- 2 tablespoons olive oil
- 1/2 cup fresh dill, chopped
- 3 large eggs, beaten
- 10 sheets filo pastry
- Salt and pepper to taste

INSTRUCTIONS:

1. Preheat your oven to 350°F (175°C).
2. In a large pan, heat olive oil over medium heat. Sauté the onion and garlic until translucent.
3. Add the spinach to the pan and cook until wilted. Remove from heat and let it cool.
4. In a large mixing bowl, combine the cooled spinach mixture with feta, dill, beaten eggs, salt, and pepper.
5. Layer 5 filo sheets in a baking dish, brushing each with olive oil. Spread the spinach mixture over the filo.
6. Top with the remaining 5 sheets of filo, brushing each with olive oil.
7. Bake in the preheated oven for 40-45 minutes or until golden brown.

Chef's Note:
Serve with Greek yogurt or a side salad for a fuller meal.

NUTRITIONAL INFORMATION (PER SERVING):
Calories: 250 kcal
Total Fat: 16 g
Monounsaturated Fat: 6 g
Total Carbohydrates: 24 g
Dietary Fiber: 3 g
Protein: 12 g
Sodium: 480 mg

CYPRIOT HALLOUMI & OLIVE SANDWICH

Indulge in a hearty sandwich made with salty halloumi cheese and Kalamata olives.
MEAL-PREP FRIENDLY

Preparation Time: 10 minutes
Cooking Time: 10 minutes
Total Time: 20 minutes
Serves: 2

INGREDIENTS:

- 4 slices of whole grain bread
- 200g halloumi cheese, sliced
- 10 Kalamata olives, pitted and sliced

- 1 small red onion, thinly sliced
- 1/2 cucumber, sliced
- 2 tablespoons olive tapenade (optional)
- Olive oil for frying

INSTRUCTIONS:
1. Heat a non-stick pan with a little olive oil over medium heat.
2. Fry the halloumi slices until golden brown on both sides.
3. Spread olive tapenade (if using) on two slices of bread.
4. Layer with fried halloumi, olives, red onion, and cucumber.
5. Top with the remaining bread slices and serve.

Chef's Note:
The sandwich can be prepared in advance and packed for a quick breakfast on the go. If you fired up some halloumi the night before for a salad just save some for this sandwich and you'll have dinner and lunch for the next day in one sitting.

NUTRITIONAL INFORMATION (PER SERVING):
Calories: 380 kcal
Total Fat: 25 g
Monounsaturated Fat: 14 g
Total Carbohydrates: 27 g
Dietary Fiber: 4 g
Protein: 15 g
Sodium: 900 mg

MALTESE FTIRA ~ TUNA SANDWICH

Experience the authentic taste of Malta with this savory tuna sandwich with Mediterranean flavors.
SO QUICK!

Preparation Time: 10 minutes
Cooking Time: 0 minutes
Total Time: 10 minutes
Serves: 2

INGREDIENTS:
- 2 Maltese ftira (or substitute with ciabatta)
- 1 can of tuna in oil, drained
- 2 tablespoons capers
- 10 black olives, pitted and chopped
- 1 small red onion, thinly sliced
- 2 tomatoes, sliced
- 1 tablespoon olive oil
- Salt and pepper to taste

INSTRUCTIONS:
1. Split the ftira or ciabatta in half horizontally.
2. Flake the tuna and spread it over the bottom half of the bread.
3. Top with capers, olives, red onion, and tomatoes.
4. Drizzle with olive oil, season with salt and pepper, and cover with the other half of the bread.

5. Press lightly and slice into halves. Serve immediately.

NUTRITIONAL INFORMATION (PER SERVING):
Calories: 320 kcal
Total Fat: 10 g
Monounsaturated Fat: 6 g
Total Carbohydrates: 35 g
Dietary Fiber: 3 g
Protein: 20 g
Sodium: 580 mg

SARDINIAN HONEY & RICOTTA TOASTS

Indulge in the sweetness of honey combined with creamy ricotta on crisp toasted bread.
KID FRIENDLY

Preparation Time: 5 minutes
Cooking Time: 5 minutes
Total Time: 10 minutes
Serves: 4

INGREDIENTS:
- 4 slices of rustic bread
- 1 cup fresh ricotta cheese
- 4 tablespoons Sardinian honey (or any available honey)
- Chopped pistachios for garnish
- Zest of 1 lemon

INSTRUCTIONS:
1. Toast the bread slices until golden brown.
2. Spread a generous layer of ricotta on each toasted slice.
3. Drizzle with honey, sprinkle with lemon zest, and top with chopped pistachios.
4. Serve immediately.

Chef's Note:
This toast can be paired with fresh fruit for a refreshing and balanced breakfast.

NUTRITIONAL INFORMATION (PER SERVING):
Calories: 250 kcal
Total Fat: 10 g
Monounsaturated Fat: 4 g
Total Carbohydrates: 32 g
Dietary Fiber: 2 g
Protein: 8 g
Sodium: 180 mg

PA AMB TOMAQUET ~ CATALAN TOMATO BREAD

Experience the simple yet flavorful Catalan classic, perfect for a quick and satisfying breakfast.
SO QUICK!

Preparation Time: 5 minutes
Cooking Time: 5 minutes

Total Time: 10 minutes
Serves: 4

INGREDIENTS:
- 4 slices of rustic bread
- 2 ripe tomatoes, halved
- 2 cloves garlic, peeled
- Extra virgin olive oil
- Salt to taste

INSTRUCTIONS:
1) Toast the bread slices until crisp and golden brown.
2) Rub the garlic cloves over the toasted sides of the bread.
3) Grate the tomatoes directly over the bread, allowing the pulp to coat the toast.
4) Drizzle with a generous amount of olive oil and sprinkle with salt.
5) Serve immediately.

Chef's Note:
I make a Mediterranean inspired Eggs Benedict adding to the tomato bread a poached egg, a dollop of ricotta cheese whipped with black pepper on top, and slices of avocado just for the kick of it!

NUTRITIONAL INFORMATION (PER SERVING):
Calories: 160 kcal
Total Fat: 6 g
Monounsaturated Fat: 4 g
Total Carbohydrates: 25 g
Dietary Fiber: 2 g
Protein: 4 g
Sodium: 270 mg

GREEK YOGURT AND HONEY POMEGRANATE SMOOTHIE

A creamy, tangy delight with a hint of sweetness and the antioxidants of pomegranate.
HEART-HEALTHY

Preparation Time: 7 minutes
Total Time: 7 minutes
Serves: 2

INGREDIENTS:
- 1 cup Greek yogurt
- 1/2 cup pomegranate juice
- 1/2 cup pomegranate seeds
- 2 tablespoons honey (or to taste)
- A pinch of ground cardamom
- Ice cubes (optional)

INSTRUCTIONS:
1. Combine Greek yogurt, pomegranate juice, pomegranate seeds, honey, and cardamom in a blender.

2. Blend until smooth.
3. If desired, add ice cubes and blend again for a cooler smoothie.
4. Pour into glasses and serve immediately.

NUTRITIONAL INFORMATION (PER SERVING):
Calories: 180 kcal
Total Fat: 1 g
Total Carbohydrates: 37 g
Dietary Fiber: 2 g
Protein: 9 g
Sodium: 45 mg

MEDITERRANEAN BREAKFAST SMOOTHIE

A vibrant blend of fruits, nuts, and Greek yogurt for a healthy start to your day.
SO QUICK!

Preparation Time: 5 minutes
Cooking Time: 0 minutes
Total Time: 5 minutes
Serves: 1

INGREDIENTS:
- 1 cup mixed berries (strawberries, blueberries, raspberries)
- 1 banana
- 1/2 cup Greek yogurt
- 1/2 cup almond milk
- 1 tablespoon honey
- 1 tablespoon chia seeds (optional)

INSTRUCTIONS:
1. Add all ingredients to a blender.
2. Blend on high speed until smooth and creamy.
3. Pour into a glass and enjoy immediately.

Chef's Note:
You can use frozen berries to make the smoothie colder and more refreshing.

NUTRITIONAL INFORMATION (PER SERVING):
Calories: 330 kcal
Total Fat: 5 g
Monounsaturated Fat: 1 g
Total Carbohydrates: 60 g
Dietary Fiber: 9 g
Protein: 14 g
Sodium: 80 mg

MEDITERRANEAN WATERMELON SMOOTHIE

Cool down and refresh yourself with this Mediterranean Watermelon Smoothie, rich in antioxidants and hydration with a hint of fresh mint and basil.

SUPER-QUICK!

Preparation Time: 10 minutes
Cooking Time: 0 minutes
Total Time: 10 minutes
Serves: 2

INGREDIENTS:

- 3 cups watermelon, cubed and chilled
- 1 cup coconut water
- 5-6 fresh mint leaves
- 5-6 fresh basil leaves
- 1 tablespoon honey or maple syrup (optional)
- 1/2 lemon, juiced
- Ice cubes (optional)

INSTRUCTIONS:

1. Add the cubed watermelon to a blender.
2. Pour in the coconut water for added hydration and a tropical twist.
3. Add fresh mint leaves and basil leaves for a Mediterranean flair.
4. If you prefer a sweeter smoothie, add honey or maple syrup at this stage.
5. Squeeze in the juice of half a lemon for a tangy kick.
6. If you like your smoothie extra cold, add some ice cubes.
7. Blend all the ingredients until smooth and creamy, about 30 seconds to 1 minute.
8. Taste and adjust the sweetness or acidity as needed. If the smoothie is too thick, add more coconut water and blend again.
9. Pour into glasses and serve immediately.

Chef's Note:
For added texture and nutrients, you could toss in a tablespoon of chia seeds or flaxseeds before blending. The smoothie is best enjoyed immediately but can be stored in the fridge for up to 24 hours.

NUTRITIONAL INFORMATION (PER SERVING):
Calories: 80 kcal
Total Fat: 0 g
    Monounsaturated Fat: 0 g
Total Carbohydrates: 20 g
    Dietary Fiber: 1 g
Protein: 1 g
Sodium: 95 mg

SMOOTHIE WITH BLUEBERRIES, SPINACH, AND ALMOND BUTTER

Energize your day with this nutrient-packed smoothie, featuring antioxidant-rich blueberries and protein-filled almond butter, with a hint of Mediterranean herbs for a unique flavor twist.

SUPER-QUICK!

Preparation Time: 5 minutes
Cooking Time: 0 minutes
Total Time: 5 minutes
Serves: 2

INGREDIENTS:

- 1 cup frozen blueberries
- 1 cup fresh spinach leaves
- 2 tablespoons almond butter
- 1 cup unsweetened almond milk (or any milk of your choice)
- 1 teaspoon fresh lemon zest
- 1/2 teaspoon dried thyme and rosemary (optional)
- 1 tablespoon chia seeds (optional)
- 1 teaspoon honey or agave nectar (optional)

INSTRUCTIONS:

1. In a blender, combine the frozen blueberries, spinach, almond butter, and almond milk.
2. Add the lemon zest and dried thyme or rosemary, if using.
3. Blend on high speed until smooth and creamy. If the smoothie is too thick, add a little more almond milk and blend again.
4. If you're using chia seeds, add them to the blender and pulse a few times to mix them in.
5. Taste the smoothie and add honey or agave nectar if you prefer it sweeter.
6. Pour into glasses and serve immediately.

Chef's Note:
For extra protein and creaminess, you can add a scoop of Greek yogurt. To switch up the flavors, try adding other Mediterranean herbs like basil or oregano, or substitute the almond butter with tahini for a different nutty twist.

NUTRITIONAL INFORMATION (PER SERVING):
Calories: 200 kcal
Total Fat: 10 g
    Monounsaturated Fat: 4 g
Total Carbohydrates: 25 g
    Dietary Fiber: 5 g
Protein: 5 g
Sodium: 100 mg

SARDINIAN FAVA BEAN SPREAD ON CROSTINI

A deliciously savory Sardinian-inspired spread made with fava beans and herbs.

VEGAN

Preparation Time: 10 minutes
Cooking Time: 30 minutes
Total Time: 40 minutes
Serves: 4

INGREDIENTS:

- 1 cup dried fava beans, soaked overnight
- 2 cloves garlic, minced
- 1/4 cup extra virgin olive oil
- Juice of 1 lemon
- Salt and pepper to taste
- 1 loaf of Italian bread, sliced and toasted

INSTRUCTIONS:

1. Boil the soaked fava beans in fresh water until soft, approximately 20-30 minutes.
2. Drain the beans and let them cool.
3. In a food processor, combine boiled fava beans, minced garlic, olive oil, lemon juice, salt, and pepper.
4. Blend until smooth.
5. Spread the fava bean mixture on toasted Italian bread slices and serve.

Chef's Note:

Garnish with a sprinkle of red pepper flakes or a drizzle of olive oil if desired.

NUTRITIONAL INFORMATION (PER SERVING):

Calories: 210 kcal
Total Fat: 12 g
Monounsaturated Fat: 6 g
Total Carbohydrates: 19 g
Dietary Fiber: 4 g
Protein: 6 g
Sodium: 150 mg

ISRAELI SABICH SANDWICH

Experience a morning in Tel Aviv with this colorful and delicious sandwich.

KID FRIENDLY

Preparation Time: 15 minutes
Cooking Time: 10 minutes
Total Time: 25 minutes
Serves: 2

INGREDIENTS:

1. 2 pita breads
2. 2 hard-boiled eggs, sliced
3. 1 small eggplant, sliced and fried
4. 1 small tomato, sliced
5. 1/4 cup tahini sauce
6. 1/4 cup hummus
7. Pickles, to taste
8. Fresh parsley, chopped, for garnish

INSTRUCTIONS:

- Spread hummus inside each pita bread.
- Layer slices of hard-boiled eggs, fried eggplant, and fresh tomato.
- Add pickles to taste.
- Drizzle tahini sauce over the ingredients.
- Garnish with fresh parsley.
- Serve immediately.

NUTRITIONAL INFORMATION (PER SERVING):

Calories: 350 kcal
Total Fat: 18 g
Monounsaturated Fat: 4 g
Total Carbohydrates: 35 g
Dietary Fiber: 6 g
Protein: 12 g
Sodium: 650 mg

MOROCCAN SPICED QUINOA PORRIDGE

Wake up to the exotic flavors of Morocco with this spiced quinoa porridge.

GLUTEN-FREE

Preparation Time: 5 minutes
Cooking Time: 15 minutes
Total Time: 20 minutes
Serves: 2

INGREDIENTS:

- 1 cup cooked quinoa
- 1 cup almond milk
- 1 teaspoon ground cinnamon
- 1/2 teaspoon ground cardamom
- 1 tablespoon honey or maple syrup
- Fresh fruits for topping (e.g., banana, berries)
- Chopped almonds for garnish

INSTRUCTIONS:

- In a saucepan, combine cooked quinoa and almond milk.
- Add the ground cinnamon and cardamom.
- Cook over medium heat, stirring frequently, until the mixture thickens, about 10 minutes.
- Stir in honey or maple syrup.
- Transfer to bowls and top with fresh fruits.
- Garnish with chopped almonds.
- Serve warm.

NUTRITIONAL INFORMATION (PER SERVING):

Calories: 250 kcal
Total Fat: 6 g
Monounsaturated Fat: 2 g

Total Carbohydrates: 40 g
Dietary Fiber: 6 g
Protein: 8 g
Sodium: 100 mg

MULTIGRAIN PANCAKES OR WAFFLES

This Mediterranean-inspired breakfast is both hearty and healthy, featuring a blend of whole grains and a touch of sweetness.

MEAL-PREP FRIENDLY

Preparation Time: 10 minutes
Cooking Time: 15 minutes
Total Time: 25 minutes
Serves: 4 (about 8 pancakes or 4 waffles)

INGREDIENTS:

- 1 cup whole-grain flour (like spelt or whole-wheat)
- 1/4 cup oat bran
- 1/4 cup cornmeal
- 1 tablespoon sugar (or substitute with a natural sweetener)
- 1 teaspoon baking powder
- 1/2 teaspoon baking soda
- 1/4 teaspoon salt
- 1 cup low-fat milk (or almond milk for a dairy-free option)
- 1 large egg (or flax egg for a vegan option)
- 2 tablespoons olive oil
- 1 teaspoon vanilla extract
- Fresh fruit for topping (like berries or sliced bananas)

INSTRUCTIONS:

1) In a large mixing bowl, whisk together the whole-grain flour, oat bran, cornmeal, sugar, baking powder, baking soda, and salt.
2) In another bowl, mix together the low-fat milk, egg, olive oil, and vanilla extract.
3) Pour the wet ingredients into the dry ingredients and stir until just combined. The batter will be lumpy.
4) Heat a non-stick skillet over medium heat for pancakes or preheat a waffle iron.
5) For pancakes: Pour 1/4 cup of the batter onto the skillet. Cook until bubbles appear on the surface, then flip and cook until golden brown. For waffles: Pour enough batter into the waffle iron to just cover the waffle grid. Close and cook as per the manufacturer's instructions until golden brown.
6) Serve warm topped with fresh fruit.

Chef's Note:

Feel free to add a sprinkle of cinnamon or a handful of nuts for extra flavor and texture. These pancakes and waffles freeze well, so you can make a larger batch and enjoy them later.

NUTRITIONAL INFORMATION (PER SERVING):

Calories: 210 kcal
Total Fat: 7 g
Monounsaturated Fat: 4 g
Total Carbohydrates: 31 g
Dietary Fiber: 4 g
Protein: 7 g
Sodium: 300 mg

WHOLE-GRAIN MEDITERRANEAN FRENCH TOAST WITH SLICED BANANAS

Indulge in a Mediterranean twist on a breakfast classic, featuring whole-grain bread and bananas for a fiber-rich and delicious start to your day.

HEART-HEALTHY

Preparation Time: 10 minutes
Cooking Time: 10 minutes
Total Time: 20 minutes
Serves: 4

INGREDIENTS:

- 8 slices whole-grain bread
- 3 large eggs
- 1 cup almond milk (or any milk of your choice)
- 1 teaspoon vanilla extract
- 1/2 teaspoon cinnamon
- 2 tablespoons olive oil
- 2 ripe bananas, sliced
- 1/4 cup chopped walnuts
- 1 tablespoon honey or maple syrup (optional)

INSTRUCTIONS:

1. In a medium-sized mixing bowl, whisk together the eggs, almond milk, vanilla extract, and cinnamon.
2. Heat a large non-stick skillet over medium heat and add a tablespoon of olive oil.
3. Dip each slice of whole-grain bread into the egg mixture, making sure both sides are well-coated.
4. Place the soaked bread slices in the skillet and cook for 3–4 minutes per side, or until golden brown.
5. Remove the French toast from the skillet and keep warm while you cook the remaining slices, adding more olive oil as needed.
6. Arrange the cooked French toast on plates and top with sliced bananas and chopped walnuts.
7. Drizzle with honey or maple syrup if desired, and serve immediately.

Chef's Note:

For extra protein, you can serve this French toast with a dollop of Greek yogurt or a sprinkle of chia seeds. This dish also pairs well with other fresh fruits like berries or apple slices for added natural sweetness.

NUTRITIONAL INFORMATION (PER SERVING):

Calories: 350 kcal
Total Fat: 15 g
　　Monounsaturated Fat: 7 g

Total Carbohydrates: 45 g
Dietary Fiber: 8 g
Protein: 12 g
Sodium: 300 mg

TOAST WITH EGG AND AVOCADO – MEDITERRANEAN STYLE

Kickstart your morning with this balanced breakfast, featuring whole-grain toast, creamy avocado, and a perfectly cooked egg, seasoned with Mediterranean herbs.
HEART-HEALTHY

Preparation Time: 5 minutes
Cooking Time: 5 minutes
Total Time: 10 minutes
Serves: 1

INGREDIENTS:
- 1 slice whole-grain bread
- 1/2 ripe avocado
- 1 large egg
- 1 tablespoon olive oil
- Salt and pepper to taste
- Optional: A sprinkle of oregano or za'atar, a pinch of red pepper flakes

INSTRUCTIONS:
1) Toast the whole-grain bread to your liking.
2) While the toast is browning, heat olive oil in a non-stick skillet over medium heat.
3) Crack the egg into the skillet and cook until the whites are set but the yolk remains runny, about 3-4 minutes. Season with salt and pepper.
4) Mash the ripe avocado and spread it over the toasted bread.
5) Gently place the cooked egg on top of the avocado.
6) Season with a sprinkle of oregano or za'atar and a pinch of red pepper flakes, if using.

Chef's Note:
To transform this into a more substantial meal, you can add sliced tomatoes, arugula, or smoked salmon on top.

NUTRITIONAL INFORMATION (PER SERVING):
Calories: 300 kcal
Total Fat: 23 g
Monounsaturated Fat: 15 g
Total Carbohydrates: 19 g
Dietary Fiber: 7 g
Protein: 9 g
Sodium: 250 mg

MEDITERRANEAN QUINOA PORRIDGE WITH FRESH BERRIES AND NUTS

Start your day with a nourishing bowl of Mediterranean Quinoa Porridge, adorned with fresh berries and a crunch of nuts. This high-protein, gluten-free breakfast option is full of flavor and will keep you satiated for hours.
VEGAN

Preparation Time: 5 minutes
Cooking Time: 20 minutes
Total Time: 25 minutes
Serves: 4

INGREDIENTS:
- 1 cup quinoa, rinsed and drained
- 2 cups almond milk (or other non-dairy milk)
- 1/4 cup honey or maple syrup (for a vegan option)
- 1 teaspoon vanilla extract
- 1/2 teaspoon ground cinnamon
- 1/4 teaspoon ground nutmeg
- 1 cup mixed fresh berries (strawberries, blueberries, raspberries, etc.)
- 1/4 cup chopped nuts (almonds, walnuts, or pecans)
- Optional: Additional almond milk for serving

INSTRUCTIONS:
1. In a medium saucepan, combine the quinoa and almond milk. Place the pan over medium-high heat and bring the mixture to a boil.
2. Once boiling, reduce the heat to low and simmer, uncovered, for about 15 minutes or until the quinoa is tender and has absorbed most of the liquid. Stir occasionally to prevent sticking.
3. Add the honey or maple syrup, vanilla extract, cinnamon, and nutmeg to the saucepan. Stir well to combine.
4. Remove the saucepan from the heat and allow the porridge to sit for 5 minutes to thicken.
5. Divide the porridge into serving bowls. Top with a generous portion of fresh berries and chopped nuts.
6. Optionally, you can add a splash of additional almond milk for a creamier texture.

Chef's Note:
Feel free to customize this recipe with your favorite fruits and nuts. You can also add some chia seeds or flaxseeds for extra fiber and nutrients.

NUTRITIONAL INFORMATION (PER SERVING):
Calories: 290 kcal
Total Fat: 8 g
Monounsaturated Fat: 4 g
Total Carbohydrates: 48 g
Dietary Fiber: 6 g
Protein: 8 g
Sodium: 95 mg

MEDITERRANEAN PISTACHIO AND OAT PORRIDGE

Start your morning with a bowl of this nourishing and flavorful porridge, which combines hearty oats with the rich texture of pistachios and a touch of natural sweetness.

SUPER-QUICK!

Preparation Time: 5 minutes
Cooking Time: 10 minutes
Total Time: 15 minutes
Serves: 2

INGREDIENTS:
- 1 cup rolled oats
- 2 cups almond milk (or any other non-dairy or dairy milk)
- 1/4 cup pistachios, shelled and roughly chopped
- 1 tablespoon honey or maple syrup
- 1/2 teaspoon ground cinnamon
- Pinch of salt
- Fresh fruit for topping (e.g., banana slices, berries)
- Additional chopped pistachios for garnish

INSTRUCTIONS:
1. In a medium saucepan, combine the rolled oats and almond milk. Place over medium heat.
2. Bring the mixture to a low boil, then reduce heat to low.
3. Add the chopped pistachios, honey (or maple syrup), ground cinnamon, and a pinch of salt.
4. Stir continuously, allowing the mixture to thicken. This should take about 7-10 minutes.
5. Once the porridge reaches your desired consistency, remove it from heat.
6. Divide the porridge into bowls, and top with fresh fruit and additional chopped pistachios.
7. Serve immediately, while warm.

Chef's Note:
For a vegan option, use non-dairy milk and maple syrup instead of honey. You can also add chia seeds or flax seeds for an extra boost of nutrients.

NUTRITIONAL INFORMATION (PER SERVING):
Calories: 270 kcal
Total Fat: 9 g
Monounsaturated Fat: 4 g
Total Carbohydrates: 40 g
Dietary Fiber: 6 g
Protein: 8 g
Sodium: 180 mg

MEDITERRANEAN BARLEY PORRIDGE WITH DRIED FRUITS

A heartwarming, fiber-rich porridge that transports you to the Mediterranean, thanks to a medley of dried fruits and a touch of spice.

HEART-HEALTHY

Preparation Time: 5 minutes
Cooking Time: 30 minutes
Total Time: 35 minutes
Serves: 4

INGREDIENTS:
- 1 cup barley
- 4 cups water
- 1/2 cup mixed dried fruits (raisins, apricots, figs), chopped
- 1/4 cup almonds or walnuts, chopped
- 1 teaspoon cinnamon
- 1/2 teaspoon cardamom powder
- 2 tablespoons honey or maple syrup
- Pinch of salt
- Zest of 1 orange for garnish (optional)

INSTRUCTIONS:
1. In a large saucepan, bring 4 cups of water to a boil.
2. Add the barley and a pinch of salt to the boiling water, stirring occasionally.
3. Reduce heat to medium-low, cover, and simmer for 25-30 minutes or until the barley is tender. Make sure to stir occasionally to prevent sticking.
4. While the barley is cooking, chop the dried fruits and nuts.
5. When the barley is done, remove it from heat and drain any excess water.
6. Stir in the chopped dried fruits, nuts, cinnamon, and cardamom powder.
7. Drizzle honey or maple syrup for sweetness. Mix well to combine all the ingredients.
8. Divide the porridge into serving bowls, and garnish with orange zest if desired.

Chef's Note:
Feel free to experiment with other dried fruits or nuts based on availability or personal preference. The porridge can be stored in an airtight container in the fridge for up to 3 days. Reheat before serving.

NUTRITIONAL INFORMATION (PER SERVING):
Calories: 250 kcal
Total Fat: 3 g
    Monounsaturated Fat: 1 g
    Polyunsaturated Fat: 1 g
Total Carbohydrates: 51 g
    Dietary Fiber: 11 g
Protein: 6 g
Sodium: 80 mg

Meat Dishes

CHICKEN SKILLET-STYLE SHAWARMA WITH TAHINI SAUCE – SHWARMA DAJAJ BIL TAHINA

This easy, quick version of Shawarma brings the Middle Eastern classic to your table in less than 30 minutes. It's a low-calorie, protein-packed dish that's perfect for a quick meal.

ONE-POT MEAL

Preparation Time: 10 minutes
Cooking Time: 8 minutes
Total Time: 18 minutes
Serves: 4 servings

INGREDIENTS:

- 2 tablespoons extra-virgin olive oil
- 1 yellow onion, finely diced
- 2 red or green bell peppers, trimmed, seeded, and cut into 1-inch pieces
- 2 cups shredded cooked chicken meat
- 1 teaspoon ground coriander
- 1/2 teaspoon ground cumin
- 1/2 teaspoon unrefined sea salt or salt
- 1/4 teaspoon freshly ground black pepper
- 2 cups diced tomatoes
- 4 pieces whole-wheat pita bread, halved, to serve
- 1 cup Tahini Sauce
- Quick Italian Pickles, to serve (optional)

INSTRUCTIONS:

1. Heat the olive oil in a large skillet over medium heat.
2. Add the diced onion and bell peppers. Sauté until lightly golden, about 3 minutes.
3. Stir in the shredded cooked chicken, ground coriander, ground cumin, salt, and pepper.
4. Add the diced tomatoes and mix well.
5. Cover and cook until peppers are tender, approximately 5 minutes.
6. When the chicken mixture is finished cooking, heat the bread. Scoop equal amounts of chicken mixture into the pockets of pita halves. Drizzle Tahini Sauce over the top.
7. Serve warm, with pickled vegetables on the side.

Chef's Note:
If you're using chicken leftovers, this is an excellent way to reimagine them into a new dish. You can also substitute the chicken with turkey or tofu for a healthier/vegetarian variation.

NUTRITIONAL INFORMATION (PER SERVING):
Calories: 250 kcal
Total Fat: 10 g
Monounsaturated Fat: 6 g
Total Carbohydrates: 20 g
Dietary Fiber: 4 g
Protein: 20 g
Sodium: 300 mg

POLPETTE ~ ITALIAN BEEF MEATBALLS

Wholesome meatballs made with lean beef, perfect as an appetizer or main course.

KID-FRIENDLY

Preparation Time: 15 minutes
Cooking Time: 15 minutes
Total Time: 30 minutes
Serves: 4

INGREDIENTS:

- 1 lb lean ground beef
- 1 egg
- 1/2 cup breadcrumbs, preferably whole-grain
- 1/4 cup grated Parmesan cheese
- 2 cloves garlic, minced
- 1 teaspoon dried oregano
- Salt and pepper to taste
- 1 tablespoon olive oil

INSTRUCTIONS:

1) In a large bowl, combine beef, egg, breadcrumbs, Parmesan, garlic, oregano, salt, and pepper. Mix well.
2) Shape the mixture into 1-inch meatballs.
3) Heat olive oil in a skillet over medium heat. Cook the meatballs for about 10-12 minutes, turning occasionally, until browned and cooked through.

Chef's Note:
These meatballs can be served with a simple tomato sauce and whole-grain spaghetti. They are also excellent in a sub sandwich with a slice of melted cheese.

NUTRITIONAL INFORMATION (PER SERVING):
Calories: 250 kcal
Total Fat: 11 g
Monounsaturated Fat: 5 g
Total Carbohydrates: 14 g
Dietary Fiber: 1 g
Protein: 25 g
Sodium: 320 mg

MOROCCAN CHICKEN COUSCOUS

SPECIAL OCCASION

Preparation Time: 20 minutes
Cooking Time: 30 minutes
Total Time: 50 minutes
Serves: 4

INGREDIENTS:

- 4 boneless, skinless chicken breasts, cut into bite-sized pieces
- 1 1/2 cups couscous
- 1 3/4 cups chicken broth, divided
- 1 tablespoon olive oil
- 1 large onion, chopped
- 2 cloves garlic, minced
- 1 teaspoon ground cumin
- 1 teaspoon ground coriander
- 1/2 teaspoon ground cinnamon
- 1/2 teaspoon turmeric
- 1/2 teaspoon paprika
- Salt and pepper, to taste
- 1 cup diced carrots
- 1 cup diced bell peppers
- 1 can (15 oz) chickpeas, drained and rinsed
- 1/4 cup raisins or dried apricots, chopped
- 1/4 cup fresh cilantro, chopped for garnish

INSTRUCTIONS:

1. In a large pan, heat olive oil over medium heat. Add the onions and garlic, sautéing until soft.
2. Add the chicken pieces to the pan, and season with cumin, coriander, cinnamon, turmeric, paprika, salt, and pepper. Cook until the chicken is browned on all sides.
3. Add the carrots, bell peppers, and 1 cup of chicken broth to the pan. Cover and simmer for about 15 minutes, or until the chicken is cooked through and the vegetables are tender.
4. While the chicken is simmering, prepare the couscous. Bring the remaining 3/4 cup of chicken broth to a boil in a separate pot. Stir in the couscous, cover, and remove from heat. Let it sit for 5 minutes, then fluff with a fork.
5. Add the cooked couscous, chickpeas, and raisins to the chicken and vegetable mixture. Stir well to combine.
6. Garnish with chopped cilantro before serving.

Chef's Note:
Feel free to substitute quinoa for couscous for a gluten-free option. You can also add other vegetables like zucchini or eggplant, depending on your preference and season. Serve with a side of Moroccan mint tea for an authentic experience.

NUTRITIONAL INFORMATION (PER SERVING):
Calories: 550 kcal
Total Fat: 8 g
Saturated Fat: 2 g
Total Carbohydrates: 80 g
Dietary Fiber: 8 g
Protein: 40 g
Sodium: 420 mg

SICILIAN STUFFED VEAL ROAST – ARROSTO DI VITELLO

A succulent stuffed veal roast inspired by Sicilian cuisine. This flavorful dish is perfect for special occasions and offers a blend of protein and Mediterranean herbs.

SPECIAL OCCASION

Preparation Time: 20 minutes
Cooking Time: 90 minutes
Total Time: 110 minutes
Serves: 6 servings

INGREDIENTS:

- 2 lbs (900g) veal roast
- 1/4 cup extra-virgin olive oil
- 1 onion, finely chopped
- 2 cloves garlic, minced
- 1 cup breadcrumbs
- 1/4 cup pine nuts
- 1/4 cup raisins
- Zest of 1 lemon
- 1 teaspoon dried oregano
- Salt and pepper to taste
- 1/2 cup white wine
- 1/2 cup beef or vegetable broth

INSTRUCTIONS:

1) Preheat the oven to 350°F (175°C).
2) In a skillet, heat 2 tablespoons of olive oil over medium heat. Add the onions and garlic and sauté until translucent, about 3 minutes.
3) Add breadcrumbs, pine nuts, and raisins to the skillet. Stir well to combine.
4) Remove the skillet from heat and add lemon zest, dried oregano, salt, and pepper. Mix thoroughly; this will be your stuffing.
5) Lay the veal roast flat on a cutting board. Spread the stuffing mixture evenly over the surface.
6) Roll up the veal tightly, securing with kitchen twine.
7) In a large oven-safe pot, heat the remaining olive oil over medium-high heat. Add the rolled veal and brown on all sides, about 5 minutes.
8) Pour in the white wine and let it reduce by half, about 2 minutes.
9) Add the beef or vegetable broth and bring to a slight simmer.
10) Cover the pot and place it in the preheated oven. Roast for 90 minutes or until the internal temperature reaches 145-150°F (63-65°C).

Chef's Note:
This dish is perfect for special occasions and holidays. The stuffing can be prepared a day in advance to save time

NUTRITIONAL INFORMATION (PER SERVING):
Calories: 420 kcal
Total Fat: 18 g
Monounsaturated Fat: 10 g
Total Carbohydrates: 20 g
Dietary Fiber: 2 g
Protein: 40 g
Sodium: 300 mg

CHICKEN CACCIATORE

Perfect for a sophisticated week night dinner.
SPECIAL OCCASION

Preparation Time: 15 minutes
Cooking Time: 45 minutes
Total Time: 60 minutes
Serves: 4
INGREDIENTS:

- 4 boneless, skinless chicken breasts (about 1.5 pounds)
- 1/2 teaspoon salt
- 1/4 teaspoon black pepper
- 2 tablespoons olive oil
- 1 medium onion, chopped
- 2 garlic cloves, minced
- 1 bell pepper, sliced
- 1 can (14.5 ounces) diced tomatoes
- 1/2 cup chicken broth
- 1 teaspoon dried oregano
- 1 teaspoon dried basil
- 1/2 teaspoon dried thyme
- 2 tablespoons capers (optional)

INSTRUCTIONS:
1. Season the chicken breasts with salt and pepper.
2. Heat olive oil in a large skillet over medium-high heat. Add the chicken breasts and brown on both sides. Remove the chicken and set aside.
3. In the same skillet, add the chopped onion, garlic, and bell pepper. Sauté until the onion is translucent.
4. Add the diced tomatoes, chicken broth, oregano, basil, and thyme to the skillet. Stir to combine.
5. Return the browned chicken to the skillet, nestling it into the vegetable mixture.
6. Reduce the heat to low, cover the skillet, and let it simmer for about 30 minutes, or until the chicken is cooked through.
7. If using capers, add them to the skillet in the last 5 minutes of cooking.
8. Check for seasoning and adjust if necessary. Serve hot.

Chef's Note:
For a complete meal, consider these recommended sides:

1. Serve over whole-grain pasta or brown rice to absorb the sauce.
2. A side of steamed vegetables like broccoli or green beans pairs well.
3. A simple side salad with a light vinaigrette complements the hearty flavors.
4. For a low-carb option, serve over cauliflower rice.
5. Crusty whole-grain bread is great for sopping up any remaining sauce.

NUTRITIONAL INFORMATION (PER SERVING):
Calories: 420 kcal
Total Fat: 14 g
    Monounsaturated Fat: 9 g
Total Carbohydrates: 20 g
    Dietary Fiber: 4 g
Protein: 48 g
Sodium: 780 mg

POLLO ALLA PUTTANESCA – CHICKEN IN SPICY TOMATO SAUCE

A low-calorie, high-flavor dish inspired by coastal Italy.
SUPER-QUICK!

Preparation Time: 10 minutes
Cooking Time: 15 minutes
Total Time: 25 minutes
Serves: 4

INGREDIENTS:
- 4 boneless, skinless chicken breasts
- 1 can of diced tomatoes
- 1/2 cup Kalamata olives, pitted and sliced
- 2 cloves garlic, minced
- 1 teaspoon chili flakes (optional)
- 2 tablespoons olive oil
- Salt and pepper to taste

INSTRUCTIONS:
1) Heat olive oil in a skillet over medium-high heat. Season chicken breasts with salt and pepper, then cook until browned on both sides. Remove and set aside.
2) In the same skillet, sauté garlic until fragrant. Add tomatoes, olives, and chili flakes.
3) Return chicken to the skillet, cover, and simmer for about 10 minutes, or until chicken is cooked through.

Chef's Note:
Serve with a side of whole-grain pasta or crusty bread to soak up the sauce.

NUTRITIONAL INFORMATION (PER SERVING):
Calories: 230 kcal
Total Fat: 10 g
Monounsaturated Fat: 6 g
Total Carbohydrates: 8 g
Dietary Fiber: 2 g
Protein: 27 g

Sodium: 300 mg

HERB-ROASTED LEG OF LAMB – LAHMA DANI FIHL FORN

A North African-inspired roasted leg of lamb dish infused with Mediterranean herbs. This protein-rich, flavorful meal is perfect for special occasions and celebrations.

SPECIAL OCCASION

Preparation Time: 20 minutes
Cooking Time: 90 minutes
Total Time: 110 minutes
Serves: 6-8 servings

INGREDIENTS:

- 1 leg of lamb, about 4-5 lbs (1.8-2.3 kg)
- 1/4 cup extra-virgin olive oil
- 4 cloves garlic, minced
- Zest of 1 lemon
- 2 tablespoons fresh rosemary, finely chopped
- 1 tablespoon fresh thyme, finely chopped
- 1 tablespoon fresh oregano, finely chopped
- Salt and freshly ground black pepper to taste
- 1 cup beef or lamb broth

INSTRUCTIONS:

1) Preheat the oven to 375°F (190°C).
2) In a small bowl, mix together the olive oil, minced garlic, lemon zest, chopped rosemary, thyme, and oregano. Add salt and pepper to taste.
3) Pat the leg of lamb dry with paper towels and place it in a roasting pan.
4) Rub the herb and oil mixture all over the leg of lamb, making sure to get it into any nooks and crannies.
5) Pour the beef or lamb broth into the bottom of the roasting pan.
6) Place the roasting pan in the preheated oven and cook for approximately 1.5 hours, or until the internal temperature reaches 135°F (57°C) for medium-rare.
7) Remove the lamb from the oven and let it rest for about 10 minutes before slicing.

Chef's Note:

If you prefer your lamb more well-done, you can adjust the cooking time. Also, the resting time allows the juices to redistribute, making for a more flavorful and moist roast. Marinate the meat at least 6 hours before starting the cooking process to ensure tender results!

NUTRITIONAL INFORMATION (PER SERVING):

Calories: 380 kcal
Total Fat: 18 g
Monounsaturated Fat: 10 g
Total Carbohydrates: 2 g
Dietary Fiber: 0 g
Protein: 48 g
Sodium: 200 mg

SOUTHERN ITALIAN GOAT AND HERB STEW – PIGNATA DI CAPRA

A hearty and nourishing stew hailing from Southern Italy, featuring goat meat and a medley of herbs. This one-pot meal is perfect for those seeking a unique, flavorful dish that's both protein-rich and comforting.

ONE-POT MEAL

Preparation Time: 20 minutes
Cooking Time: 120 minutes
Total Time: 140 minutes
Serves: 4-6 servings

INGREDIENTS:

- 2 lbs (900g) goat meat, cut into cubes
- 2 tablespoons extra-virgin olive oil
- 1 large onion, chopped
- 4 cloves garlic, minced
- 1 carrot, diced
- 1 stalk celery, diced
- 1 cup white wine
- 4 cups beef or vegetable broth
- 1 bay leaf
- 1 tablespoon fresh rosemary, finely chopped
- 1 tablespoon fresh thyme, finely chopped
- 1 tablespoon fresh oregano, finely chopped
- Salt and freshly ground black pepper to taste
- 1 can (14.5 oz) diced tomatoes
- Zest of 1 lemon

INSTRUCTIONS:

1) In a large pot or Dutch oven, heat the olive oil over medium heat. Add the onion and garlic and sauté until translucent, about 5 minutes.
2) Add the diced carrot and celery to the pot and cook for another 3 minutes.
3) Add the goat meat to the pot and brown on all sides, about 7-10 minutes.
4) Pour in the white wine and allow it to reduce by half, about 3 minutes.
5) Add the beef or vegetable broth, bay leaf, rosemary, thyme, and oregano. Season with salt and black pepper to taste.
6) Bring the mixture to a boil, then reduce heat to low and simmer for 90 minutes, stirring occasionally.
7) Add the diced tomatoes and lemon zest, and continue to simmer for an additional 30 minutes.
8) Check for seasoning and adjust as necessary before serving.

Chef's Note:

This stew is excellent when made a day ahead, as the flavors meld together even better. It also freezes well, so feel free to make a large batch for meal-prepping.

NUTRITIONAL INFORMATION (PER SERVING):
Calories: 400 kcal
Total Fat: 12 g
Monounsaturated Fat: 6 g
Total Carbohydrates: 12 g
Dietary Fiber: 3 g
Protein: 55 g
Sodium: 400 mg

HUMMUS~BI~LAHM – HUMMUS WITH GROUND LAMB

A luxurious yet simple dish featuring rich hummus topped with seasoned ground lamb.
SUPER-QUICK!

Preparation Time: 15 minutes
Cooking Time: 15 minutes
Total Time: 30 minutes
Serves: 4

INGREDIENTS:
- 2 cups hummus, store-bought or homemade
- 1 lb ground lamb
- 2 cloves garlic, minced
- 1 teaspoon ground cumin
- 1 teaspoon ground coriander
- 2 tablespoons olive oil
- Chopped parsley for garnish

INSTRUCTIONS:
1) Heat olive oil in a skillet over medium heat. Add garlic and sauté until fragrant.
2) Add ground lamb, breaking it apart with a spoon. Cook until browned.
3) Add cumin and coriander to the lamb, stir well to combine.
4) Spread hummus on a serving platter, then top with the cooked lamb.
5) Garnish with chopped parsley before serving.

Chef's Note:
If lamb is not to your taste, you can substitute it with ground turkey or beef.

NUTRITIONAL INFORMATION (PER SERVING):
Calories: 480 kcal
Total Fat: 35 g
Monounsaturated Fat: 18 g
Total Carbohydrates: 15 g
Dietary Fiber: 4 g
Protein: 30 g
Sodium: 500 mg

ITALIAN PORK SCALLOPINI

Thin pork slices sautéed in a zesty lemon-caper sauce.
SUPER-QUICK!

Preparation Time: 5 minutes
Cooking Time: 10 minutes
Total Time: 15 minutes
Serves: 4

INGREDIENTS:
- 4 thin pork cutlets
- 1/4 cup flour for dredging
- 2 tablespoons olive oil
- Juice of 1 lemon
- 2 tablespoons capers, drained
- Salt and pepper to taste

INSTRUCTIONS:
1) Lightly dredge pork cutlets in flour, shaking off excess.
2) In a skillet, heat olive oil over medium-high heat. Add pork and sauté until browned, about 3 minutes per side.
3) Add lemon juice and capers to the skillet. Cook for another 2 minutes.
4) Season with salt and pepper. Serve immediately.

NUTRITIONAL INFORMATION (PER SERVING):
Calories: 250 kcal
Total Fat: 15 g
Monounsaturated Fat: 9 g
Total Carbohydrates: 8 g
Protein: 22 g
Sodium: 150 mg

ITALIAN CHICKEN MARSALA

Delicious Italian-style chicken in a rich Marsala wine sauce.
ONE-POT MEAL

Preparation Time: 10 minutes
Cooking Time: 25 minutes
Total Time: 35 minutes
Serves: 4

INGREDIENTS:
- 4 boneless, skinless chicken breasts
- 1 cup Marsala wine
- 8 oz cremini mushrooms, sliced
- 1/4 cup olive oil
- Salt and pepper to taste

INSTRUCTIONS:
1) Season chicken breasts with salt and pepper.
2) In a large skillet, heat olive oil over medium heat. Add chicken breasts and cook until browned on both sides, about 5 minutes per side.
3) Remove chicken and set aside.

4) In the same skillet, add mushrooms and sauté until tender.
5) Add Marsala wine and bring to a boil, scraping up any brown bits from the pan.
6) Return chicken to the skillet, reduce heat, and simmer for about 10 minutes, until chicken is cooked through and sauce has thickened.
7) Serve hot with a side of roasted vegetables.

NUTRITIONAL INFORMATION (PER SERVING):
Calories: 320 kcal
Total Fat: 14 g
Monounsaturated Fat: 8 g
Total Carbohydrates: 12 g
Dietary Fiber: 1 g
Protein: 28 g
Sodium: 110 mg

MEDITERRANEAN TURKEY STUFFED PEPPERS
Bell peppers filled with a hearty mixture of meat and veggies.
GLUTEN-FREE

Preparation Time: 20 minutes
Cooking Time: 20 minutes
Total Time: 40 minutes
Serves: 4

INGREDIENTS:
- 4 bell peppers, halved and seeded
- 1/2 lb ground turkey
- 1 cup cooked quinoa
- 1 zucchini, diced
- 1 cup cherry tomatoes, halved
- 2 garlic cloves, minced
- 2 tablespoons olive oil
- Salt and pepper to taste

INSTRUCTIONS:
1) Preheat oven to 375°F (190°C).
2) In a skillet, heat olive oil over medium heat. Add ground turkey and garlic, cooking until meat is no longer pink.
3) Add zucchini and cherry tomatoes to the skillet. Cook for another 5 minutes.
4) Stir in cooked quinoa, salt, and pepper.
5) Stuff each bell pepper half with the turkey and quinoa mixture.
6) Place stuffed peppers in a baking dish and cover with aluminum foil.
7) Bake for 20 minutes or until peppers are tender.
8) Serve hot, optionally garnished with fresh basil.

NUTRITIONAL INFORMATION (PER SERVING):
Calories: 260 kcal
Total Fat: 10 g
Monounsaturated Fat: 6 g
Total Carbohydrates: 25 g

Dietary Fiber: 5 g
Protein: 20 g
Sodium: 90 mg

GREEK STIFADO
A delicious Greek stew featuring beef and aromatic spices.
ONE-POT MEAL

Preparation Time: 15 minutes
Cooking Time: 45 minutes
Total Time: 60 minutes
Serves: 4

INGREDIENTS:
- 1 lb beef stew meat, cubed
- 1 large onion, chopped
- 2 cloves garlic, minced
- 1 cinnamon stick
- 1/4 teaspoon allspice
- 1 can (14 oz) diced tomatoes
- 2 tablespoons olive oil
- Salt and pepper to taste

INSTRUCTIONS:
1) Heat olive oil in a large pot over medium-high heat.
2) Add the beef and brown on all sides. Remove and set aside.
3) In the same pot, sauté onion and garlic until translucent.
4) Add cinnamon stick and allspice. Stir for 1 minute.
5) Add diced tomatoes, salt, and pepper. Bring to a simmer.
6) Return beef to the pot, cover, and simmer for 45 minutes until tender.
7) Serve with a side of steamed vegetables or brown rice.

NUTRITIONAL INFORMATION (PER SERVING):
Calories: 350 kcal
Total Fat: 18 g
Monounsaturated Fat: 8 g
Total Carbohydrates: 15 g
Dietary Fiber: 3 g
Protein: 30 g
Sodium: 120 mg

BIFTEKI
Burgers, Mediterranean style!
KID FRIENDLY

Preparation Time: 15 minutes
Cooking Time: 15 minutes
Total Time: 30 minutes
Serves: 4

INGREDIENTS:
- 1 lb ground beef or pork

- 1 onion, finely chopped
- 1 egg
- 1/2 cup breadcrumbs
- ½ cup feta
- 2 cloves garlic, minced
- Salt and pepper to taste
- 1 tablespoon olive oil for frying

INSTRUCTIONS:
1) In a bowl, mix together the meat, onion, egg, feta breadcrumbs, garlic, salt, and pepper. Don't overmix.
2) Shape into patties.
3) Heat olive oil in a skillet over medium heat.
4) Fry the patties for about 7 minutes per side, or until fully cooked. You can also bake or grill them
5) Serve with a side of Greek salad or tzatziki sauce.

Chef's Note: The type of feta you use can make a significant difference. For a creamier texture and a tangier flavor, use Greek feta made from sheep's milk.

NUTRITIONAL INFORMATION (PER SERVING):
Calories: 310 kcal
Total Fat: 15 g
Monounsaturated Fat: 5 g
Total Carbohydrates: 15 g
Dietary Fiber: 1 g
Protein: 30 g
Sodium: 200 mg

MOUSSAKA

A classic dish, elaborate to make, but easy to store!
MEAL-PREP FRIENDLY

Preparation Time: 30 minutes
Cooking Time: 1 hour
Total Time: 1 hour 30 minutes
Serves: 6

INGREDIENTS:
- 2 medium eggplants, sliced 1/4-inch thick
- 1 lb lean ground beef
- 1 medium onion, finely chopped
- 2 cloves garlic, minced
- 1 14.5-oz can of diced tomatoes, drained
- 2 tbsp tomato paste
- 1/2 tsp ground cinnamon
- 1/2 tsp oregano
- Salt and pepper to taste
- 2 tbsp olive oil for sautéing

For the Béchamel Sauce:
- 2 cups skim milk
- 2 tbsp olive oil
- 2 tbsp all-purpose flour
- 1/4 tsp nutmeg
- Salt and pepper to taste

- 1/2 cup grated Parmesan cheese

INSTRUCTIONS:
1. Preheat oven to 375°F (190°C). Arrange the eggplant slices in a single layer on a baking sheet, sprinkle with salt, and set aside for 15 minutes to draw out moisture. Rinse and pat dry.
2. In a skillet over medium heat, sauté the ground beef, breaking it into small pieces until browned. Remove beef from the skillet and set aside.
3. In the same skillet, add chopped onion and garlic. Sauté until onion is translucent.
4. Add the cooked ground beef back into the skillet along with diced tomatoes, tomato paste, cinnamon, and oregano. Season with salt and pepper, mix well, and let it simmer for about 10 minutes.
5. In a separate saucepan, heat the olive oil for the Béchamel sauce over medium heat. Add the flour and whisk continuously for a couple of minutes. Slowly add in the milk while whisking to avoid lumps. Add nutmeg, salt, and pepper, and keep stirring until the sauce thickens.
6. In a 9x13-inch baking dish, arrange a layer of eggplant slices. Spoon half of the meat mixture over it. Repeat layers, finishing with a layer of eggplant slices.
7. Pour the Béchamel sauce over the top layer, spreading it evenly. Sprinkle the grated Parmesan cheese on top.
8. Bake in the preheated oven for 40-45 minutes or until the top turns golden brown.
9. Allow to rest for 10-15 minutes before slicing and serving.

Chef's Note:
- Moussaka pairs well with a side salad of greens and a glass of red wine for a complete Mediterranean feast.

NUTRITIONAL INFORMATION (PER SERVING):
Calories: 600 kcal
Total Fat: 32 g
    Monounsaturated Fat: 15 g
Total Carbohydrates: 42 g
    Dietary Fiber: 10 g
Protein: 35 g
Sodium: 450 mg

GYROS

Greek seasoned and cooked meat usually served in pita bread with vegetables and sauces.
KID FRIENDLY

Preparation Time: 20 minutes
Cooking Time: 45 minutes
Total Time: 1 hour 5 minutes
Serves: 4

INGREDIENTS:
- 1 lb ground lamb or beef
- 1 medium onion, grated

- 3 garlic cloves, minced
- 1 teaspoon oregano
- 1 teaspoon thyme
- 1 teaspoon rosemary
- 1 teaspoon salt
- 1/2 teaspoon black pepper
- 2 tablespoons olive oil

INSTRUCTIONS:
1) Preheat the oven to 375°F (190°C).
2) In a mixing bowl, combine the ground meat, grated onion, minced garlic, oregano, thyme, rosemary, salt, and pepper.
3) Mix the ingredients thoroughly until well combined.
4) Shape the mixture into a loaf and place it on a baking sheet.
5) Drizzle olive oil over the loaf.
6) Bake for 45 minutes or until the internal temperature reaches 160°F (71°C).
7) Allow to cool slightly before serving

Chef's Note: You can double the batch and save leftovers to mix in a salad or use the next day for a quick lunch sandwich in pita bread with sliced cucumbers and tomatoes and a dollop of Greek Yogurt.

NUTRITIONAL INFORMATION (PER SERVING):
Calories: 380 kcal
Total Fat: 28 g
Monounsaturated Fat: 10 g
Total Carbohydrates: 4 g
Dietary Fiber: 1 g
Protein: 26 g
Sodium: 610 mg

GREEK BRAISED LAMB WITH ARTICHOKES — ARNI ME AGKINARES

A luxurious yet easy Greek-inspired dish featuring tender lamb and artichokes, braised to perfection. This one-pot meal provides a high-protein, low-carb dinner option that's both nourishing and flavorful.
ONE-POT MEAL

Preparation Time: 20 minutes
Cooking Time: 90 minutes
Total Time: 110 minutes
Serves: 4-6 servings

INGREDIENTS:
- 2 lbs (900g) lamb shoulder, cut into cubes
- 2 tablespoons extra-virgin olive oil
- 1 onion, finely chopped
- 4 cloves garlic, minced
- 1 cup white wine
- 3 cups chicken broth
- 1 bay leaf

- 1 teaspoon dried oregano
- Salt and freshly ground black pepper to taste
- 1 can (14 oz) artichoke hearts, drained and halved
- Juice of 1 lemon
- Zest of 1 lemon

INSTRUCTIONS:
1) In a large pot or Dutch oven, heat the olive oil over medium heat. Add the chopped onion and minced garlic, sautéing until translucent, about 5 minutes.
2) Add the lamb cubes and brown them on all sides, around 7-10 minutes.
3) Pour in the white wine to deglaze the pot, allowing it to reduce by half, approximately 3 minutes.
4) Add chicken broth, bay leaf, and dried oregano. Season with salt and freshly ground black pepper.
5) Bring the mixture to a boil, then reduce the heat to low, cover, and let it simmer for 60 minutes.
6) Add the artichoke hearts, lemon juice, and lemon zest to the pot. Continue to simmer for another 30 minutes, uncovered.
7) Check for seasoning and adjust as needed before serving.

Chef's Note:
If you can't find canned artichoke hearts, frozen ones work just as well. Thaw and drain them before adding to the pot. This dish can also be made a day ahead to allow the flavors to meld even better.

NUTRITIONAL INFORMATION (PER SERVING):
Calories: 420 kcal
Total Fat: 16 g
Monounsaturated Fat: 8 g
Total Carbohydrates: 10 g
Dietary Fiber: 3 g
Protein: 55 g
Sodium: 250 mg

NORTH AFRICAN SPICED CHICKEN STEW — DJEJ BIL-BASAL

A hearty and aromatic chicken stew that captures the essence of North African cuisine, featuring a blend of spices and herbs. This one-pot meal is low in calories but rich in flavors and protein.
MEAL PREP FRIENDLY

Preparation Time: 20 minutes
Cooking Time: 40 minutes
Total Time: 60 minutes
Serves: 4-6 servings

INGREDIENTS:
- 2 lbs (900g) chicken thighs, bone-in and skin-on
- 2 tablespoons olive oil
- 1 large onion, thinly sliced
- 3 cloves garlic, minced

- 1 teaspoon ground cumin
- 1 teaspoon ground coriander
- 1/2 teaspoon ground cinnamon
- 1/4 teaspoon ground turmeric
- 4 cups chicken broth
- 1 can (14.5 oz) chickpeas, drained and rinsed
- 2 large carrots, diced
- Salt and pepper to taste
- Fresh cilantro, chopped, for garnish

INSTRUCTIONS:

1) In a large pot or Dutch oven, heat the olive oil over medium heat. Add the chicken thighs, skin-side down, and cook until the skin is browned, about 5 minutes. Remove and set aside.
2) In the same pot, add the sliced onion and garlic. Sauté until the onions become translucent, around 5 minutes.
3) Stir in the ground cumin, coriander, cinnamon, and turmeric, and cook for another 2 minutes to release the flavors.
4) Return the chicken thighs to the pot, and add the chicken broth. Bring the mixture to a boil, then reduce the heat to low and cover. Simmer for 20 minutes.
5) Add the chickpeas and diced carrots to the pot. Continue to simmer for another 20 minutes, until the chicken is cooked through and the carrots are tender.
6) Season with salt and pepper to taste. Garnish with fresh cilantro before serving.

Chef's Note:

This stew can be made a day in advance to allow the flavors to meld. It's also freezer-friendly and perfect for meal prep.

NUTRITIONAL INFORMATION (PER SERVING):

Calories: 320 kcal
Total Fat: 14 g
Monounsaturated Fat: 8 g
Total Carbohydrates: 20 g
Dietary Fiber: 5 g
Protein: 28 g
Sodium: 300 mg

ROSEMARY LAMB CHOPS WITH ROASTED VEGETABLES

A deceptively easy week night dinner. Prep your vegetables before hand and let the lamb marinate all day, so when you get home you'll just have to pop the vegetables in the oven and cook the lamb chops and the kids will love it.

KID-FRIENDLY

Preparation Time: 15 minutes
Cooking Time: 30 minutes
Total Time: 45 minutes
Serves: 4

INGREDIENTS:

- 4 lamb chops, about 1-inch thick

- 2 tablespoons olive oil
- 4 sprigs of fresh rosemary
- 3 cloves garlic, minced
- Salt and pepper, to taste
- 2 medium zucchinis, sliced
- 1 red bell pepper, sliced
- 1 yellow bell pepper, sliced
- 1 medium red onion, sliced
- 2 medium carrots, sliced

INSTRUCTIONS:

1. Preheat your oven to 400°F (200°C). Line a baking sheet with parchment paper.
2. In a large bowl, combine zucchinis, bell peppers, onion, and carrots. Drizzle 1 tablespoon of olive oil and season with salt and pepper. Toss to coat the vegetables evenly.
3. Spread the seasoned vegetables on the prepared baking sheet in a single layer. Roast in the preheated oven for 20-25 minutes or until tender, stirring halfway through.
4. While the vegetables are roasting, prepare the lamb chops. In a small bowl, mix together the minced garlic, remaining olive oil, and leaves from 2 sprigs of rosemary. Season with salt and pepper.
5. Rub the garlic-rosemary mixture on both sides of each lamb chop. If you can, do this at least 2 hours in advance, or even the night before.
6. Heat a grill pan or skillet over medium-high heat. Once hot, add the lamb chops and cook for 4-5 minutes per side for medium-rare, or until your desired level of doneness is reached.
7. Remove the lamb chops from the grill pan and let them rest for 5 minutes.
8. Serve the lamb chops hot, alongside the roasted vegetables. Garnish with remaining rosemary sprigs.

Chef's Note:

- This dish pairs well with a light red wine like Pinot Noir or a robust white like Chardonnay.
- The roasted vegetables also make a great side for other meat or fish dishes.

NUTRITIONAL INFORMATION (PER SERVING):

Calories: 420 kcal
Total Fat: 24 g
    Monounsaturated Fat: 12 g
Total Carbohydrates: 16 g
    Dietary Fiber: 4 g
Protein: 36 g
Sodium: 90 mg

HERB~CRUSTED LAMB CHOPS

Perfect for a romantic dinner, these lamb chops are tender and rich in flavor.

SPECIAL OCCASION

Preparation Time: 20 minutes
Cooking Time: 12 minutes
Total Time: 32 minutes
Serves: 2

INGREDIENTS:

- 4 lamb chops
- 1 cup Olive Tapenade Marinade (refer to chef's note for recipe)
- Salt and pepper to taste

INSTRUCTIONS:

- Marinate the lamb chops in Olive Tapenade Marinade for at least 6 hours, better if overnight.
- Preheat the oven to high heat.
- Roast the lamb chops for 6 minutes per side for medium-rare, or until desired doneness.
- Rest for a few minutes before serving.

Chef's Note:
Olive Tapenade Marinade Recipe

INGREDIENTS:

1 cup black or green olives, pitted
2 tbsp capers, drained
2-3 garlic cloves
1 lemon, zest and juice
1/4 cup extra-virgin olive oil
Salt and pepper to taste
Optional: a handful of fresh herbs like basil or parsley.

Steps:
Combine olives, capers, and garlic in a food processor.
Pulse until finely chopped but not fully puréed.
Add lemon zest and juice.
While processing, slowly drizzle in olive oil.
Season with salt, pepper, and optional herbs.
Use immediately as a marinade, or store in an airtight container in the fridge.

NUTRITIONAL INFORMATION (PER SERVING):
Calories: 350 kcal
Total Fat: 24 g
Monounsaturated Fat: 11 g
Total Carbohydrates: 2 g
Dietary Fiber: 0 g
Protein: 28 g
Sodium: 220 mg

OSSO BUCO

A classic Italian dish, Osso Buco features braised veal shanks cooked in a rich, flavorful sauce. The name literally means "bone with a hole," referring to the marrow-filled bone in the center of each veal shank.

GLUTEN-FREE

Preparation Time: 20 minutes
Cooking Time: 2 hours

Total Time: 2 hours 20 minutes
Serves: 4
INGREDIENTS:

- 4 veal shanks, about 2 inches thick each
- Salt and freshly ground black pepper, to taste
- 1/4 cup all-purpose flour (for dredging)
- 1/4 cup olive oil
- 1 onion, finely chopped
- 2 carrots, peeled and finely chopped
- 2 celery stalks, finely chopped
- 4 cloves garlic, minced
- 1 cup dry white wine
- 1 can (14 oz) diced tomatoes
- 2 cups beef or chicken broth
- 1 bay leaf
- 2 sprigs fresh thyme
- 2 sprigs fresh rosemary

INSTRUCTIONS:

1. Preheat the oven to 325°F (160°C).
2. Season the veal shanks with salt and freshly ground black pepper. Dredge each shank in flour, shaking off the excess.
3. In a large, ovenproof skillet or Dutch oven, heat the olive oil over medium-high heat. Add the veal shanks and sear until browned on all sides. Remove the shanks and set aside.
4. In the same skillet, add the onion, carrots, celery, and garlic. Sauté for about 5 minutes, or until the vegetables are softened.
5. Add the white wine to the skillet, scraping up any browned bits from the bottom of the pan.
6. Stir in the diced tomatoes, including the juice.
7. Return the veal shanks to the skillet, and add the beef or chicken broth, bay leaf, thyme, and rosemary.
8. Bring the mixture to a simmer, then cover the skillet with a lid or foil. Transfer to the preheated oven and braise for about 1.5 to 2 hours, or until the meat is fork-tender.
9. Remove the bay leaf and herb sprigs before serving. Serve the osso buco hot, ideally over creamy risotto or mashed potatoes.

Chef's Note:
Traditionally, osso buco is served with a gremolata—a mix of lemon zest, garlic, and parsley—sprinkled on top for added flavor and freshness.

NUTRITIONAL INFORMATION (PER SERVING):
Calories: 650 kcal
Total Fat: 28 g
　　　Monounsaturated Fat: 16 g
　　　Polyunsaturated Fat: 2 g
Total Carbohydrates: 15 g
　　　Dietary Fiber: 2 g
Protein: 50 g
Sodium: 900 mg

OLIVE AND FIG CHICKEN RAGÙ

A fusion of Italian and North African flavors with the sweetness of figs and the richness of olives. A comforting and hearty meat sauce.

KID-FRIENDLY

Preparation Time: 10 minutes
Cooking Time: 20 minutes
Total Time: 30 minutes
Serves: 4

INGREDIENTS:

- 4 boneless, skinless chicken breasts, cut into cubes
- 1 onion, finely chopped
- 3 cloves garlic, minced
- 4 fresh figs, diced
- 1 cup pitted Kalamata olives
- 1 can (14 oz) crushed tomatoes
- 2 tbsp olive oil
- Salt and pepper to taste
- 1 tsp ground cumin
- Fresh parsley, for garnish

INSTRUCTIONS:

1) Heat olive oil in a skillet over medium heat. Add onions and garlic, sauté until translucent.
2) Add the chicken cubes to the skillet. Cook until no longer pink.
3) Stir in the figs and olives, sauté for 3-4 minutes.
4) Add crushed tomatoes, ground cumin, salt, and pepper. Simmer for 10 minutes.
5) Garnish with fresh parsley and serve with whole wheat couscous or quinoa (for a gluten-free option)

NUTRITIONAL INFORMATION (PER SERVING):

Calories: 350 kcal
Total Fat: 12 g
Monounsaturated Fat: 8 g
Total Carbohydrates: 25 g
Dietary Fiber: 6 g
Protein: 35 g
Sodium: 400 mg

LAMB TAGINE WITH APRICOTS

A sweet and savory blend of lamb, apricots, and spices, evoking the taste of Greek island life.

ONE-POT MEAL

Preparation Time: 15 minutes
Cooking Time: 45 minutes
Total Time: 60 minutes
Serves: 4

INGREDIENTS:

- 1 lb lamb, cut into chunks
- 8 dried apricots, cut into halves
- 1 onion, sliced
- 2 cups chicken or lamb broth
- 1 tsp ground cinnamon
- 1 tsp ground coriander
- Salt and pepper to taste
- 2 tbsp olive oil

INSTRUCTIONS:

1) Heat olive oil in a pot over medium heat. Add the onion and sauté until translucent.
2) Add lamb chunks to the pot. Brown on all sides.
3) Add the apricots, ground cinnamon, ground coriander, salt, and pepper.
4) Pour in the broth and bring to a boil.
5) Reduce heat and let simmer for 45 minutes or until the meat is tender.

NUTRITIONAL INFORMATION (PER SERVING):

Calories: 360 kcal
Total Fat: 18 g
Monounsaturated Fat: 10 g
Total Carbohydrates: 20 g
Dietary Fiber: 3 g
Protein: 28 g
Sodium: 300 mg

SICILIAN-INSPIRED PORK WITH CAPERS & ALMONDS

An aromatic dish featuring pork tenderloin enhanced by briny capers and crunchy almonds.

GLUTEN-FREE

Preparation Time: 10 minutes
Cooking Time: 25 minutes
Total Time: 35 minutes
Serves: 4

INGREDIENTS:

- 1 pork tenderloin, about 1 lb, sliced into medallions
- ¼ cup almonds, toasted and roughly chopped
- 3 tbsp capers, drained
- 1 orange, zest and juice
- 2 tbsp olive oil
- Salt and pepper to taste

INSTRUCTIONS:

1) Preheat your oven to 400°F (200°C).
2) In a skillet, heat olive oil over medium heat. Add pork medallions and brown on both sides. Remove and set aside.
3) In the same skillet, add capers and almonds, sauté for 2-3 minutes.
4) Return pork to the skillet. Add orange zest and juice.
5) Transfer skillet to the preheated oven. Bake for 10-15 minutes or until pork is cooked through.

Chef's Note:
Serve over a bed of arugula for added freshness and a peppery kick.

NUTRITIONAL INFORMATION (PER SERVING):
Calories: 280 kcal
Total Fat: 16 g
Monounsaturated Fat: 9 g
Total Carbohydrates: 10 g
Dietary Fiber: 2 g
Protein: 25 g
Sodium: 250 mg

SOUTZOUKAKIA ~ GREEK CINNAMON–SCENTED LAMB MEATBALLS

A classic Greek meatball recipe infused with aromatic cinnamon, perfect for a cozy family dinner. This dish is rich in protein and healthy fats.
KID FRIENDLY

Preparation Time: 15 minutes
Cooking Time: 20 minutes
Total Time: 35 minutes
Serves: 4 servings

INGREDIENTS:

- 1 lb (450g) ground lamb
- 1 medium onion, finely grated
- 2 cloves garlic, minced
- 1 teaspoon ground cinnamon
- 1/2 teaspoon ground cumin
- 1/4 teaspoon ground allspice
- Salt and pepper to taste
- 1 large egg, beaten
- 2 tablespoons breadcrumbs
- 2 tablespoons olive oil
- 1 can (14 oz) crushed tomatoes
- Fresh parsley, for garnish

INSTRUCTIONS:

1) In a large mixing bowl, combine ground lamb, grated onion, minced garlic, cinnamon, cumin, and allspice. Season with salt and pepper.
2) Add the beaten egg and breadcrumbs to the meat mixture. Mix until well incorporated.
3) Shape the mixture into 1.5-inch meatballs.
4) Heat olive oil in a large skillet over medium heat. Add the meatballs and cook until browned on all sides, about 5 minutes. Remove meatballs and set aside.
5) In the same skillet, add the crushed tomatoes and bring to a simmer.
6) Return the meatballs to the skillet, cover, and cook in the tomato sauce for about 15 minutes, or until fully cooked through.
7) Garnish with fresh parsley before serving.

Chef's Note:
These meatballs pair wonderfully with orzo or a simple Greek salad. For a gluten-free option, substitute breadcrumbs with almond meal.

NUTRITIONAL INFORMATION (PER SERVING):
Calories: 320 kcal
Total Fat: 20 g
Monounsaturated Fat: 8 g
Total Carbohydrates: 12 g
Dietary Fiber: 3 g
Protein: 24 g
Sodium: 320 mg

SHEET~PAN CHICKEN WITH ROASTED SPRING VEGETABLES & LEMON VINAIGRETTE

This one-pan dish is a burst of fresh flavors, featuring juicy chicken and vibrant spring vegetables, all unified by a tangy lemon vinaigrette.
ONE-POT MEAL

Preparation Time: 10 minutes
Cooking Time: 20 minutes
Total Time: 30 minutes
Serves: 4

INGREDIENTS:

- 4 boneless, skinless chicken breasts
- 2 cups asparagus, trimmed
- 1 cup cherry tomatoes
- 1 zucchini, sliced
- 1/4 cup olive oil
- Juice of 1 lemon
- Salt and pepper to taste

INSTRUCTIONS:

1) Preheat the oven to 400°F (200°C).
2) Place chicken breasts and vegetables on a large sheet pan.
3) In a small bowl, whisk together the olive oil and lemon juice. Drizzle over the chicken and vegetables.
4) Season with salt and pepper.
5) Roast for 20-25 minutes or until chicken is cooked through and vegetables are tender.

Chef's Note:
You can switch out the vegetables according to the season or your personal preference.

NUTRITIONAL INFORMATION (PER SERVING):
Calories: 310 kcal
Total Fat: 14 g
Monounsaturated Fat: 9 g
Total Carbohydrates: 8 g

Dietary Fiber: 2 g
Protein: 35 g
Sodium: 200 mg

PAELLA WITH CHICKEN AND RABBIT

Dive into the rich, authentic flavors of Spanish cuisine with this Paella featuring both chicken and rabbit. A medley of rice, saffron, and an array of fresh vegetables brings this dish to life.

SPECIAL OCCASION

Preparation Time: 30 minutes
Cooking Time: 1 hour
Total Time: 1 hour 30 minutes
Serves: 6-8

INGREDIENTS:

- 1.5 cups paella rice (short-grain)
- 1 rabbit, cut into pieces
- 1 whole chicken, cut into pieces
- 1 red bell pepper, sliced
- 1 medium onion, chopped
- 4 cloves garlic, minced
- 4 cups chicken stock, warmed
- 1/2 cup white wine
- 1/2 teaspoon saffron threads, soaked in warm water
- 1 cup green beans, cut into 2-inch pieces
- 1/2 cup canned or fresh tomatoes, diced
- 1 teaspoon smoked paprika
- 1/4 cup extra-virgin olive oil
- Salt and pepper to taste
- Lemon wedges and parsley for garnish

INSTRUCTIONS:

1. In a large, wide pan (preferably a paella pan), heat the olive oil over medium-high heat.
2. Add the pieces of chicken and rabbit to the pan, browning them evenly on all sides. Remove the meat and set it aside.
3. In the same pan, add the chopped onion, garlic, and bell pepper. Sauté until the onions become translucent.
4. Add the paella rice to the pan and stir for about 2-3 minutes, ensuring each grain is coated with the oil and vegetable mixture.
5. Pour in the white wine and let it evaporate, stirring continuously.
6. Stir in the tomatoes and smoked paprika.
7. Begin adding the warmed chicken stock, one ladle at a time, to the rice mixture. Add the saffron threads and their soaking water.
8. Return the browned chicken and rabbit pieces to the pan, nestling them into the rice.
9. Add the green beans and gently stir to combine all the ingredients.
10. Reduce the heat to medium-low, cover the pan, and let it cook for about 20-25 minutes, or until the rice is tender and the liquid is mostly absorbed.
11. Check for seasoning and add salt and pepper as needed.
12. Remove the pan from the heat and let it sit for about 5 minutes before serving.
13. Garnish with lemon wedges and fresh parsley.

Chef's Note:

Traditional paella is often cooked uncovered. If you wish to follow this method, keep an eye on the liquid level and add more warmed stock as needed.

NUTRITIONAL INFORMATION (PER SERVING):

Calories: 580 kcal
Total Fat: 20 g
Monounsaturated Fat: 10 g
Total Carbohydrates: 45 g
Dietary Fiber: 3 g
Protein: 55 g
Sodium: 390 mg

HOW TO GRILL MEAT THE MEDITERRANEAN WAY

Grilling is a cornerstone of Mediterranean cuisine, emphasizing simplicity and bold, fresh flavors. Marinades are key and usually combine olive oil, acid like lemon juice or vinegar, and herbs such as oregano, rosemary, and thyme, to both tenderize and flavor the meat. The acid breaks down meat fibers, while the herbs and spices infuse it with robust taste. Chicken should marinate for 2-4 hours, pork for 2-8 hours, and beef and lamb for 4-24 hours, depending on the cut's toughness and fat content. As a rule of thumb the fatter and tougher the meat, the longer the marinade time should be. Once your meat is marinated, preheat the grill to get a good sear and use a meat thermometer to ensure the perfect level of doneness. Control any flare-ups to prevent charring and let the meat rest post-grilling to redistribute juices. Finally, serve your grilled delicacies with Mediterranean staples like fresh salads or dips such as tzatziki or hummus for an authentic dining experience.

Of course, grilling is not always an option, but you can easily convert the following grill recipes in everyday recipe with two alternative methods that will allow you to emulate the grilled texture and health benefits:

Oven Broiling

Move your oven rack to the highest level, closest to the broiler. Preheat the broiler for 5-10 minutes. While preheating, prepare your foods by lightly coating them in extra virgin olive oil and your choice of herbs and spices (or the amazing marinades below). Place the items on a broiling pan, which allows the heat to circulate around the food, mimicking the effect of an outdoor grill. Broil the food, keeping a watchful eye to prevent burning. Turn the meat once, as you would on a grill.

Broiling, like grilling, allows excess fat to drain away, effectively reducing the calorie and saturated fat content in meats. For plant-based foods like vegetables, broiling can caramelize the natural sugars, enhancing the flavors without the need for additional fats or sugars. The high heat and quick cooking time also preserve many of the nutrients in your foods.

Oven Roasting

Preheat your oven to a high temperature, generally around 425°F (220°C). Prepare your meats or vegetables by tossing them in a minimal amount of extra virgin olive oil along with herbs and spices. Place them on a baking sheet or roasting pan and roast until cooked to your liking.

Roasting at a high temperature for a shorter time can provide some of the benefits of broiling. The high heat seals in the juices, often eliminating the need for additional fats or oils. The quick cooking can also help preserve nutrient content, much like grilling.

MEDITERRANEAN CHICKEN MARINADE

INGREDIENTS:
1/2 cup olive oil
Juice of 1 lemon
4 cloves garlic, minced
2 teaspoons dried oregano or 2 tablespoons fresh oregano, chopped
Salt and pepper to taste

Procedure:
Whisk together olive oil, lemon juice, garlic, oregano, salt, and pepper in a bowl.
Place the chicken in a Ziplock bag or a glass container.
Pour the marinade over the chicken, ensuring all pieces are coated.
Seal and refrigerate for 30 minutes to 4 hours.

MEDITERRANEAN BEEF MARINADE

INGREDIENTS:
1/2 cup olive oil
1/4 cup red wine vinegar
3-4 cloves garlic, minced
2 teaspoons dried rosemary or 2 tablespoons fresh rosemary, chopped
Salt and pepper to taste

Procedure:
Combine olive oil, red wine vinegar, garlic, rosemary, salt, and pepper in a bowl and mix well.
Place the beef in a Ziplock bag or a glass container.
Add the marinade, making sure the meat is fully coated.
Seal and refrigerate for 2 to 8 hours.

MEDITERRANEAN PORK MARINADE

INGREDIENTS:
1/2 cup olive oil
1/4 cup white wine vinegar
3-4 cloves garlic, minced
1 teaspoon dried thyme or 1 tablespoon fresh thyme, chopped
Salt and pepper to taste

Procedure:
In a bowl, mix together olive oil, white wine vinegar, garlic, thyme, salt, and pepper.
Place the pork in a Ziplock bag or glass container.
Add the marinade, ensuring the meat is fully coated.
Seal and refrigerate for 2 to 8 hours.

MEDITERRANEAN LAMB MARINADE

INGREDIENTS:
1/2 cup olive oil
Juice of 1 lemon
3-4 cloves garlic, minced
2 teaspoons dried mint or 2 tablespoons fresh mint, chopped
Salt and pepper to taste

Procedure:
Combine olive oil, lemon juice, garlic, mint, salt, and pepper in a bowl.
Place the lamb in a Ziplock bag or glass container.
Pour in the marinade, making sure the meat is fully coated.
Seal and refrigerate for 2 to 8 hours.

TRADITIONAL MARINADES:

Herb and Lemon Marinade:
Olive oil
Lemon zest and juice
Garlic, minced
Rosemary/thyme/oregano
Salt and pepper
Best For: Chicken, fish, and pork

Spicy Yogurt Marinade:
Greek yogurt
Olive oil
Garlic, minced
Chili flakes
Lemon juice
Salt and pepper
Best For: Chicken, lamb, and beef

Tomato and Basil Marinade:
Tomato puree
Olive oil
Fresh basil, chopped
Garlic, minced
Salt and pepper
Best For: Beef and lamb

Red Wine and Garlic Marinade:
Red wine
Olive oil
Garlic, minced
Rosemary
Salt and pepper
Best For: Beef and lamb

Balsamic and Fig Marinade:
Balsamic vinegar
Olive oil
Dried figs, finely chopped
Garlic, minced
Salt and pepper
Best For: Lamb

Citrus and Coriander Marinade:
INGREDIENTS:
Orange juice and zest
Lemon juice
Olive oil
Fresh coriander, chopped
Garlic, minced
Salt and pepper
Best For: Chicken and lamb

Olive Tapenade Marinade:
INGREDIENTS:
Black olives, pitted and chopped
Olive oil
Lemon juice
Garlic, minced
Capers
Fresh parsley, chopped
Salt and pepper
Best for: Chicken and lamb

Honey and Mustard Marinade:
INGREDIENTS:
Honey
Dijon mustard
Olive oil
Garlic, minced
Thyme
Salt and pepper
Best for: Pork

Mint and Cumin Yogurt Marinade:
INGREDIENTS:
Greek yogurt
Fresh mint, chopped
Cumin, ground
Lemon juice
Garlic, minced
Salt and pepper
Best for: Lamb and beef

MEDITERRANEAN HERB-GRILLED CHICKEN

A heart-healthy recipe full of Mediterranean flavors like rosemary, thyme, and lemon zest.

HEART-HEALTHY

Preparation Time: 15 minutes
Cooking Time: 20 minutes
Total Time: 35 minutes
Serves: 4

INGREDIENTS:
- 4 boneless, skinless chicken breasts
- 1 cup Herb and Lemon Marinade
- Salt and pepper to taste
- Optional: lemon wedges for garnish

INSTRUCTIONS:
1) Marinate the chicken breasts in Herb and Lemon Marinade for at least 30 minutes.
2) Preheat the grill to medium-high heat.
3) Grill chicken for about 10 minutes per side or until it reaches an internal temperature of 165°F.
4) Optional: Garnish with lemon wedges.

NUTRITIONAL INFORMATION (PER SERVING):
Calories: 200 kcal
Total Fat: 9 g
Monounsaturated Fat: 4 g
Total Carbohydrates: 3 g
Dietary Fiber: 0 g
Protein: 28 g
Sodium: 180 mg

BALSAMIC FIG PORK TENDERLOIN

This pork tenderloin has a sweet and tangy flavor, making it a sophisticated choice for dinner parties.

SPECIAL OCCASION

Preparation Time: 15 minutes
Cooking Time: 20 minutes
Total Time: 35 minutes
Serves: 4

INGREDIENTS:
- 1 pork tenderloin, about 1 lb
- 1 cup Balsamic and Fig Marinade
- Salt and pepper to taste

INSTRUCTIONS:
1) Marinate the pork tenderloin in Balsamic and Fig Marinade for at least 1 hour.
2) Preheat the grill to medium heat.
3) Grill the pork for about 20 minutes, turning occasionally, until it reaches an internal temperature of 145°F.
4) Let rest for a few minutes before slicing.

NUTRITIONAL INFORMATION (PER SERVING):
Calories: 210 kcal
Total Fat: 7 g

Monounsaturated Fat: 3 g
Total Carbohydrates: 5 g
Dietary Fiber: 0 g
Protein: 30 g
Sodium: 180 mg

SOUVLAKI – GREEK GRILLED CHICKEN

Fire up the grill for these Greek chicken skewers, marinated in olive oil, garlic, and herbs.

KID-FRIENDLY

Preparation Time: 15 minutes (plus marinating time)
Cooking Time: 10 minutes
Total Time: 25 minutes
Serves: 4

INGREDIENTS:
- 1 lb chicken breast, cut into cubes
- 1/4 cup olive oil
- 2 cloves garlic, minced
- 1 tablespoon oregano
- Juice of 1 lemon
- Salt and pepper to taste

INSTRUCTIONS:
1) In a bowl, mix together olive oil, garlic, oregano, lemon juice, salt, and pepper.
2) Add chicken cubes to the marinade, cover, and refrigerate for at least 1 hour.
3) Preheat grill to medium-high heat.
4) Thread the marinated chicken cubes onto skewers.
5) Grill for 8-10 minutes, turning occasionally, until chicken is cooked through.

Chef's Note:
Serve with a side of tzatziki sauce and a fresh Greek salad for a complete meal.

NUTRITIONAL INFORMATION (PER SERVING):
Calories: 220 kcal
Total Fat: 12 g
Monounsaturated Fat: 8 g
Total Carbohydrates: 2 g
Dietary Fiber: 0 g
Protein: 25 g
Sodium: 150 mg

HONEY GLAZED GRILLED CHICKEN THIGHS

A sweet and savory blend perfect for BBQs and picnics.

DAIRY-FREE

Preparation Time: 20 minutes
Cooking Time: 20 minutes
Total Time: 40 minutes
Serves: 4

INGREDIENTS:
- 8 chicken thighs
- 1 cup Herb and Lemon Marinade, with 2 tablespoons honey added
- Salt and pepper to taste

INSTRUCTIONS:
1) Marinate the chicken thighs in the modified Herb and Lemon Marinade for 1 hour.
2) Preheat the grill to medium-high heat.
3) Grill thighs for about 20 minutes, turning occasionally.
4) Serve hot.

Chef's Note:
Complements well with corn on the cob and potato salad.

NUTRITIONAL INFORMATION (PER SERVING):
Calories: 410 kcal
Total Fat: 30 g
Monounsaturated Fat: 12 g
Total Carbohydrates: 12 g
Dietary Fiber: 0 g
Protein: 28 g
Sodium: 270 mg

SPICY YOGURT-MARINATED BEEF SKEWERS

These beef skewers are a crowd-pleaser, making them great for family gatherings or barbecues.

KID FRIENDLY

Preparation Time: 25 minutes
Cooking Time: 10 minutes
Total Time: 35 minutes
Serves: 4

INGREDIENTS:
- 1 lb beef sirloin, cut into 1-inch cubes
- 1 cup Spicy Yogurt Marinade
- Salt and pepper to taste

INSTRUCTIONS:
1) Marinate the beef cubes in Spicy Yogurt Marinade for at least 2 hours.
2) Preheat the grill to medium-high heat.
3) Thread beef onto skewers and grill for 4-5 minutes per side or until desired doneness.
4) Serve immediately.

NUTRITIONAL INFORMATION (PER SERVING):
Calories: 280 kcal
Total Fat: 12 g
Monounsaturated Fat: 5 g
Total Carbohydrates: 3 g
Dietary Fiber: 0 g
Protein: 35 g
Sodium: 200 mg

GRILLED BEEF KOFTA

Middle Eastern flavors meet the grill in this savory dish.

SPECIAL OCCASION

Preparation Time: 25 minutes
Cooking Time: 15 minutes
Total Time: 40 minutes
Serves: 4

INGREDIENTS:
- 1 lb ground beef
- 1 cup Spicy Yogurt Marinade
- Salt and pepper to taste

INSTRUCTIONS:
1) Mix ground beef with Spicy Yogurt Marinade and form into sausage shapes around skewers.
2) Preheat the grill to medium heat.
3) Grill koftas for about 15 minutes, turning occasionally.
4) Serve immediately with flatbreads.

NUTRITIONAL INFORMATION (PER SERVING):
Calories: 320 kcal
Total Fat: 20 g
Monounsaturated Fat: 8 g
Total Carbohydrates: 5 g
Dietary Fiber: 1 g
Protein: 29 g
Sodium: 240 mg

KALOPRESTI GALOPOULA ~ GRILLED HERB~ STUFFED TURKEY TENDERLOINS

A low-calorie, lean protein option that pairs well with a variety of Mediterranean sides. This turkey dish is infused with fresh herbs and is light on the palate.

LOW-CALORIES

Preparation Time: 10 minutes
Cooking Time: 20 minutes
Total Time: 30 minutes
Serves: 4 servings

INGREDIENTS:
- 2 turkey tenderloins, about 1 lb each
- 1/4 cup fresh basil leaves, chopped
- 1/4 cup fresh parsley leaves, chopped
- 2 cloves garlic, minced
- Zest of 1 lemon
- 1 tablespoon olive oil
- Salt and pepper to taste

INSTRUCTIONS:
1) Preheat grill to medium-high heat.
2) In a bowl, combine chopped basil, parsley, minced garlic, and lemon zest.

3) Make small slits in the turkey tenderloins and stuff them with the herb mixture.
4) Rub olive oil over the tenderloins and season with salt and pepper.
5) Grill the tenderloins for about 10 minutes per side, or until the internal temperature reaches 165°F (74°C).
6) Allow to rest for a few minutes before slicing and serving.

Chef's Note:
Serve with a side of steamed vegetables or a quinoa salad for a complete meal.

NUTRITIONAL INFORMATION (PER SERVING):
Calories: 180 kcal
Total Fat: 4 g
Monounsaturated Fat: 2 g
Total Carbohydrates: 2 g
Dietary Fiber: 1 g
Protein: 35 g
Sodium: 100 mg

TURKISH LAMB KEBABS

If you grill just one thing this summer, grilld this, juicy and spicy, they will be the hit of the BBQ party.

SPECIAL OCCASION

Preparation Time: 15 minutes
Cooking Time: 10 minutes
Marinating Time: at least 2 hours
Total Time: 2 hours 25 minutes
Serves: 4

INGREDIENTS:
- 1.5 pounds lamb shoulder, cut into 1-inch cubes
- 1 medium onion, grated
- 3 cloves garlic, minced
- 1/4 cup olive oil
- 2 tablespoons lemon juice
- 1 teaspoon ground cumin
- 1 teaspoon ground coriander
- 1/2 teaspoon ground paprika
- Salt and pepper, to taste
- 8 wooden or metal skewers

INSTRUCTIONS:
1. In a large mixing bowl, combine grated onion, minced garlic, olive oil, lemon juice, cumin, coriander, paprika, salt, and pepper.
2. Add the cubed lamb to the marinade and mix thoroughly to coat each piece well. Cover the bowl and refrigerate for at least 2 hours, up to overnight for better flavor.
3. If using wooden skewers, soak them in water for at least 30 minutes prior to grilling to prevent burning.
4. Preheat the grill to medium-high heat.

5. Thread the marinated lamb cubes onto the skewers, leaving a small gap between each piece.
6. Grill the skewers for 4-5 minutes on each side or until the lamb reaches your desired level of doneness.
7. Remove the kebabs from the grill and let them rest for a few minutes before serving.

Chef's Note:
Serve the lamb kebabs with flatbread, tzatziki sauce, and a side of grilled vegetables or a fresh salad. You can also serve them over a bed of rice pilaf. If you are feeling fanciful, try pairing them with grilled fig skewers (use rosemary to skewer the figs and grill 2 minutes per part) and a glass of red wine.

NUTRITIONAL INFORMATION (PER SERVING):
Calories: 420 kcal
Total Fat: 30 g
    Monounsaturated Fat: 14 g
Total Carbohydrates: 4 g
    Dietary Fiber: 1 g
Protein: 35 g
Sodium: 400 mg

TURKISH LAMB KOFTA

Juicy inside and charred on the outside, this meal will enjoyed by both chidren and their parents!
KID FRIENDLY

Preparation Time: 20 minutes (plus 1 hour for marinating)
Cooking Time: 10 minutes
Total Time: 30 minutes (plus 1 hour for marinating)
Serves: 4

INGREDIENTS:
- 1 lb ground lamb
- 1 medium onion, grated
- 2 cloves garlic, minced
- 1/4 cup fresh parsley, finely chopped
- 1/4 cup fresh mint, finely chopped
- 1 teaspoon ground cumin
- 1/2 teaspoon ground coriander
- 1/2 teaspoon paprika
- Salt and pepper, to taste
- 4 wooden or metal skewers (if using wooden, soak in water for at least 30 minutes)
- 1 tablespoon olive oil, for brushing

INSTRUCTIONS:
1. In a large mixing bowl, combine the ground lamb, grated onion, minced garlic, chopped parsley and mint, cumin, coriander, paprika, salt, and pepper. Mix until all ingredients are well incorporated.
2. Cover the mixture and place it in the refrigerator to marinate for at least 1 hour.
3. Preheat your grill to medium-high heat.
4. Divide the lamb mixture into 8 equal portions. Shape each portion into an elongated oval and thread onto skewers.
5. Brush the koftas lightly with olive oil.
6. Place the skewers on the preheated grill and cook for 4-5 minutes per side, or until the internal temperature reaches at least 160°F (71°C).
7. Remove the koftas from the grill and let them rest for a few minutes before serving.

Chef's Note:
You can serve these lamb koftas with pita bread, yogurt sauce, and a side of fresh salad for a complete Turkish-inspired meal. They also go well with rice pilaf or grilled vegetables.

NUTRITIONAL INFORMATION (PER SERVING):
Calories: 310 kcal
Total Fat: 23 g
Saturated Fat: 9 g
Total Carbohydrates: 4 g
Dietary Fiber: 1 g
Protein: 21 g
Sodium: 110 mg

Fish and Seafood Dishes

LEMON GARLIC BAKED COD

Simple, clean flavors make this cod dish shine.
HEART-HEALTHY

Preparation Time: 10 minutes
Cooking Time: 20 minutes
Total Time: 30 minutes
Serves: 4

INGREDIENTS:
- 4 cod fillets
- 4 tablespoons olive oil
- 2 cloves garlic, minced
- Zest and juice of 1 lemon
- Salt and pepper to taste

INSTRUCTIONS:
1) Preheat the oven to 375°F (190°C).
2) Place cod fillets in a baking dish.
3) Mix olive oil, garlic, lemon zest, and juice in a bowl.
4) Pour mixture over cod, season with salt and pepper.
5) Bake for 18-20 minutes, or until cod flakes easily.

NUTRITIONAL INFORMATION (PER SERVING):
Calories: 270 kcal
Total Fat: 14 g
Monounsaturated Fat: 10 g
Total Carbohydrates: 1 g
Dietary Fiber: 0 g
Protein: 32 g
Sodium: 90 mg

CREAMY SEAFOOD RISOTTO

A luxurious dish featuring a medley of seafood.
SPECIAL OCCASION

Preparation Time: 20 minutes
Cooking Time: 40 minutes
Total Time: 60 minutes
Serves: 4

INGREDIENTS:
- 1 cup Arborio rice
- 4 cups seafood stock
- 1 cup mixed seafood (shrimp, squid, mussels)
- 1/2 cup white wine
- 2 tablespoons olive oil
- 1 small onion, chopped
- Salt and pepper to taste

INSTRUCTIONS:
1) Heat olive oil in a pot and sauté onion until translucent.
2) Add rice and cook for 2 minutes.
3) Pour in white wine and cook until mostly absorbed.
4) Gradually add stock, stirring constantly.
5) When rice is almost done, add mixed seafood.
6) Cook until seafood is cooked through, season with salt and pepper.

Chef's Note:
Finish with a drizzle of truffle oil for extra decadence.

NUTRITIONAL INFORMATION (PER SERVING):
Calories: 440 kcal
Total Fat: 12 g
Monounsaturated Fat: 8 g
Total Carbohydrates: 54 g
Dietary Fiber: 2 g
Protein: 22 g
Sodium: 810 mg

SHRIMP AND ASPARAGUS RISOTTO

A luxurious and comforting Italian dish featuring tender shrimp and crisp asparagus, all brought together in a creamy Arborio rice base.
GLUTEN-FREE

Preparation Time: 15 minutes
Cooking Time: 30 minutes
Total Time: 45 minutes
Serves: 4

INGREDIENTS:
- 1 pound large shrimp, peeled and deveined
- 1 bunch asparagus, trimmed and cut into 1-inch pieces
- 1 1/2 cups Arborio rice
- 4 cups chicken or vegetable broth, warmed
- 1 cup dry white wine
- 1 medium onion, finely chopped
- 3 cloves garlic, minced
- 2 tablespoons olive oil
- 1/2 cup Parmesan cheese, grated
- Salt and pepper, to taste
- Zest of 1 lemon
- 2 tablespoons fresh parsley, chopped (for garnish)

INSTRUCTIONS:
1. In a large skillet or saucepan, heat the olive oil over medium heat.
2. Add the chopped onion and garlic, sautéing until they become translucent, about 3-4 minutes.

3. Stir in the Arborio rice and cook for another 1-2 minutes, until the rice is well-coated with the oil and has a translucent edge.
4. Pour in the white wine and cook until it is mostly evaporated.
5. Start adding the warmed broth, one ladleful at a time, stirring constantly. Wait until the liquid is mostly absorbed before adding the next ladleful.
6. When the rice is halfway cooked (about 10 minutes), add the asparagus pieces. Continue adding broth and stirring.
7. When the rice is almost fully cooked and the asparagus is tender, add the shrimp. Cook until the shrimp are pink and cooked through, about 3-5 minutes.
8. Stir in the grated Parmesan cheese and lemon zest. Season with salt and pepper to taste.
9. Remove from heat and garnish with chopped parsley before serving.

Chef's Note:
The lemon zest brings out the flavor of the shrimp and asparagus, making it an integral part of the dish. For a different twist, you could substitute the asparagus with peas or add some saffron for a luxurious touch.

NUTRITIONAL INFORMATION (PER SERVING):
Calories: 420 kcal
Total Fat: 12 g
    Monounsaturated Fat: 4 g
Total Carbohydrates: 50 g
    Dietary Fiber: 3 g
Protein: 25 g
Sodium: 650 mg

SPAGHETTI ALLE VONGOLE
Classic Italian dish spotlighting fresh clams in a garlicky white wine sauce.
DAIRY-FREE

Preparation Time: 15 minutes
Cooking Time: 20 minutes
Total Time: 35 minutes
Serves: 4

INGREDIENTS:
- 1 lb spaghetti
- 2 lbs fresh clams, cleaned
- 1/4 cup olive oil
- 4 cloves garlic, thinly sliced
- 1/2 cup white wine
- Red pepper flakes (optional)
- Salt and pepper to taste

INSTRUCTIONS:
1) Cook spaghetti according to package instructions.
2) In a large pan, heat olive oil and add garlic (and red pepper flakes if using).
3) Add clams and white wine, cover, and steam until clams open.
4) Toss cooked spaghetti into the pan with clams.
5) Season with salt and pepper and serve.

NUTRITIONAL INFORMATION (PER SERVING):
Calories: 520 kcal
Total Fat: 14 g
Monounsaturated Fat: 9 g
Total Carbohydrates: 70 g
Dietary Fiber: 3 g
Protein: 25 g
Sodium: 640 mg

GAMBAS AL AJILLO ~ SPANISH GARLIC SHRIMP
A classic Spanish tapas dish featuring succulent shrimp sautéed in garlic and chili flakes.
GLUTEN-FREE

Preparation Time: 10 minutes
Cooking Time: 5 minutes
Total Time: 15 minutes
Serves: 4

INGREDIENTS:
- 1 pound large shrimp, peeled and deveined
- 1/4 cup olive oil
- 5 cloves garlic, thinly sliced
- 1 teaspoon red chili flakes
- Salt to taste
- Chopped parsley for garnish

INSTRUCTIONS:
1) Heat olive oil in a skillet over medium heat.
2) Add garlic and red chili flakes. Sauté for about 1 minute, until garlic is fragrant.
3) Add shrimp to the skillet. Cook for 2-3 minutes per side, until pink and cooked through.
4) Season with salt, garnish with chopped parsley, and serve immediately.

NUTRITIONAL INFORMATION (PER SERVING):
Calories: 230 kcal
Total Fat: 15 g
Total Carbohydrates: 2 g
Dietary Fiber: 0 g
Protein: 21 g
Sodium: 320 mg

PSARI PLAKI ~ GREEK–STYLE ROASTED FISH AND VEGETABLES

A wholesome dish inspired by the islands of Greece, this fish recipe is brimming with Mediterranean flavors and essential nutrients.

HEART-HEALTHY

Preparation Time: 15 minutes
Cooking Time: 25 minutes
Total Time: 40 minutes
Serves: 4 servings

INGREDIENTS:

- 4 fish fillets (e.g., cod, snapper, or tilapia), about 6 oz each
- 1 medium zucchini, sliced
- 1 bell pepper, sliced
- 1 onion, thinly sliced
- 2 tomatoes, sliced
- 1/4 cup extra virgin olive oil
- Juice of 1 lemon
- 3 cloves garlic, minced
- 1 teaspoon dried oregano
- Salt and pepper to taste
- Fresh parsley for garnish

INSTRUCTIONS:

1) Preheat oven to 400°F (200°C).
2) In a large baking dish, lay out the fish fillets and surround them with the zucchini, bell pepper, onion, and tomato slices.
3) In a small bowl, whisk together olive oil, lemon juice, minced garlic, dried oregano, salt, and pepper.
4) Drizzle the olive oil mixture over the fish and vegetables, making sure to coat them evenly.
5) Place the baking dish in the preheated oven and roast for 20-25 minutes, or until the fish flakes easily with a fork and the vegetables are tender.
6) Remove from oven, garnish with fresh parsley, and serve immediately.

Chef's Note:
This dish pairs well with a side of whole-grain rice or quinoa to make it a more filling meal. You can also add olives or capers for an extra Mediterranean touch.

NUTRITIONAL INFORMATION (PER SERVING):
Calories: 260 kcal
Total Fat: 14 g
Monounsaturated Fat: 10 g
Total Carbohydrates: 10 g
Dietary Fiber: 2 g
Protein: 25 g
Sodium: 120 mg

ITALIAN HALIBUT WITH GRAPES AND OLIVE OIL / PESCE AL FORNO CON L'UVA

This simple yet sophisticated dish showcases the flavors of coastal Italy. The halibut is rich in protein and omega-3 fatty acids, making it a heart-healthy choice.

HEART-HEALTHY

Preparation Time: 10 minutes
Cooking Time: 15 minutes
Total Time: 25 minutes
Serves: 4 servings

INGREDIENTS:

- 4 halibut fillets, about 6 oz each
- 1 cup seedless red grapes, halved
- 3 tablespoons extra-virgin olive oil
- Juice of 1 lemon
- 2 cloves garlic, minced
- 1 teaspoon fresh rosemary, finely chopped
- Salt and pepper to taste
- Fresh basil leaves for garnish

INSTRUCTIONS:

1) Preheat the oven to 400°F (200°C).
2) In a baking dish, lay the halibut fillets skin-side down and scatter the halved grapes around them.
3) In a small bowl, whisk together the olive oil, lemon juice, minced garlic, and rosemary.
4) Drizzle the olive oil mixture over the halibut and grapes, ensuring that the fillets are well-coated.
5) Season with salt and pepper to taste.
6) Bake for 12-15 minutes, or until the fish is opaque and flakes easily with a fork.
7) Remove from the oven, garnish with fresh basil leaves, and serve immediately.

Chef's Note:
This dish pairs wonderfully with a side of steamed asparagus or sautéed spinach. For a more indulgent touch, a drizzle of aged balsamic vinegar works wonders.

NUTRITIONAL INFORMATION (PER SERVING):
Calories: 240 kcal
Total Fat: 10 g
Monounsaturated Fat: 7 g
Polyunsaturated Fat: 1 g (omega-3 fatty acids)
Total Carbohydrates: 10 g
Dietary Fiber: 1 g
Protein: 28 g
Sodium: 100 mg

POLPO ALLA TOSCANA ~ TUSCAN~STYLE OCTOPUS STEW

This dish brings the Tuscan coast to your table. Featuring tender octopus in a tomato and herb stew, it's a low-fat, protein-rich choice.

ONE-POT MEAL

Preparation Time: 15 minutes
Cooking Time: 45 minutes
Total Time: 60 minutes
Serves: 4 servings

INGREDIENTS:

- 1 medium octopus (about 2 pounds), cleaned, cooked (see instructions in the introduction) and cut into pieces
- 1 can (14 oz) diced tomatoes
- 1 medium onion, finely chopped
- 2 cloves garlic, minced
- 2 tablespoons olive oil
- 1 teaspoon dried thyme
- 1 teaspoon dried oregano
- Salt and pepper to taste
- Fresh parsley for garnish

INSTRUCTIONS:

1) In a large pot, heat olive oil over medium heat. Add onion and garlic and sauté until translucent.
2) Add the octopus pieces to the pot and sauté for another 5 minutes.
3) Stir in the diced tomatoes, thyme, oregano, salt, and pepper.
4) Cover and let simmer on low heat for 40 minutes or until the octopus is tender.
5) Check for seasoning and adjust if necessary. Garnish with fresh parsley before serving.

Chef's Note:

Serve this stew with crusty whole-grain bread to soak up the delicious tomato-based sauce.

NUTRITIONAL INFORMATION (PER SERVING):

Calories: 230 kcal
Total Fat: 8 g
Monounsaturated Fat: 5 g
Total Carbohydrates: 10 g
Dietary Fiber: 3 g
Protein: 30 g
Sodium: 300 mg

CLASSIC SEAFOOD PAELLA

A Spanish culinary masterpiece, this Seafood Paella is a sumptuous mix of saffron rice and various seafood, perfect for impressing guests or enjoying a festive family meal.

PAELLA

Preparation Time: 30 minutes
Cooking Time: 40 minutes
Total Time: 70 minutes
Serves: 6

INGREDIENTS:

- 2 cups Arborio or short-grain rice
- 4 cups chicken or seafood broth
- 1 cup white wine
- 1/2 teaspoon saffron threads
- 1/4 cup olive oil
- 1 onion, finely chopped
- 1 red bell pepper, sliced
- 1 yellow bell pepper, sliced
- 3 cloves garlic, minced
- 1 teaspoon smoked paprika
- 1 teaspoon cayenne pepper (optional)
- 1 pound large shrimp, peeled and deveined
- 1 pound mussels, cleaned
- 1 pound clams, cleaned
- 1/2 pound squid, cut into rings
- Salt and pepper, to taste
- Lemon wedges and chopped parsley, for garnish

INSTRUCTIONS:

1. In a small saucepan, warm the broth and add the saffron threads. Allow it to sit for 10 minutes to infuse.
2. In a large paella pan or wide, shallow skillet, heat the olive oil over medium heat. Add the onions and bell peppers, sautéing until softened.
3. Add the garlic, smoked paprika, and cayenne pepper, if using, and cook for another minute.
4. Stir in the rice, making sure to coat it with the oil and spices.
5. Pour in the white wine and simmer until it's mostly evaporated.
6. Gradually add the saffron-infused broth, one cup at a time, stirring occasionally. Allow the liquid to be absorbed before adding more.
7. When the rice is almost cooked (about 20 minutes), arrange the shrimp, mussels, clams, and squid on top of the rice. Cover the pan with a lid or foil.
8. Cook for another 10–15 minutes, or until the seafood is cooked and the mussels and clams have opened.
9. Discard any mussels or clams that did not open.
10. Season with salt and pepper, and garnish with lemon wedges and chopped parsley before serving.

Chef's Note:

For a more traditional touch, you might want to avoid stirring the rice after the seafood is added. This allows the rice to form a slightly crusty bottom layer known as "socarrat."

NUTRITIONAL INFORMATION (PER SERVING):
Calories: 450 kcal
Total Fat: 12 g
    Monounsaturated Fat: 7 g
Total Carbohydrates: 50 g
    Dietary Fiber: 2 g
Protein: 35 g
Sodium: 600 mg

SAFFRON SEAFOOD PAELLA WITH SCALLOPS

A luxurious take on traditional Spanish Paella, featuring succulent scallops infused with the aroma of saffron.
SPECIAL OCCASION

Preparation Time: 20 minutes
Cooking Time: 40 minutes
Total Time: 60 minutes
Serves: 6

INGREDIENTS:
- 1 cup Arborio rice
- 4 cups seafood broth
- 1 pinch saffron threads
- 1/2 lb scallops
- 1 bell pepper, sliced
- 1 onion, chopped
- 2 cloves garlic, minced
- 2 tablespoons olive oil
- Salt and pepper to taste
- Lemon wedges and fresh parsley for garnish

INSTRUCTIONS:
1) In a paella pan or large skillet, heat the olive oil over medium heat.
2) Add the chopped onion, minced garlic, and sliced bell pepper. Sauté until the vegetables are softened, about 5 minutes.
3) Stir in the Arborio rice, making sure it's well-coated with the oil and vegetable mixture.
4) In a separate pot, warm the seafood broth and add the saffron threads to infuse.
5) Add the saffron-infused broth to the rice mixture and stir well.
6) When the rice is about halfway cooked (roughly 15 minutes), arrange the scallops on top.
7) Cover the pan and let it simmer for another 20-25 minutes, or until the rice is fully cooked and the scallops are opaque and cooked through.
8) Season with salt and pepper to taste.

Chef's Note:
Garnish with lemon wedges and a sprinkle of fresh parsley

before serving. For a varied seafood experience, you can also add shrimp or mussels to the mix.

NUTRITIONAL INFORMATION (PER SERVING):
Calories: 320 kcal
Total Fat: 8 g
Monounsaturated Fat: 5 g
Total Carbohydrates: 40 g
Dietary Fiber: 2 g
Protein: 22 g
Sodium: 600 mg

SHELL SEAFOOD AU GRATIN

This luxurious dish features an assortment of seafood, including swordfish, tuna, and shrimp, baked to perfection in scallop shells and topped with a flavorful breadcrumb mixture.
SPECIAL OCCASION

Preparation Time: 25 minutes (plus 30 minutes for marinating)
Cooking Time: 10 minutes
Total Time: 65 minutes
Serves: 6-8

INGREDIENTS:
- 150 g swordfish, cut into small pieces
- 100 g fresh tuna, cut into small pieces
- 75 g peeled shrimp, cut into small pieces
- 50 g fresh salmon, cut into small pieces
- 60 ml dry white wine
- 2 tablespoons vegetable broth
- 1 slice of bread, processed into crumbs
- 1 tablespoon grated Parmesan cheese
- 1/2 tablespoon chopped parsley
- 1 clove garlic, minced
- 1.5 tablespoons extra-virgin olive oil
- Salt and pepper to taste
- Large scallop shells for serving

INSTRUCTIONS:
1) In a bowl, combine the swordfish, tuna, shrimp, and salmon. Drizzle with 1/2 tablespoon of olive oil, season with salt and pepper, and mix well. Let the mixture marinate in the refrigerator for 30 minutes.
2) Preheat the oven to 200°C (392°F).
3) In another bowl, mix the bread crumbs, Parmesan cheese, minced garlic, chopped parsley, salt, and pepper.
4) Use a kitchen brush to lightly oil the insides of the large scallop shells.
5) Place one piece of each type of marinated fish into each shell.
6) Sprinkle each shell with a tablespoon of vegetable broth.
7) Top the seafood mixture in each shell with the flavored breadcrumb mixture.

8) Drizzle with the remaining olive oil.
9) Place the shells on a baking sheet and bake for 8-10 minutes, or until the seafood is cooked through and the breadcrumbs are golden.

Chef's Note:
For added richness, you may add a splash of dry white wine over the seafood before baking. Pair this dish with a chilled glass of white wine for a complete dining experience.

NUTRITIONAL INFORMATION (PER SERVING):
Calories: 220 kcal
Total Fat: 9 g
Monounsaturated Fat: 6 g
Total Carbohydrates: 5 g
Dietary Fiber: 0 g
Protein: 28 g
Sodium: 320 mg

SQUID INK PASTA WITH SEAFOOD

Elevate your pasta night with squid ink pasta and a medley of seafood.
DAIRY-FREE

Preparation Time: 20 minutes
Cooking Time: 20 minutes
Total Time: 40 minutes
Serves: 4

INGREDIENTS:
- 1 lb squid ink pasta
- 1/2 lb shrimp, peeled and deveined
- 1/2 lb squid, cleaned and sliced into rings
- 1/4 cup olive oil
- 3 cloves garlic, minced
- 1/4 teaspoon red pepper flakes
- 1/2 cup white wine
- Salt and pepper to taste

INSTRUCTIONS:
- Cook pasta according to package instructions.
- In a large skillet, heat olive oil over medium heat. Add garlic and red pepper flakes and sauté until fragrant.
- Add shrimp and squid to the skillet. Cook until just opaque.
- Deglaze the skillet with white wine and let it reduce by half.
- Toss the cooked pasta into the skillet, mixing well to combine.
- Season with salt and pepper to taste.

Chef's Note:
This dish pairs well with a crisp glass of white wine.

NUTRITIONAL INFORMATION (PER SERVING):
Calories: 490 kcal
Total Fat: 15 g

Monounsaturated Fat: 10 g
Total Carbohydrates: 50 g
Dietary Fiber: 2 g
Protein: 30 g
Sodium: 400 mg

POLENTA AND SARDINES

This dish pairs the rich flavors of sardines with the earthy, creamy texture of polenta, creating a unique and satisfying meal.
GLUTEN-FREE

Preparation Time: 40 minutes (plus 30 minutes for soaking sardines)
Cooking Time: 40 minutes
Total Time: 1 hour 50 minutes
Serves: 6-8

INGREDIENTS:
- 220 g corn flour
- 1 L water
- 1 tablespoon chives, finely chopped
- 250 g sardine fillets
- 150 ml milk
- 2 tablespoons extra-virgin olive oil, divided
- 200 g finely chopped onion
- 20 g pine nuts
- 20 g raisins
- 100 ml white vinegar
- 100 ml dry white wine
- Salt and pepper to taste
- Vegetable leaves for serving (e.g., green lettuce)

INSTRUCTIONS:
1) Bring 1 L of salted water to a boil. Slowly pour in the corn flour while stirring constantly. Cook for about 40 minutes, stirring frequently.
2) Add the chopped chives to the cooked polenta, mix well. Pour the polenta into a baking dish and let it cool. Once cool, turn it onto a cutting board.
3) Use a round pastry cutter to cut the polenta into square pieces, 3 cm high and 6 cm wide. Place the pieces in a greased pan. Carve a cup-like groove on top of each piece using a spoon.
4) Cut the sardine fillets into strips and soak them in milk for 30 minutes. Drain and pat dry with paper towels. Lightly dust the sardines with flour.
5) Heat 1 tablespoon of olive oil in a pan, fry the sardine strips for a few minutes, and then transfer them to a baking dish.
6) In the same pan, sauté the chopped onion in 1 tablespoon of olive oil until soft. Add the vinegar and wine, and allow the mixture to reduce slowly. Remove from heat.
7) Add pine nuts and raisins to the onion mixture and stir well.

8) Fill each groove in the polenta pieces with sardine strips. Top with the onion, pine nut, and raisin mixture.
9) Preheat the oven to 180°C (350°F) and bake for 10 minutes.
10) Serve the polenta and sardines on a bed of vegetable leaves, like green lettuce.

Chef's Note:
To make the dish even more special, consider garnishing with additional chives or a sprinkle of Parmesan cheese before serving.

NUTRITIONAL INFORMATION (PER SERVING):
Calories: 310 kcal
Total Fat: 12 g
Monounsaturated Fat: 8 g
Total Carbohydrates: 37 g
Dietary Fiber: 3 g
Protein: 14 g
Sodium: 400 mg

MEDITERRANEAN SEA BASS

A simple yet flavorful dish that celebrates the natural flavors of sea bass, enriched with the tastes of cherry tomatoes, olives, and capers.
ONE POT MEAL

Preparation Time: 10 minutes
Cooking Time: 30 minutes
Total Time: 40 minutes
Serves: 6-8

INGREDIENTS:
- 1 sea bass, approximately 0.5 kg
- 100 g cherry tomatoes, halved
- 10 olives, pitted
- 0.5 tablespoon salted capers, rinsed and drained
- Oregano to taste
- 2.5 tablespoons of extra-virgin olive oil, divided
- 2 bay leaves
- Fennel bunch for decoration
- Salt and pepper to taste

INSTRUCTIONS:
1) Preheat the oven to 200°C (390°F).
2) Scale the fish using a knife or scaling tool. Clean and rinse the fish, then pat dry with paper towels.
3) Rub salt on both the inside and outside of the fish.
4) Place the fish in the middle of a large sheet of baking paper.
5) Sprinkle oregano over the fish.
6) Scatter the halved cherry tomatoes, olives, and drained capers over and around the fish.
7) Drizzle 1 tablespoon of the olive oil over the ingredients.
8) Place the bay leaves beside the fish.

9) Close the foil tightly, creating a parcel.
10) Bake for approximately 30 minutes, or until the fish is cooked through.
11) Serve warm, decorated with a bunch of fennel and drizzled with the remaining extra-virgin olive oil.

Chef's Note:
For an extra burst of flavor, you can add a splash of white wine to the fish before sealing the foil parcel.

NUTRITIONAL INFORMATION (PER SERVING):
Calories: 230 kcal
Total Fat: 13 g
Monounsaturated Fat: 9 g
Total Carbohydrates: 5 g
Dietary Fiber: 1 g
Protein: 25 g
Sodium: 350 mg

CAPESANTE MARINATE AL LIMONE ~ CITRUS–MARINATED SCALLOPS

A vibrant Italian-inspired dish, these scallops are marinated in citrus juices for a burst of fresh flavor and a healthy dose of vitamin C.
LOW-CALORIES

Preparation Time: 10 minutes
Cooking Time: 5 minutes
Total Time: 15 minutes
Serves: 4 servings

INGREDIENTS:
- 1 lb scallops
- Juice of 1 lemon
- Juice of 1 orange
- 3 cloves garlic, minced
- Salt and pepper to taste
- 2 tablespoons extra-virgin olive oil
- Fresh parsley for garnish

INSTRUCTIONS:
1) In a bowl, combine lemon juice, orange juice, minced garlic, salt, and pepper.
2) Add the scallops to the bowl and marinate for 10 minutes.
3) Heat olive oil in a skillet over medium-high heat.
4) Add the scallops and cook for 2–3 minutes on each side, or until they turn opaque.
5) Garnish with fresh parsley and serve immediately.

Chef's Note: Perfect as an appetizer or served over a bed of mixed greens for a light, healthy meal.

NUTRITIONAL INFORMATION (PER SERVING):
Calories: 180 kcal
Total Fat: 8 g
Monounsaturated Fat: 6 g

Total Carbohydrates: 8 g
Dietary Fiber: 1 g
Protein: 20 g
Sodium: 200 mg

CIOPPINO ~ ITALIAN SEAFOOD STEW

This Cioppino recipe brings together a variety of seafood in a rich tomato-based broth, giving you the flavors of Italy in every spoonful. Ideal for a special occasion and heart-healthy due to its omega-3 rich ingredients.
MIX-AND-MATCH

Preparation Time: 20 minutes
Cooking Time: 50 minutes
Total Time: 70 minutes
Serves: 6

INGREDIENTS:

- 3 tbsp olive oil
- 1 large onion, finely chopped
- 4 garlic cloves, minced
- 1 bell pepper, chopped
- 1 cup dry white wine
- 1 can (28 oz) crushed tomatoes
- 4 cups fish stock
- 1 bay leaf
- Salt and pepper to taste
- 1 lb mixed seafood (e.g., shrimp, mussels, squid)
- 1 lb firm white fish (e.g., cod, halibut)
- Fresh parsley for garnish

INSTRUCTIONS:

1) In a large pot, heat olive oil over medium heat. Add onions, garlic, and bell pepper. Sauté until onions are translucent, about 5 minutes.
2) Add dry white wine and let it reduce by half, around 3-4 minutes.
3) Add crushed tomatoes, fish stock, bay leaf, salt, and pepper. Bring to a simmer and cook for 30-40 minutes.
4) Add the mixed seafood and white fish. Cook until the seafood is done, usually around 5 minutes.
5) Remove the bay leaf, garnish with fresh parsley, and serve hot.

Variations:

Shellfish Lovers: Use a variety of shellfish like mussels, clams, and crab legs.
Mediterranean Flavors: Add fennel and orange zest for an extra Mediterranean twist.
Low-Calorie: Use a chicken or vegetable broth instead of fish stock, and skip the wine.
Winter Warmth: Add some winter vegetables like carrots and potatoes for more body.
The Spicy Kick: Add 1-2 teaspoons of red pepper flakes for some heat.

NUTRITIONAL INFORMATION (PER SERVING):

Calories: 280 kcal
Total Fat: 10 g
Monounsaturated Fat: 6 g
Polyunsaturated Fat: 1 g (0.3 g omega-3 fatty acids)
Total Carbohydrates: 16 g
Dietary Fiber: 3 g
Protein: 30 g
Sodium: 800 mg

TUNISIAN FISH & COUSCOUS ONE~POT MEAL

A North African-inspired one-pot meal that's meal-prep friendly and teeming with spices and flavors.
ONE-POT MEAL

Preparation Time: 15 minutes
Cooking Time: 30 minutes
Total Time: 45 minutes
Serves: 4

INGREDIENTS:

- 2 tbsp olive oil
- 1 onion, chopped
- 3 cloves garlic, minced
- 1 lb white fish fillets (e.g., cod, tilapia)
- 1 can (14 oz) chickpeas, drained
- 1 cup couscous
- 2 cups chicken or vegetable broth
- 1 tsp cumin
- 1 tsp paprika
- Salt and pepper to taste
- Fresh cilantro for garnish

INSTRUCTIONS:

1) In a large pot, heat olive oil over medium heat. Add onions and garlic, sauté until soft.
2) Add spices (cumin, paprika, salt, and pepper) and stir for about 1 minute.
3) Add fish fillets and chickpeas, stirring gently.
4) Pour in the broth and bring to a simmer.
5) Add couscous, cover the pot, and remove from heat. Let it sit for 5 minutes to cook the couscous.
6) Fluff couscous with a fork, garnish with fresh cilantro, and serve.

NUTRITIONAL INFORMATION (PER SERVING):

Calories: 400 kcal
Total Fat: 10 g
Monounsaturated Fat: 6 g
Total Carbohydrates: 50 g
Dietary Fiber: 8 g
Protein: 25 g
Sodium: 500 mg

SHRIMP AND FETA SAGANAKI

A Greek-inspired dish that pairs succulent shrimp with tangy feta cheese, perfect for a special occasion.

SPECIAL OCCASION

Preparation Time: 15 minutes
Cooking Time: 20 minutes
Total Time: 35 minutes
Serves: 4

INGREDIENTS:

- 1 lb large shrimp, peeled and deveined
- 3 tbsp olive oil
- 1 onion, finely chopped
- 3 cloves garlic, minced
- 1 can (14 oz) diced tomatoes
- 1/4 cup white wine (optional)
- 1/4 cup fresh parsley, chopped
- 1 cup feta cheese, crumbled
- Salt and pepper to taste

INSTRUCTIONS:

1) Preheat your oven to 400°F (200°C).
2) In a skillet, heat the olive oil over medium heat. Add the onion and garlic, sautéing until soft and translucent.
3) Add the diced tomatoes, wine (if using), and half of the chopped parsley. Simmer for 10 minutes.
4) Season the shrimp with salt and pepper, and add them to the skillet. Cook for 2-3 minutes.
5) Transfer the shrimp and tomato mixture to an oven-safe dish. Top with crumbled feta cheese.
6) Bake for 10-12 minutes, or until the shrimp are cooked through and the feta is slightly golden.
7) Garnish with the remaining parsley before serving.

Chef's Note:

For added flavor, consider serving with crusty bread to soak up the rich sauce.

Variations:

Spicy Kick: Add a teaspoon of red pepper flakes to the tomato sauce.
Vegetable Boost: Incorporate some spinach or bell peppers into the dish.
Mediterranean Flavors: Add olives and capers for a more Mediterranean twist.
Alcohol-Free: Replace the white wine with vegetable broth.
Cheese Variation: Use ricotta or goat cheese instead of feta for a different flavor profile.

NUTRITIONAL INFORMATION (PER SERVING):

Calories: 310 kcal
Total Fat: 18 g
Monounsaturated Fat: 11 g
Total Carbohydrates: 10 g
Dietary Fiber: 2 g
Protein: 25 g

Sodium: 800 mg

MEDITERRANEAN PAN~SEARED SALMON WITH ASPARAGUS

Elevate your dinner with this Mediterranean-inspired pan-seared salmon, perfectly paired with crisp asparagus for a healthy and delicious meal.

HEART-HEALTHY

Preparation Time: 10 minutes
Cooking Time: 15 minutes
Total Time: 25 minutes
Serves: 4

INGREDIENTS:

- 4 (6-ounce) salmon fillets
- 1 bunch of asparagus, ends trimmed
- 1/4 cup extra-virgin olive oil
- 1 lemon, zested and juiced
- 4 cloves garlic, minced
- 1 teaspoon dried oregano
- 1 teaspoon dried thyme
- Salt and pepper to taste

INSTRUCTIONS:

1. Preheat a non-stick skillet over medium-high heat.
2. In a bowl, mix together the olive oil, lemon zest, lemon juice, minced garlic, oregano, and thyme.
3. Season the salmon fillets and asparagus with salt and pepper.
4. Add half of the olive oil mixture to the skillet and place the salmon fillets skin-side down. Cook for about 4-5 minutes per side or until the salmon is cooked to your desired doneness.
5. Remove the salmon fillets from the skillet and set aside.
6. In the same skillet, add the remaining olive oil mixture and toss in the asparagus. Sauté for about 5 minutes, or until the asparagus is tender but still crisp.
7. Serve the pan-seared salmon hot, topped with the sautéed asparagus.

Chef's Note:

The lemon and herb-infused olive oil also works wonderfully with other types of fish or even chicken. Consider pairing this dish with a glass of white wine or a light salad for a complete Mediterranean experience.

NUTRITIONAL INFORMATION (PER SERVING):

Calories: 410 kcal
Total Fat: 28 g
Monounsaturated Fat: 18 g
Total Carbohydrates: 6 g
Dietary Fiber: 2 g
Protein: 35 g
Sodium: 125 mg

SIZZLING ROSEMARY SHRIMP OVER POLENTA / GAMBERI AL ROSMARINO CON POLENTA

A classic fusion of Italian flavors, this dish combines the richness of polenta with the zesty aroma of rosemary-marinated shrimp.

GLUTEN-FREE

Preparation Time: 15 minutes
Cooking Time: 30 minutes
Total Time: 45 minutes
Serves: 4 servings

INGREDIENTS:

- 1 lb large shrimp, peeled and deveined
- 2 tablespoons olive oil
- 2 sprigs fresh rosemary, minced
- 4 cups water
- 1 cup cornmeal (for polenta)
- 2 cloves garlic, minced
- Salt and pepper to taste
- Grated Parmesan cheese for garnish

INSTRUCTIONS:

1) In a bowl, marinate shrimp with olive oil, minced rosemary, garlic, salt, and pepper. Set aside for 15 minutes.
2) In a saucepan, bring water to a boil. Gradually whisk in the cornmeal. Reduce heat and cook, stirring continuously, until the mixture thickens.
3) Season the polenta with salt and pepper and set aside, keeping it warm.
4) In a skillet, cook the marinated shrimp over medium-high heat for 2-3 minutes on each side, or until pink and opaque.
5) Serve the shrimp over the warm polenta and garnish with grated Parmesan cheese.

Chef's Note:

For added flavor, consider stirring in sun-dried tomatoes or sautéed mushrooms into the polenta.

NUTRITIONAL INFORMATION (PER SERVING):

Calories: 320 kcal
Total Fat: 10 g
Monounsaturated Fat: 6 g
Total Carbohydrates: 35 g
Dietary Fiber: 4 g
Protein: 25 g
Sodium: 400 mg

MUSSELS IN TOMATO–SAFFRON BROTH / MOULES PROVENÇALES

A Provençal dish that combines the earthy flavors of saffron with succulent mussels, offering a high-protein, low-fat feast.

HEART-HEALTHY

Preparation Time: 10 minutes
Cooking Time: 20 minutes
Total Time: 30 minutes
Serves: 4 servings

INGREDIENTS:

- 2 lbs fresh mussels, cleaned
- 1 can (14 oz) diced tomatoes
- 2 cups vegetable broth
- 1 small onion, finely chopped
- 3 cloves garlic, minced
- 1 pinch saffron threads
- 1 tablespoon olive oil
- Salt and pepper to taste
- Fresh parsley, for garnish

INSTRUCTIONS:

1) In a large pot, heat olive oil over medium heat. Add onion and garlic, and sauté until softened.
2) Add diced tomatoes, vegetable broth, and saffron threads. Bring to a simmer.
3) Add cleaned mussels to the pot and cover. Cook for about 10 minutes or until mussels have opened.
4) Discard any mussels that did not open. Season with salt and pepper.
5) Garnish with fresh parsley before serving.

Chef's Note:

Perfect as an appetizer or main course, serve with whole-grain bread to soak up the flavorful broth.

NUTRITIONAL INFORMATION (PER SERVING):

Calories: 220 kcal
Total Fat: 5 g
Monounsaturated Fat: 3 g
Total Carbohydrates: 16 g
Dietary Fiber: 2 g
Protein: 24 g
Sodium: 460 mg

CITRUS–MARINATED SALMON WITH FENNEL CREAM / SALMONE AGLI AGRUMI CON CREMA DI FINOCCHIO

Delight in the mingling of citrus-marinated salmon and a creamy fennel sauce, capturing a light yet flavorful Italian essence.

MEAL-PREP FRIENDLY

Preparation Time: 15 minutes
Cooking Time: 25 minutes
Total Time: 40 minutes
Serves: 4 servings

INGREDIENTS:

- 4 salmon fillets
- Juice of 1 lemon
- Juice of 1 orange
- 1 fennel bulb, sliced
- 1 cup low-fat Greek yogurt
- Salt and pepper to taste
- 1 tablespoon olive oil

INSTRUCTIONS:

1) Marinate salmon fillets in a mixture of lemon and orange juice for 15 minutes.
2) Meanwhile, sauté fennel slices in olive oil until soft. Blend with Greek yogurt to make fennel cream. Season with salt and pepper.
3) Preheat the oven to 400°F (200°C). Place the marinated salmon on a baking sheet lined with parchment paper.
4) Bake for 12–15 minutes, or until salmon is cooked to your liking.
5) Serve salmon with a dollop of fennel cream on top.

Chef's Note:

You can prepare the fennel cream in advance for a quick weekday meal and use it in other dishes as well, like a sandwich or as a dip for vegetables

NUTRITIONAL INFORMATION (PER SERVING):

Calories: 340 kcal
Total Fat: 15 g
Monounsaturated Fat: 9 g
Total Carbohydrates: 10 g
Dietary Fiber: 2 g
Protein: 40 g
Sodium: 260 mg

TROUT COOKED IN PARCHMENT / TROTA AL CARTOCCIO

Experience the lightness and delicate flavor of trout in this Italian classic, enveloped in parchment for a moist, low-fat finish.

SUPER-QUICK!

Preparation Time: 10 minutes
Cooking Time: 15 minutes
Total Time: 25 minutes
Serves: 4 servings

INGREDIENTS:

- 4 trout fillets
- 1 lemon, sliced
- 4 sprigs of fresh thyme
- Salt and pepper to taste
- 1 tablespoon olive oil

INSTRUCTIONS:

1) Preheat your oven to 400°F (200°C).
2) Cut four large pieces of parchment paper. Place a trout fillet on each.
3) Drizzle a little olive oil over each fillet. Season with salt and pepper.
4) Place lemon slices and a sprig of thyme on top of each fillet.
5) Fold the parchment paper over the trout, sealing the edges to create a pouch.
6) Place the parchment packets on a baking sheet and bake for 12–15 minutes.
7) Carefully open the packets (watch for steam) and serve immediately.

Chef's Note:

This is a great dish for entertaining, as each guest can have their own individual serving.

NUTRITIONAL INFORMATION (PER SERVING):

Calories: 220 kcal
Total Fat: 8 g
Monounsaturated Fat: 4 g
Total Carbohydrates: 2 g
Dietary Fiber: 1 g
Protein: 34 g
Sodium: 210 mg

SICILIAN SWORDFISH BUNDLES / INVOLTINI DI PESCE SPADA

Indulge in a Sicilian specialty featuring swordfish rolled with herbs and cheese, all within a rich tomato sauce. Light and elegant, this dish is perfect for a low-fat Mediterranean meal.

HEART-HEALTHY

Preparation Time: 20 minutes
Cooking Time: 20 minutes
Total Time: 40 minutes
Serves: 4 servings

INGREDIENTS:

- 4 swordfish steaks, thinly sliced
- 1 cup low-fat ricotta cheese
- 2 tablespoons capers, drained
- 1 cup diced tomatoes (canned or fresh)
- 1 clove garlic, minced
- 1 tablespoon olive oil
- Zest of 1 lemon
- Salt and pepper to taste
- Fresh basil leaves for garnish

INSTRUCTIONS:

1) Preheat your oven to 350°F (175°C).
2) In a bowl, mix low-fat ricotta, capers, and lemon zest. Season with salt and pepper.
3) Lay out the swordfish slices and spread the ricotta mixture on each. Roll up the slices and secure with toothpicks.
4) Heat olive oil in a skillet over medium heat. Add garlic and sauté until fragrant.
5) Add diced tomatoes and bring to a simmer.
6) Carefully place the swordfish bundles in the skillet, seam-side down.
7) Cover and transfer the skillet to the preheated oven. Bake for 15-20 minutes.
8) Garnish with fresh basil leaves before serving.

Chef's Note:
Serve with a side of steamed vegetables or whole-grain rice to make it a complete meal.

NUTRITIONAL INFORMATION (PER SERVING):

Calories: 250 kcal
Total Fat: 8 g
Monounsaturated Fat: 4 g
Total Carbohydrates: 7 g
Dietary Fiber: 2 g
Protein: 35 g
Sodium: 220 mg

BAKED SARDINES WITH TOMATOES AND CAPERS

Experience the authentic taste of Mediterranean cuisine with this simple yet flavorful dish. Fresh sardines are baked to perfection with juicy tomatoes and zesty capers, offering a delightful blend of taste and texture.

HEART-HEALTHY

Preparation Time: 15 minutes
Cooking Time: 20 minutes
Total Time: 35 minutes
Serves: 4

INGREDIENTS:

- 12 fresh sardines, cleaned and gutted
- 2 cups cherry tomatoes, halved
- 1/4 cup capers, drained
- 4 cloves garlic, thinly sliced
- 1 lemon, thinly sliced
- 1/4 cup extra-virgin olive oil
- 1 teaspoon dried oregano
- Salt and pepper to taste
- Fresh parsley for garnish

INSTRUCTIONS:

1. Preheat your oven to 375°F (190°C).
2. In a baking dish, arrange the sardines side by side.
3. Scatter the halved cherry tomatoes, capers, and sliced garlic around and on top of the sardines.
4. Place lemon slices over the sardines for added flavor.
5. Drizzle the extra-virgin olive oil over the entire dish.
6. Sprinkle the dried oregano, salt, and pepper over the sardines and vegetables.
7. Place the baking dish in the preheated oven and bake for about 20 minutes, or until the sardines are cooked through and the tomatoes are soft.
8. Remove from the oven and let rest for a few minutes before serving.

To Serve:
1. Garnish with fresh parsley and additional lemon slices if desired.
2. Serve hot, directly from the baking dish or plated individually.

Chef's Note:
You can substitute fresh sardines with canned ones, but adjust the cooking time accordingly. If using canned, baking for 10-12 minutes should suffice.

NUTRITIONAL INFORMATION (PER SERVING):

Calories: 260 kcal
Total Fat: 16 g
Monounsaturated Fat: 9 g
Total Carbohydrates: 7 g
Dietary Fiber: 2 g
Protein: 22 g
Sodium: 450 mg

PORTUGUESE FISH STEW

Delight in the rich, comforting flavors of the Iberian coast with this Portuguese Fish Stew, featuring a medley of seafood and aromatic herbs.

SPECIAL OCCASION

Preparation Time: 20 minutes
Cooking Time: 40 minutes
Total Time: 60 minutes
Serves: 4

INGREDIENTS:

- 1 lb white fish (cod, haddock, or snapper), cut into chunks
- 1/2 lb shrimp, peeled and deveined
- 1/2 lb clams, scrubbed
- 1 medium onion, finely chopped
- 3 cloves garlic, minced
- 1 can (14.5 oz) diced tomatoes
- 4 cups fish stock or vegetable broth
- 1 cup dry white wine
- 1/4 cup olive oil
- 1 bay leaf
- 1 tsp paprika
- 1/2 tsp crushed red pepper flakes
- Salt and pepper to taste
- Chopped parsley for garnish
- Lemon wedges for serving

INSTRUCTIONS:

1. In a large pot, heat the olive oil over medium heat. Add the chopped onion and garlic and sauté until translucent, about 5 minutes.
2. Stir in the paprika and crushed red pepper flakes, followed by the diced tomatoes. Cook for another 3-4 minutes, allowing the flavors to meld.
3. Add the white wine and let it reduce by half, about 5 minutes.
4. Pour in the fish stock or vegetable broth and add the bay leaf. Bring the mixture to a simmer and cook for 15 minutes.
5. Add the white fish chunks to the pot, and simmer for 5 minutes.
6. Add the shrimp and clams, cover the pot, and cook for an additional 10 minutes, or until the clams have opened and the shrimp are pink.
7. Remove the bay leaf, and season the stew with salt and pepper to taste.
8. Ladle the stew into bowls, garnish with chopped parsley, and serve with lemon wedges on the side.

Chef's Note:

Feel free to include other seafood like mussels or squid for added variety. This stew is excellent served with crusty bread to soak up the broth.

NUTRITIONAL INFORMATION (PER SERVING):

Calories: 420 kcal
Total Fat: 16 g
Monounsaturated Fat: 9 g
Total Carbohydrates: 20 g
Dietary Fiber: 2 g
Protein: 45 g
Sodium: 800 mg

SWORDFISH A LA SICILIANA

Experience the vibrant flavors of Sicily with this swordfish dish featuring cherry tomatoes, olives, and capers.

HEART-HEALTHY

Preparation Time: 15 minutes
Cooking Time: 20 minutes
Total Time: 35 minutes
Serves: 4

INGREDIENTS:

- 4 swordfish steaks, about 6 oz each
- 1 pint cherry tomatoes, halved
- 1/2 cup green olives, pitted and chopped
- 1/4 cup capers, drained
- 1/4 cup fresh basil leaves, chopped
- 2 cloves garlic, minced
- 1/4 cup extra-virgin olive oil
- Juice of 1 lemon
- Salt and pepper to taste
- Additional basil leaves for garnish

INSTRUCTIONS:

1. Preheat your oven to 400°F (200°C).
2. In a bowl, mix together the cherry tomatoes, olives, capers, chopped basil, and garlic.
3. In an oven-safe skillet, heat 2 tablespoons of olive oil over medium-high heat. Season the swordfish steaks with salt and pepper.
4. Add the swordfish to the skillet and sear for about 2 minutes on each side, until slightly browned.
5. Remove the skillet from heat and spoon the tomato-olive mixture around the swordfish.
6. Drizzle the remaining olive oil and lemon juice over the fish and the tomato-olive mixture.
7. Place the skillet in the preheated oven and bake for 12-15 minutes, or until the swordfish is cooked through but still moist.
8. Remove from oven, garnish with additional basil leaves, and serve immediately.

Chef's Note:

You can also add a touch of white wine to the tomato-olive mixture for extra flavor. This dish pairs wonderfully with a side of couscous.

NUTRITIONAL INFORMATION (PER SERVING):

- Calories: 490 kcal
- Total Fat: 28 g
- Monounsaturated Fat: 16 g
- Total Carbohydrates: 10 g
- Dietary Fiber: 2 g
- Protein: 45 g
- Sodium: 680 mg

HOW TO GRILL FISH THE MEDITERRANEAN WAY

Grilling fish is a wonderful way to enjoy its flavors, textures, and nutritional benefits. However, cooking fish on the grill can be a bit tricky, especially given its tendency to stick or break apart. Here's a comprehensive guide on how to grill fish like a pro the Mediterranean way!

Choosing the Right Fish
- **Firm Fish:** Tuna, swordfish, and salmon are excellent for grilling as they are more robust and won't flake easily.
- **Delicate Fish:** Fish like tilapia, cod, and flounder are best avoided on the grill unless you're using a fish basket or foil, as they tend to fall apart.

Prepping the Fish
- **Marinate or Season:** Depending on your recipe, marinate the fish for at least 30 minutes or simply season it with salt, pepper, and your choice of herbs or spices. Don't marinate for too long, especially with acidic marinades, because the fish will "cook".
- **Oil it Up:** Lightly oil the fish to prevent it from sticking to the grill. Alternatively, you can oil the grill grates.

Prepping the Grill
- **Clean the Grill:** Always start with a clean grill to prevent sticking and any off-flavors.
- **High Heat for High Fats:** Fatty fish like salmon do well on high heat.
- **Medium Heat for Lean Fish:** Leaner fish like tilapia or cod should be cooked on medium heat to avoid drying out.

Grilling Techniques
- **Direct Heat:** Best for firm, thick cuts. Place the fish directly over the heat source.
- **Indirect Heat:** For more delicate or thinly sliced fish, use indirect heat.
- **Fish Basket/Foil:** A fish basket or a layer of foil can help keep more delicate fish intact.

Cooking Times
- **Thick Fillets (1-1.5 inches):** About 4-5 minutes per side on high heat
- **Medium Fillets (0.5-1 inch):** 3-4 minutes per side on medium-high heat
- **Thin Fillets:** 2-3 minutes per side on medium heat

Pairings
- **White Wines:** Lighter fish pairs wonderfully with crisp white wines like Pinot Grigio or Chardonnay.
- **Red Wines:** For hearty, meaty fish like tuna or swordfish, consider lighter reds like Pinot Noir.
- **Sides:** Grilled vegetables, coleslaw, or a fresh salad are excellent accompaniments.
- **Sauces:** A lemon butter sauce, aioli, or a fresh salsa can add a burst of flavor.

Common Mistakes to Avoid
- **Overcooking:** Fish cooks quickly. Keep an eye on it to avoid overcooking.
- **Flipping Too Soon:** Wait for a good sear to form before flipping to avoid sticking.
- **Ignoring Grill Temp:** Make sure the grill is adequately preheated to the correct temperature.

Tips
- **Skin On:** Cooking skin-on helps keep the fish moist.
- **The Flake Test:** Fish is done when it easily flakes with a fork but still has a moist appearance.

GRILLED LEMON-HERB SALMON

A simple yet flavorful recipe that brings out the richness of salmon with a zesty lemon-herb marinade.
KID-FRIENDLY

Preparation Time: 10 minutes
Cooking Time: 10 minutes
Total Time: 20 minutes
Serves: 4

INGREDIENTS:
- 4 salmon fillets
- 2 lemons, juiced
- 3 tbsp olive oil
- 2 cloves garlic, minced
- 1 tbsp chopped fresh herbs (dill, parsley, or thyme)
- Salt and pepper to taste

INSTRUCTIONS:
1) Mix lemon juice, olive oil, garlic, herbs, salt, and pepper in a bowl.
2) Marinate the salmon fillets for at least 30 minutes.
3) Preheat the grill to high heat.
4) Grill the salmon for 4-5 minutes per side, or until it easily flakes with a fork.

Variations:
- Citrus Twist: Use lime or orange juice instead of lemon.

- Asian Flair: Add a dash of soy sauce and ginger to the marinade.
- Spicy Kick: Include a teaspoon of red pepper flakes or cayenne pepper in the marinade.
- Mediterranean Style: Add chopped olives and capers.
- Garlic Lovers: Double the amount of garlic for a stronger flavor.

Chef's Note:
Serve with grilled vegetables for a complete meal.

NUTRITIONAL INFORMATION (PER SERVING):
Calories: 320 kcal
Total Fat: 22 g
Monounsaturated Fat: 12 g
Polyunsaturated Fat: 6 g (2 g omega-3 fatty acids)
Total Carbohydrates: 4 g
Dietary Fiber: 1 g
Protein: 28 g
Sodium: 100 mg

TRADITIONAL GRILLED SWORDFISH

A classic grilled swordfish recipe that highlights the meaty, rich flavor of the fish, perfect for a quick and nutritious meal.
SUPER-QUICK!

Preparation Time: 10 minutes
Cooking Time: 10 minutes
Total Time: 20 minutes
Serves: 4

INGREDIENTS:
- 4 swordfish steaks (about 6 ounces each)
- 1/4 cup olive oil
- 2 cloves garlic, minced
- Zest and juice of 1 lemon
- 1 tablespoon fresh parsley, chopped
- Salt and freshly ground black pepper, to taste

INSTRUCTIONS:
1. Preheat the grill to medium-high heat.
2. In a small bowl, whisk together the olive oil, minced garlic, lemon zest, lemon juice, and chopped parsley.
3. Season the swordfish steaks with salt and freshly ground black pepper.
4. Generously brush each side of the swordfish steaks with the olive oil mixture.
5. Place the seasoned swordfish steaks on the preheated grill.
6. Grill for about 4 to 5 minutes per side, or until the fish flakes easily with a fork.
7. Remove the swordfish steaks from the grill and let them rest for a couple of minutes before serving.

Chef's Note:
Swordfish can be a little dry if overcooked, so make sure to keep an eye on it. This dish pairs well with a side of grilled vegetables or a fresh salad.

NUTRITIONAL INFORMATION (PER SERVING):
Calories: 280 kcal
Total Fat: 14 g
Monounsaturated Fat: 9 g
Total Carbohydrates: 2 g
Dietary Fiber: 0 g
Protein: 35 g
Sodium: 100 mg

SAMAK BIL CHERMOULA ~ MOROCCAN~ STYLE GRILLED TUNA

A succulent grilled tuna dish infused with chermoula, a Moroccan herb and spice marinade. This low-calorie, low-fat recipe offers a burst of flavors while keeping things light and healthy.
HEART HEALTHY

Preparation Time: 15 minutes
Marination Time: 30 minutes
Cooking Time: 8 minutes
Total Time: 53 minutes
Serves: 4

INGREDIENTS:
- 4 tuna steaks, each about 150g
- 2 cloves garlic, minced
- Juice of 1 lemon
- 2 tablespoons olive oil
- 1 teaspoon ground cumin
- 1 teaspoon ground coriander
- 1/2 teaspoon paprika
- Salt and black pepper to taste
- 1/4 cup chopped fresh cilantro
- 1/4 cup chopped fresh parsley

INSTRUCTIONS:
1) In a bowl, combine the minced garlic, lemon juice, olive oil, cumin, coriander, paprika, salt, and black pepper. Stir well to make the chermoula marinade.
2) Add the chopped cilantro and parsley to the chermoula and mix.
3) Place the tuna steaks in a shallow dish and pour the chermoula marinade over them, ensuring all sides are well coated.
4) Cover the dish with plastic wrap and refrigerate for at least 30 minutes to marinate.
5) Preheat a grill or grill pan over medium-high heat.
6) Once hot, place the marinated tuna steaks on the grill.

7) Cook for about 3-4 minutes on each side or until done to your liking.
8) Serve hot, garnished with extra fresh herbs if desired.

Chef's Note:
You can also use the chermoula as a sauce by setting aside a portion before marinating the fish. Serve it alongside the grilled tuna for added flavor.

NUTRITIONAL INFORMATION (PER SERVING):
Calories: 250 kcal
Total Fat: 8 g
Monounsaturated Fat: 5 g
Total Carbohydrates: 3 g
Dietary Fiber: 1 g
Protein: 35 g
Sodium: 160 mg

CHARRED HERB~CRUSTED MACKEREL

A delightful dish, where the smoky flavor of grilled mackerel meets the freshness of herbs.
SPECIAL OCCASION

Preparation Time: 10 minutes
Cooking Time: 8 minutes
Total Time: 18 minutes
Serves: 4

INGREDIENTS:
- 4 mackerel fillets
- 3 tbsp olive oil
- 1 clove garlic, minced
- 1 tbsp chopped fresh parsley
- 1 tbsp chopped fresh dill
- Salt and pepper to taste

INSTRUCTIONS:
1) In a bowl, mix olive oil, garlic, parsley, dill, salt, and pepper.
2) Brush the herb mixture onto the mackerel fillets.
3) Preheat the grill to medium-high heat.
4) Grill the fillets for 3-4 minutes per side until the skin is crispy and the fish is cooked through.

NUTRITIONAL INFORMATION (PER SERVING):
Calories: 290 kcal
Total Fat: 20 g
Monounsaturated Fat: 8 g
Polyunsaturated Fat: 3 g
Total Carbohydrates: 1 g
Dietary Fiber: 0 g
Protein: 25 g
Sodium: 90 mg

SPICED GRILLED TROUT WITH LEMON

A rustic dish with spiced trout that's elevated with a drizzle of lemon.
KID FRIENDLY

Preparation Time: 10 minutes
Cooking Time: 12 minutes
Total Time: 22 minutes
Serves: 4

INGREDIENTS:
- 4 trout fillets
- 2 tbsp olive oil
- 1 tsp smoked paprika
- 1/2 tsp ground cumin
- Salt and pepper to taste
- Zest and juice of 1 lemon

INSTRUCTIONS:
- Mix olive oil, paprika, cumin, salt, and pepper in a bowl.
- Brush the spice mixture onto the trout fillets.
- Preheat grill to medium heat.
- Grill the fillets for 5-6 minutes per side until the fish is cooked through.
- Drizzle the lemon zest over the grilled trout before serving.

Chef's Note:
Enjoy with a light couscous salad or roasted potatoes on the side.

NUTRITIONAL INFORMATION (PER SERVING):
Calories: 310 kcal
Total Fat: 22 g
Monounsaturated Fat: 10 g
Polyunsaturated Fat: 3 g
Total Carbohydrates: 2 g
Dietary Fiber: 0 g
Protein: 28 g
Sodium: 90 mg

GRILLED SPICY GARLIC SHRIMP

A quick and easy dish that brings together the smokiness of the grill with spicy garlic flavors.
SUPER-QUICK!

Preparation Time: 5 minutes
Cooking Time: 6 minutes
Total Time: 11 minutes
Serves: 4

INGREDIENTS:
- 1 lb large shrimp, peeled and deveined
- 3 tbsp olive oil

- 2 cloves garlic, minced
- 1 tsp red pepper flakes
- Salt to taste

INSTRUCTIONS:
1) In a bowl, mix olive oil, minced garlic, red pepper flakes, and salt.
2) Toss the shrimp in the spicy garlic oil mixture.
3) Preheat the grill to high heat.
4) Grill the shrimp for 2-3 minutes per side until they turn pink.

Chef's Note:
This shrimp pairs well with grilled corn on the cob or a side of coleslaw.

NUTRITIONAL INFORMATION (PER SERVING):
Calories: 220 kcal
Total Fat: 14 g
Monounsaturated Fat: 10 g
Total Carbohydrates: 1 g
Dietary Fiber: 0 g
Protein: 22 g
Sodium: 180 mg

GRILLED CLAMS WITH LEMON-HERB SAUCE

A simple and elegant dish where the briny clams are highlighted by a zesty lemon-herb sauce.
LOW-CALORIES

Preparation Time: 10 minutes
Cooking Time: 10 minutes
Total Time: 20 minutes
Serves: 4

INGREDIENTS:
- 2 dozen small clams, scrubbed
- 1/4 cup olive oil
- Juice and zest of 1 lemon
- 1 tbsp chopped fresh basil
- 1 tbsp chopped fresh thyme
- Salt and pepper to taste

INSTRUCTIONS:
1) Preheat the grill to medium-high heat.
2) In a bowl, mix olive oil, lemon juice, lemon zest, basil, thyme, salt, and pepper.
3) Place the clams directly on the grill grates.
4) Cover and grill for 6-10 minutes until the clams have opened.
5) Discard any unopened clams and drizzle the lemon-herb sauce over the opened ones.

Chef's Note:
Serve with a side of grilled vegetables or a simple salad.

NUTRITIONAL INFORMATION (PER SERVING):
Calories: 160 kcal
Total Fat: 14 g
Monounsaturated Fat: 10 g
Total Carbohydrates: 2 g
Dietary Fiber: 0 g
Protein: 6 g
Sodium: 50 mg

15-MINUTE GREEK GRILLED SARDINES

Enjoy the authentic flavors of the Mediterranean with these simple yet delicious grilled sardines, packed with omega-3 fatty acids.
SUPER-QUICK!

Preparation Time: 5 minutes
Cooking Time: 10 minutes
Total Time: 15 minutes
Serves: 4

INGREDIENTS:
- 12 fresh sardines, cleaned and gutted
- 4 tbsp olive oil
- Juice and zest of 1 lemon
- 2 cloves garlic, minced
- Salt and pepper to taste
- Fresh oregano leaves for garnish

INSTRUCTIONS:
1) In a small bowl, mix olive oil, lemon juice, lemon zest, minced garlic, salt, and pepper.
2) Preheat grill to medium-high heat.
3) Brush the sardines with the olive oil mixture.
4) Place the sardines on the grill and cook for about 4-5 minutes on each side, until the skin is crispy and the fish is cooked through.
5) Garnish with fresh oregano leaves before serving.

Chef's Note:
Excellent with a side of Greek salad or tzatziki sauce.

NUTRITIONAL INFORMATION (PER SERVING):
Calories: 230 kcal
Total Fat: 17 g
Monounsaturated Fat: 11 g
Total Carbohydrates: 2 g
Dietary Fiber: 0 g
Protein: 18 g
Sodium: 90 mg

GRILLED FISH WITH WALNUT GREMOLADA

Upgrade your grilled fish game with this aromatic walnut gremolada, bringing nuttiness and zest to every bite.

HEART-HEALTHY

Preparation Time: 10 minutes
Cooking Time: 10 minutes
Total Time: 20 minutes
Serves: 4

INGREDIENTS:

- 4 fish fillets (salmon, cod, or sea bass)
- 2 tbsp olive oil
- Salt and pepper to taste
- 1/2 cup walnuts, finely chopped
- Zest of 1 lemon
- 2 cloves garlic, minced
- 2 tbsp fresh parsley, chopped

INSTRUCTIONS:

1) Preheat the grill to medium-high heat.
2) Drizzle fish fillets with olive oil and season with salt and pepper.
3) In a small bowl, combine walnuts, lemon zest, garlic, and parsley to make the gremolada.
4) Place fish on the grill and cook for about 4-5 minutes per side, depending on thickness, or until fish is opaque and flakes easily.
5) Once cooked, top each fish fillet with a generous spoonful of walnut gremolada.

Chef's Note:
This dish pairs well with grilled vegetables or a light, mixed greens salad.

NUTRITIONAL INFORMATION (PER SERVING):
Calories: 280 kcal
Total Fat: 18 g
Monounsaturated Fat: 10 g
Total Carbohydrates: 3 g
Dietary Fiber: 1 g
Protein: 25 g
Sodium: 120 mg

SHAWIA ~ MOROCCAN GRILLED OCTOPUS

This North African-inspired dish infuses the octopus with a blend of spices, offering an exquisite taste and richness in protein.

SPECIAL OCCASION

Preparation Time: 20 minutes
Cooking Time: 40 minutes
Total Time: 60 minutes
Serves: 4

INGREDIENTS:

- 1 octopus (~1.5 kg), cleaned and prepared
- 1/4 cup olive oil
- 1 teaspoon ground cumin
- 1 teaspoon paprika
- 2 cloves garlic, minced
- Salt and pepper to taste

INSTRUCTIONS:

1) Boil the octopus in a pot of salted water for about 30 minutes or until tender. Let it cool in the water to tenderize further.
2) Preheat the grill to medium-high heat.
3) In a bowl, mix olive oil, cumin, paprika, minced garlic, salt, and pepper.
4) Rub the octopus with the spice mixture, making sure it's well coated.
5) Grill for about 5 minutes per side, or until the octopus gets a nice char.
6) Serve immediately.

Chef's Note:
To serve, you can slice the octopus and toss it in a salad with fresh herbs, olive oil, and lemon juice.

NUTRITIONAL INFORMATION (PER SERVING):
Calories: 260 kcal
Total Fat: 14 g
Monounsaturated Fat: 10 g
Total Carbohydrates: 5 g
Dietary Fiber: 0 g
Protein: 28 g
Sodium: 200 mg

GRILLED CALAMARI WITH LEMON AND HERBS

KID-FRIENDLY

Preparation Time: 20 minutes (plus 1 hour marinating)
Cooking Time: 10 minutes
Total Time: 30 minutes (plus 1 hour marinating)
Serves: 4

INGREDIENTS:

- 1.5 pounds fresh calamari tubes and tentacles, cleaned
- 3 cloves garlic, minced
- Zest and juice of 1 lemon
- 1/4 cup extra-virgin olive oil
- 2 tablespoons fresh parsley, finely chopped
- 2 tablespoons fresh basil, finely chopped
- Salt and freshly ground black pepper, to taste
- Lemon wedges for serving

INSTRUCTIONS:

1. In a mixing bowl, combine the garlic, lemon zest and juice, olive oil, parsley, basil, salt, and pepper.

2. Add the calamari to the marinade and toss well to coat. Cover and refrigerate for at least 1 hour, or up to 4 hours.
3. Preheat the grill to high heat. If using a charcoal grill, wait until the coals are covered with white ash.
4. Remove the calamari from the marinade, allowing excess to drip off. Grill the calamari for 4-5 minutes per side, or until they are opaque and slightly charred.
5. Transfer the grilled calamari to a serving platter and sprinkle with additional salt, if needed. Garnish with lemon wedges and extra herbs if desired.
6. Serve immediately, with lemon wedges on the side for squeezing.

Chef's Note:
This grilled calamari dish is great for outdoor gatherings and pairs wonderfully with a crisp, white wine or a cold beer. You can also serve it as an appetizer or incorporate it into a Mediterranean-style salad.

NUTRITIONAL INFORMATION (PER SERVING):
Calories: 220 kcal
Total Fat: 12 g
Saturated Fat: 2 g
Total Carbohydrates: 4 g
Dietary Fiber: 0 g
Protein: 25 g
Sodium: 110 mg

GRILLED CALAMARI STUFFED WITH FETA AND SPINACH

Indulge in a Greek-inspired delicacy that melds fresh calamari with creamy feta and nutritious spinach. A high-protein, low-carb dish that's simply unforgettable.
MEAL-PREP FRIENDLY

Preparation Time: 20 minutes
Cooking Time: 10 minutes
Total Time: 30 minutes
Serves: 4

INGREDIENTS:
1) 4 whole squid (calamari), cleaned, tentacles removed
2) 200g feta cheese, crumbled
3) 100g fresh spinach, chopped
4) 1 small red onion, finely chopped
5) 1 clove garlic, minced
6) 2 tablespoons pine nuts
7) 2 tablespoons extra-virgin olive oil
8) Zest of 1 lemon
9) Salt and pepper to taste
10) 1 tablespoon fresh oregano, chopped (for garnish)

INSTRUCTIONS:
1) Preheat the grill to medium-high heat.
2) In a pan over medium heat, sauté the chopped onion and garlic in 1 tablespoon of olive oil until translucent.

3) Add the spinach to the pan and cook until wilted. Remove from heat.
4) In a bowl, combine the sautéed spinach mixture, crumbled feta, pine nuts, and lemon zest. Season with a pinch of salt and pepper.
5) Carefully stuff each calamari with the feta and spinach mixture. Use toothpicks to seal the open end.
6) Drizzle the stuffed calamari with the remaining olive oil and season with a bit more salt and pepper.
7) Place the calamari on the preheated grill and cook for about 4-5 minutes per side, turning once, until the calamari is cooked through and slightly charred.
8) Garnish with fresh oregano before serving.

Chef's Note:
This dish can be prepared ahead and kept refrigerated until ready to grill. Just make sure to bring it to room temperature before grilling for even cooking.

NUTRITIONAL INFORMATION (PER SERVING):
Calories: 270 kcal
Total Fat: 17 g
Monounsaturated Fat: 8 g
Total Carbohydrates: 8 g
Dietary Fiber: 1 g
Protein: 23 g
Sodium: 420 mg

MEDITERRANEAN GRILLED SEA BASS WITH OLIVE RELISH

Dive into the flavors of the Mediterranean with this succulent Grilled Sea Bass, complemented by a vibrant olive relish. This easy-to-make, nutritious dish is perfect for a summer cookout or a sophisticated dinner.
SPECIAL OCCASION

Preparation Time: 20 minutes
Cooking Time: 10 minutes
Total Time: 30 minutes
Serves: 4

INGREDIENTS:
For the Sea Bass:
*   4 sea bass fillets (about 6-8 oz each)
*   2 tablespoons extra-virgin olive oil
*   Salt and pepper to taste
*   1 lemon, cut into wedges
For the Olive Relish:
*   1 cup pitted Kalamata olives, finely chopped
*   1/2 cup cherry tomatoes, quartered
*   1/4 cup fresh parsley, chopped
*   2 tablespoons capers, drained
*   1 clove garlic, minced
*   Zest of 1 lemon
*   2 tablespoons extra-virgin olive oil
*   Salt and pepper to taste

INSTRUCTIONS:

For the Olive Relish:

1. In a medium bowl, combine the chopped olives, cherry tomatoes, parsley, capers, minced garlic, and lemon zest.
2. Drizzle with olive oil and season with salt and pepper. Stir well and set aside to let the flavors meld together.

For the Sea Bass:

1. Preheat the grill to medium-high heat.
2. Pat the sea bass fillets dry with a paper towel, and then rub them with olive oil. Season with salt and pepper.
3. Place the fillets on the preheated grill and cook for about 4-5 minutes per side, or until the fish flakes easily with a fork.
4. Remove the fillets from the grill and place them on serving plates.

To Serve:

1. Spoon a generous amount of olive relish over each sea bass fillet.
2. Serve with lemon wedges on the side.

Chef's Note:

If you can't find sea bass, you can substitute it with another firm, white-fleshed fish like halibut or cod.

NUTRITIONAL INFORMATION (PER SERVING):

Calories: 320 kcal
Total Fat: 18 g
Monounsaturated Fat: 10 g
Total Carbohydrates: 6 g
Dietary Fiber: 2 g
Protein: 35 g
Sodium: 680 mg

GRILLED TROUT WITH MEDITERRANEAN RELISH

This amazing relish made with olives, capers, and sun-dried tomatoes goes well with everything so make a double batch and keep it in the fridge forup to three days, you can use it a snack on multigrain crackers, over grilled chicken or tofu, or even mixed in a frittata

MEAL-PREP FRIENDLY

Preparation Time: 20 minutes
Cooking Time: 10 minutes
Total Time: 30 minutes
Serves: 4

INGREDIENTS:

- 4 trout fillets, about 6 oz each
- 2 tablespoons olive oil
- Salt and pepper to taste

For the Mediterranean Relish:

- 1 cup cherry tomatoes, halved
- 1/2 cup Kalamata olives, pitted and chopped
- 1/4 cup sun-dried tomatoes, chopped
- 2 tablespoons capers, drained
- 1 garlic clove, minced
- 2 tablespoons fresh basil, chopped
- Zest of 1 lemon
- 1 tablespoon lemon juice
- 2 tablespoons olive oil
- Salt and pepper to taste

INSTRUCTIONS:

1. Preheat the grill to medium-high heat. Clean and oil the grill grates.
2. Drizzle olive oil over the trout fillets and season with salt and pepper. Set aside.
3. In a medium bowl, combine all the ingredients for the Mediterranean relish. Stir well and set aside.
4. Place the trout fillets on the grill, skin-side down. Cook for 4-5 minutes per side or until the fish is cooked through and flakes easily with a fork.
5. Once the trout is cooked, remove from the grill and place on serving plates.
6. Spoon a generous amount of Mediterranean relish over each trout fillet.
7. Serve immediately, garnished with additional basil leaves if desired.

Chef's Note:

This dish pairs beautifully with a side of grilled asparagus or steamed green beans. The Mediterranean relish can also be made in advance and stored in the fridge for up to 2 days.

NUTRITIONAL INFORMATION (PER SERVING):

Calories: 350 kcal
Total Fat: 18 g
Monounsaturated Fat: 8 g
Total Carbohydrates: 6 g
Dietary Fiber: 2 g
Protein: 35 g
Sodium: 420 mg

Vegetarian Dishes

LENTIL-STUFFED BELL PEPPERS

Easy to make, easy to store, and a crowd-pleaser!
KID-FRIENDLY

Preparation Time: 20 minutes
Cooking Time: 50 minutes
Total Time: 70 minutes
Serves: 4

INGREDIENTS:

- 4 large bell peppers, halved and seeds removed
- 1 cup dried green lentils, rinsed and drained
- 2 1/2 cups vegetable broth
- 1 tablespoon olive oil
- 1 small onion, finely chopped
- 2 cloves garlic, minced
- 1 medium carrot, grated
- 1 teaspoon ground cumin
- 1 teaspoon ground paprika
- Salt and pepper to taste
- 1 can (14.5 oz) diced tomatoes, drained
- 1/4 cup chopped fresh parsley
- 1 cup shredded mozzarella cheese (optional)

INSTRUCTIONS:

1. Preheat your oven to 375°F (190°C).
2. In a medium saucepan, bring vegetable broth to a boil. Add lentils, reduce heat to low, and simmer until tender, about 20 minutes. Drain any excess liquid.
3. While the lentils are cooking, heat olive oil in a skillet over medium heat. Add chopped onions and garlic, sautéing until softened.
4. Stir in grated carrots, ground cumin, and paprika. Cook for an additional 2-3 minutes.
5. Combine the cooked lentils with the sautéed vegetable mixture in a large bowl. Stir in diced tomatoes and fresh parsley. Season with salt and pepper.
6. Place the halved bell peppers in a baking dish, open side up.
7. Stuff the bell pepper halves with the lentil mixture. Cover the baking dish with aluminum foil.
8. Bake for about 30 minutes, or until the peppers are tender.
9. If using cheese, remove foil and sprinkle shredded mozzarella on top of each stuffed pepper. Return to oven and bake for an additional 5 minutes, or until the cheese is melted.

Chef's Note:

These lentil-stuffed bell peppers are excellent as is, but they also work well with a variety of accompaniments:

1. Serve with a dollop of Greek yogurt or tzatziki.
2. A simple side salad complements the dish nicely.
3. They can also be enjoyed with a serving of whole-grain rice or quinoa.
4. For a meaty version, you could add some crumbled feta cheese.
5. For a vegan option, use vegan cheese or omit the cheese entirely.

NUTRITIONAL INFORMATION (PER SERVING):

Calories: 260 kcal
Total Fat: 6 g
    Monounsaturated Fat: 3 g
Total Carbohydrates: 40 g
    Dietary Fiber: 15 g
Protein: 14 g
Sodium: 560 mg

ZUCCHINI LASAGNA

Indulge in this low-carb, gluten-free version of lasagna that uses zucchini slices in place of pasta for a healthy, veggie-packed meal.
GLUTEN-FREE

Preparation Time: 30 minutes
Cooking Time: 40 minutes
Total Time: 1 hour 10 minutes
Serves: 4

INGREDIENTS:

- 2 large zucchinis, thinly sliced lengthwise
- 1 tablespoon olive oil
- 1 pound ground turkey or beef
- 1 small onion, finely chopped
- 3 cloves garlic, minced
- 1 cup marinara sauce
- 1 teaspoon Italian seasoning
- Salt and pepper, to taste
- 1 cup ricotta cheese
- 1 cup shredded mozzarella cheese
- 1/4 cup grated Parmesan cheese

INSTRUCTIONS:

1. Preheat the oven to 375°F (190°C).
2. Use paper towels to blot excess moisture from the zucchini slices. Lay them out on a baking sheet and bake for 10 minutes to remove additional moisture. Remove and set aside.
3. While the zucchini is baking, heat olive oil in a skillet over medium heat. Add the ground meat, chopped onion, and garlic. Cook until the meat is browned.
4. Stir in the marinara sauce, Italian seasoning, salt, and pepper. Simmer for 5 minutes.

5. In a 9x13-inch baking dish, spread a thin layer of the meat sauce.
6. Arrange a layer of zucchini slices over the meat sauce.
7. Spread half of the ricotta cheese over the zucchini slices, then sprinkle with one-third of the shredded mozzarella.
8. Repeat layers: meat sauce, zucchini slices, and remaining ricotta.
9. Top the final layer with the remaining meat sauce and sprinkle the rest of the mozzarella and Parmesan cheese on top.
10. Bake in the preheated oven for 25-30 minutes or until the cheese is melted and bubbly.

Chef's Note:
If you prefer more veggies, feel free to add layers of sautéed spinach or bell peppers. This dish is great fresh but also reheats well for leftovers. Serve with a side of green salad for a complete meal.

NUTRITIONAL INFORMATION (PER SERVING):
Calories: 400 kcal
Total Fat: 24 g
    Monounsaturated Fat: 8 g
Total Carbohydrates: 10 g
    Dietary Fiber: 2 g
Protein: 35 g
Sodium: 700 mg

MEDITERRANEAN GRILLED VEGETABLES

Mix and match your veggies according to what you have on hand. Great as a side and even better as a main with some tzatziki or a luscious aioli.
VEGAN

Preparation Time: 15 minutes
Cooking Time: 10 minutes
Total Time: 25 minutes
Serves: 4

INGREDIENTS:
- 2 zucchinis, sliced lengthwise
- 2 bell peppers, quartered
- 1 red onion, sliced into 1/2-inch rings
- 1 eggplant, sliced into 1/2-inch rounds
- 4 tablespoons olive oil
- 2 cloves garlic, minced
- 1 teaspoon dried oregano
- 1 teaspoon dried basil
- Salt and pepper to taste
- Lemon wedges for serving

INSTRUCTIONS:
1. Preheat the grill to medium-high heat.
2. In a small bowl, mix together the olive oil, minced garlic, oregano, basil, salt, and pepper.

3. Brush the vegetable slices on both sides with the olive oil mixture.
4. Place the vegetables on the preheated grill. Cook for about 4-5 minutes per side or until they have nice grill marks and are tender.
5. Remove the vegetables from the grill and arrange them on a platter. Serve with lemon wedges on the side.

Chef's Note:
These grilled vegetables are versatile and can be enjoyed as a side dish with grilled chicken or fish. Alternatively, you can chop them up to use as a topping for pizzas or toss them into a pasta salad.

NUTRITIONAL INFORMATION (PER SERVING):
Calories: 160 kcal
Total Fat: 10 g
    Monounsaturated Fat: 7 g
Total Carbohydrates: 18 g
    Dietary Fiber: 5 g
Protein: 3 g
Sodium: 50 mg

SPANISH VEGAN PAELLA

A vegetarian twist on the classic Spanish dish, filled with colorful vegetables and aromatic spices.
ONE-POT MEAL

Preparation Time: 15 minutes
Cooking Time: 40 minutes
Total Time: 55 minutes
Serves: 4-6

INGREDIENTS:
- 1 1/2 cups Arborio rice
- 3 cups vegetable broth
- 1 onion, chopped
- 1 red bell pepper, chopped
- 1 green bell pepper, chopped
- 2 cloves garlic, minced
- 1 cup cherry tomatoes, halved
- 1/2 cup artichoke hearts, chopped
- 1/2 cup green peas
- 1/4 cup olive oil
- 1 tsp saffron threads or turmeric
- Salt and pepper to taste

INSTRUCTIONS:
1) In a large skillet or paella pan, heat olive oil over medium heat.
2) Sauté onions and garlic until translucent.
3) Add bell peppers and cook until softened.
4) Stir in rice, making sure it's well-coated with the oil and veggies.
5) Add vegetable broth, saffron threads, and bring to a simmer.

6) Add cherry tomatoes, artichoke hearts, and green peas.
7) Cover and cook for 20-25 minutes or until the rice is cooked through.
8) Season with salt and pepper to taste before serving.

Chef's Note:
Feel free to substitute the vegetables based on what's in season or to your liking.

NUTRITIONAL INFORMATION (PER SERVING):
Calories: 370 kcal
Total Fat: 12 g
Monounsaturated Fat: 8 g
Total Carbohydrates: 58 g
Dietary Fiber: 6 g
Protein: 8 g
Sodium: 460 mg

MOROCCAN VEGETABLE COUSCOUS

Infused with aromatic spices and brimming with vegetables, this Moroccan Vegetable Couscous is a feast for the senses. Enjoy it as a standalone vegetarian meal or as a side dish to grilled meats or fish.

VEGAN

Preparation Time: 15 minutes
Cooking Time: 25 minutes
Total Time: 40 minutes
Serves: 6

INGREDIENTS:
- 1 1/2 cups couscous
- 2 cups vegetable broth
- 2 tablespoons olive oil
- 1 onion, diced
- 2 cloves garlic, minced
- 1 red bell pepper, diced
- 1 zucchini, diced
- 1 carrot, diced
- 1 cup canned chickpeas, drained and rinsed
- 1 teaspoon ground cumin
- 1 teaspoon ground coriander
- 1/2 teaspoon paprika
- Salt and pepper, to taste
- Optional: chopped fresh parsley or cilantro, for garnish

INSTRUCTIONS:
1. In a medium saucepan, bring the vegetable broth to a boil. Stir in the couscous, cover, and remove from heat. Let it sit for 5 minutes, then fluff with a fork.
2. Heat olive oil in a large skillet over medium heat. Add the diced onion and minced garlic, cooking until the onion becomes translucent.
3. Add the diced red bell pepper, zucchini, and carrot to the skillet. Sauté for about 5 minutes, or until the vegetables are tender but still vibrant.

4. Stir in the chickpeas, ground cumin, ground coriander, and paprika. Cook for another 2-3 minutes, allowing the flavors to meld.
5. Add the cooked couscous to the skillet and stir to combine with the vegetables and spices. Season with salt and pepper to taste.
6. Garnish with chopped fresh parsley or cilantro before serving, if desired.

Chef's Note:
You can add other vegetables such as eggplant or cauliflower for added texture and flavor. For a non-vegetarian option, consider serving this couscous with grilled chicken or lamb skewers.

NUTRITIONAL INFORMATION (PER SERVING):
Calories: 300 kcal
Total Fat: 6 g
    Monounsaturated Fat: 3 g
Total Carbohydrates: 52 g
    Dietary Fiber: 6 g
Protein: 9 g
Sodium: 370 mg

MEDITERRANEAN QUINOA SALAD

It takes a bit of chopping, but is well worth the effort, especially if you make a double batch and keep it ready in the fridge for a busy day. It will keep well for up to 4 days.

HEART-HEALTHY

Preparation Time: 15 minutes
Cooking Time: 20 minutes
Total Time: 35 minutes
Serves: 4

INGREDIENTS:
- 1 cup uncooked quinoa
- 2 cups water or vegetable broth
- 1 cup cherry tomatoes, halved
- 1 cucumber, diced
- 1/2 red bell pepper, diced
- 1/2 cup Kalamata olives, pitted and sliced
- 1/4 cup feta cheese, crumbled
- 1/4 cup fresh parsley, chopped
- 2 tablespoons fresh mint, chopped
- 2 tablespoons olive oil
- Juice of 1 lemon
- Salt and pepper, to taste

INSTRUCTIONS:
1. In a medium saucepan, bring 2 cups of water or vegetable broth to a boil. Add quinoa and a pinch of salt. Reduce the heat to low, cover, and simmer for 15 minutes or until the quinoa is cooked and water is absorbed.

2. Remove the saucepan from heat and let it sit for 5 minutes, then fluff the quinoa with a fork. Transfer to a large mixing bowl and allow it to cool.
3. While the quinoa is cooling, prepare the vegetables and herbs.
4. Add the halved cherry tomatoes, diced cucumber, diced red bell pepper, sliced Kalamata olives, chopped parsley, and chopped mint to the bowl with quinoa.
5. In a small bowl, whisk together olive oil, lemon juice, salt, and pepper to make the dressing.
6. Pour the dressing over the quinoa and vegetable mixture. Toss well to combine all ingredients.
7. Sprinkle crumbled feta cheese on top before serving.

Chef's Note:
This Mediterranean Quinoa Salad can be served as a standalone meal or as a side dish to grilled chicken or fish. It can also be customized with other Mediterranean ingredients like artichokes or roasted red peppers.

NUTRITIONAL INFORMATION (PER SERVING):
Calories: 280 kcal
Total Fat: 11 g
    Monounsaturated Fat: 7 g
Total Carbohydrates: 35 g
    Dietary Fiber: 5 g
Protein: 10 g
Sodium: 350 mg

LENTIL SOUP CASSEROLE
Healthy like a soup, hearthy like a casserole. Easy to prep and store.
DAIRY-FREE

Preparation Time: 20 minutes
Cooking Time: 45 minutes
Total Time: 65 minutes
Serves: 6

INGREDIENTS:
- 1 cup green lentils, rinsed
- 2 1/2 cups vegetable broth
- 1 onion, diced
- 2 cloves garlic, minced
- 1 zucchini, diced
- 1 carrot, diced
- 1 can (14 oz) diced tomatoes
- 2 tbsp olive oil
- 1 tsp dried oregano
- 1 tsp dried thyme
- Salt and pepper to taste

INSTRUCTIONS:
1) Preheat the oven to 375°F (190°C).
2) In a large skillet, heat olive oil over medium heat.
3) Sauté onion and garlic until translucent.
4) Add carrots and zucchini, and cook until softened.

5) Add lentils, vegetable broth, diced tomatoes, oregano, and thyme.
6) Bring the mixture to a boil, then reduce heat and simmer for 20 minutes, or until lentils are almost cooked.
7) Transfer the mixture to a casserole dish and bake for 25 minutes, or until the lentils are fully cooked and the top is slightly crispy.
8) Season with salt and pepper to taste.

NUTRITIONAL INFORMATION (PER SERVING):
Calories: 250 kcal
Total Fat: 8 g
Monounsaturated Fat: 5 g
Total Carbohydrates: 36 g
Dietary Fiber: 15 g
Protein: 12 g
Sodium: 310 mg

EGGPLANT PARMESAN
An Italian classic reimagined with Mediterranean flair, featuring layers of baked eggplant, tomato sauce, and cheese.
KID-FRIENDLY

Preparation Time: 20 minutes
Cooking Time: 40 minutes
Total Time: 60 minutes
Serves: 4

INGREDIENTS:
- 2 large eggplants, sliced into 1/2-inch rounds
- 1 jar (16 oz) marinara sauce
- 1 1/2 cups shredded mozzarella cheese
- 1/2 cup grated Parmesan cheese
- 1/4 cup fresh basil leaves
- 2 tbsp olive oil
- Salt and pepper to taste

INSTRUCTIONS:
1) Preheat your oven to 400°F (200°C).
2) Brush eggplant slices with olive oil on both sides and season with salt and pepper.
3) Place on a baking sheet and bake for 20 minutes, flipping halfway through.
4) In a baking dish, layer a scoop of marinara sauce, followed by a layer of baked eggplant slices, then mozzarella and Parmesan cheese.
5) Repeat the layers until all ingredients are used, finishing with a layer of cheese on top.
6) Bake in the preheated oven for 20 minutes, or until cheese is melted and bubbly.
7) Garnish with fresh basil leaves before serving.

Chef's Note:
Excellent when paired with a glass of red wine and a side of crusty bread.

NUTRITIONAL INFORMATION (PER SERVING):
Calories: 350 kcal
Total Fat: 18 g
Monounsaturated Fat: 6 g
Total Carbohydrates: 35 g
Dietary Fiber: 9 g
Protein: 16 g
Sodium: 800 mg

MOROCCAN CHICKPEA STEW

A hearty and flavorful stew packed with chickpeas, tomatoes, and aromatic spices.
ONE-POT MEAL

Preparation Time: 10 minutes
Cooking Time: 30 minutes
Total Time: 40 minutes
Serves: 4

INGREDIENTS:
- 2 cans (14 oz each) chickpeas, drained and rinsed
- 1 can (14 oz) diced tomatoes
- 1 onion, chopped
- 3 cloves garlic, minced
- 2 tbsp olive oil
- 2 tsp cumin
- 1 tsp paprika
- Salt and pepper to taste

INSTRUCTIONS:
1) Heat olive oil in a large pot over medium heat.
2) Sauté onions and garlic until translucent.
3) Add cumin and paprika, stirring well to coat the onions and garlic.
4) Add chickpeas and diced tomatoes, including the juice from the can.
5) Bring to a simmer and cook for about 20-25 minutes, allowing flavors to meld.
6) Season with salt and pepper to taste.

NUTRITIONAL INFORMATION (PER SERVING):
Calories: 290 kcal
Total Fat: 9 g
Monounsaturated Fat: 5 g
Total Carbohydrates: 40 g
Dietary Fiber: 12 g
Protein: 12 g
Sodium: 420 mg

LENTIL~STUFFED PORTOBELLO MUSHROOMS

A delicious and hearty plant-based meal featuring large Portobello mushrooms filled with a savory lentil mixture.
MEAL-PREP FRIENDLY

Preparation Time: 20 minutes
Cooking Time: 25 minutes
Total Time: 45 minutes
Serves: 4

INGREDIENTS:
- 4 large Portobello mushrooms, stems removed
- 1 cup cooked lentils
- 1 onion, chopped
- 2 cloves garlic, minced
- 1 medium tomato, chopped
- 1 tsp oregano
- 1 tsp thyme
- Salt and pepper to taste
- 2 tbsp olive oil

INSTRUCTIONS:
1) Preheat the oven to 375°F (190°C).
2) In a skillet, heat olive oil and sauté onion and garlic until translucent.
3) Add cooked lentils, chopped tomato, oregano, thyme, salt, and pepper. Cook for 5-7 minutes.
4) Place the Portobello mushrooms, gill-side up, on a baking sheet.
5) Fill each mushroom cap with the lentil mixture.
6) Bake for 20-25 minutes, or until the mushrooms are tender.

NUTRITIONAL INFORMATION (PER SERVING):
Calories: 220 kcal
Total Fat: 8 g
Monounsaturated Fat: 5 g
Total Carbohydrates: 26 g
Dietary Fiber: 10 g
Protein: 12 g
Sodium: 300 mg

LENTIL AND MUSHROOM STUFFED TOMATOES

Umami rich and dense with nutrients for a complete vegetarian meal.
MEAL-PREP FRIENDLY

Preparation Time: 20 minutes
Cooking Time: 40 minutes
Total Time: 1 hour
Serves: 4

INGREDIENTS:

- 4 large tomatoes
- 1 cup cooked green lentils
- 1 cup mushrooms, finely chopped
- 1 small onion, finely chopped
- 2 cloves garlic, minced
- 2 tablespoons olive oil
- 1 teaspoon dried thyme
- 1 teaspoon dried oregano
- Salt and pepper, to taste
- 1/4 cup breadcrumbs
- 1/4 cup grated Parmesan cheese (optional)

INSTRUCTIONS:

1. Preheat the oven to 350°F (175°C).
2. Cut the tops off the tomatoes and scoop out the pulp, leaving a hollow shell. Reserve the pulp and chop it up for the filling.
3. In a medium skillet, heat the olive oil over medium heat. Add the onions and garlic, sautéing until translucent.
4. Add the mushrooms to the skillet and cook until softened, about 5 minutes.
5. Stir in the chopped tomato pulp, cooked lentils, thyme, and oregano. Cook for another 5–7 minutes. Season with salt and pepper to taste.
6. Carefully stuff each tomato with the lentil-mushroom mixture.
7. Place the stuffed tomatoes in a baking dish. Sprinkle breadcrumbs over the tops, and if you're using it, add grated Parmesan cheese.
8. Cover the dish with aluminum foil and bake for 20 minutes. Remove the foil and continue to bake for an additional 10–15 minutes, or until the tomatoes are soft and the tops are slightly browned.

Chef's Note:

Feel free to use brown rice or quinoa as a substitute for lentils for different textures and flavors. For a gluten-free version, you can replace breadcrumbs with almond meal or gluten-free breadcrumbs.

NUTRITIONAL INFORMATION (PER SERVING):

Calories: 460 kcal
Total Fat: 12 g
    Monounsaturated Fat: 6 g
Total Carbohydrates: 65 g
    Dietary Fiber: 20 g
Protein: 20 g
Sodium: 350 mg

BUCATINI WITH TOMATO, BASIL, AND MOZZARELLA

KID-FRIENDLY

Preparation Time: 15 minutes
Cooking Time: 20 minutes

Total Time: 35 minutes
Serves: 4

INGREDIENTS:

- 12 oz bucatini pasta
- 1 tablespoon olive oil
- 3 cloves garlic, minced
- 1 (28-ounce) can of whole tomatoes, crushed by hand
- 1/2 teaspoon red pepper flakes (optional)
- Salt and pepper, to taste
- 1/2 cup fresh basil leaves, torn
- 8 oz fresh mozzarella, diced or torn into small pieces
- Grated Parmesan cheese, for serving (optional)

INSTRUCTIONS:

1. Bring a large pot of salted water to a boil. Add the bucatini and cook according to package instructions until al dente. Drain and set aside.
2. While the pasta is cooking, heat the olive oil in a large skillet over medium heat. Add the minced garlic and sauté until fragrant, about 1 minute.
3. Add the crushed tomatoes, red pepper flakes if using, salt, and pepper. Simmer the sauce for 10-15 minutes, allowing it to thicken.
4. Stir in the torn basil leaves and cook for another 2 minutes.
5. Add the cooked bucatini to the skillet, tossing it in the sauce to combine.
6. Remove the skillet from heat, add the diced mozzarella, and gently mix it in.
7. Serve immediately, garnished with additional fresh basil and grated Parmesan cheese if desired.

NUTRITIONAL INFORMATION (PER SERVING):

Calories: 510 kcal
Total Fat: 15 g
Saturated Fat: 6 g
Total Carbohydrates: 72 g
Dietary Fiber: 4 g
Protein: 20 g
Sodium: 490 mg

GREEK ZOODLE BOWL

A light and refreshing dish featuring zucchini noodles tossed in a garlicky olive oil sauce with Mediterranean flavors.

SUPER-QUICK!

Preparation Time: 10 minutes
Cooking Time: 5 minutes
Total Time: 15 minutes
Serves: 2

INGREDIENTS:

- 2 medium zucchinis, spiralized into noodles
- 1/4 cup olive oil
- 3 cloves garlic, minced
- 1/4 cup Kalamata olives, pitted and sliced

- 1/4 cup cherry tomatoes, halved
- Salt and pepper to taste
- 1 tbsp lemon juice
- Fresh basil leaves for garnish

INSTRUCTIONS:

1) Heat olive oil in a large pan over medium heat. Add minced garlic and cook until fragrant.
2) Add zucchini noodles to the pan and sauté for 2-3 minutes.
3) Stir in the olives and cherry tomatoes.
4) Season with salt, pepper, and lemon juice.
5) Garnish with fresh basil before serving.

Chef's Note:

This dish is best served immediately to enjoy the crunch of the zucchini noodles.

NUTRITIONAL INFORMATION (PER SERVING):

Calories: 280 kcal
Total Fat: 25 g
Monounsaturated Fat: 18 g
Total Carbohydrates: 12 g
Dietary Fiber: 4 g
Protein: 4 g
Sodium: 350 mg

RISOTTO WITH PORCINI MUSHROOMS

Indulge in this creamy, savory risotto featuring porcini mushrooms for an authentic Italian dining experience right at home.
SPECIAL OCCASION

Preparation Time: 10 minutes
Cooking Time: 30 minutes
Total Time: 40 minutes
Serves: 4

INGREDIENTS:

- 1.5 cups Arborio rice
- 4 cups chicken or vegetable broth, warmed
- 1 cup dried porcini mushrooms, rehydrated in hot water
- 1/2 cup white wine
- 1 medium onion, finely chopped
- 2 cloves garlic, minced
- 2 tablespoons extra-virgin olive oil
- 1/2 cup grated Parmesan cheese
- Salt and pepper to taste

INSTRUCTIONS:

1. In a large pan, heat the olive oil over medium heat. Add the chopped onion and garlic, and sauté until translucent.
2. Add the Arborio rice to the pan and stir for about 2 minutes, making sure each grain is coated with the oil.

3. Pour in the white wine and let it evaporate, stirring continuously.
4. Begin adding the warmed broth, one ladle at a time, to the rice. Stir continuously and wait until the liquid is mostly absorbed before adding more broth.
5. After about 15 minutes of cooking, add the rehydrated porcini mushrooms to the rice. Continue adding broth and stirring until the rice is tender but still al dente, about 15 more minutes.
6. Once the rice is cooked, remove from heat and stir in the grated Parmesan cheese. Season with salt and pepper to taste.
7. Serve hot, garnished with additional Parmesan if desired.

Chef's Note:

Feel free to use fresh porcini mushrooms if they're available. You can also add some sautéed spinach or peas for extra color and nutrients. This risotto pairs well with a glass of dry white wine.

NUTRITIONAL INFORMATION (PER SERVING):

Calories: 420 kcal
Total Fat: 12 g
    Monounsaturated Fat: 6 g
Total Carbohydrates: 62 g
    Dietary Fiber: 3 g
Protein: 12 g
Sodium: 380 mg

QUINOA STUFFED EGGPLANT

This dish features eggplants filled with a mix of hearty grains and flavorful veggies, making for a satisfying meal.
GUTEN-FREE

Preparation Time: 20 minutes
Cooking Time: 40 minutes
Total Time: 60 minutes
Serves: 4

INGREDIENTS:

- 2 large eggplants, halved lengthwise
- 1 cup cooked quinoa (or rice)
- 1 can (14 oz) chickpeas, drained and rinsed
- 1 red bell pepper, diced
- 1 onion, diced
- 2 cloves garlic, minced
- 1 cup tomato sauce
- 2 tbsp olive oil
- Salt and pepper to taste
- Fresh basil leaves for garnish

INSTRUCTIONS:

1) Preheat the oven to 400°F (200°C).
2) Scoop out the flesh of the eggplants, leaving about 1/2-inch border.

3) In a skillet, heat olive oil and sauté onion, garlic, and bell pepper until softened.
4) Add chickpeas, the scooped-out eggplant flesh, and tomato sauce. Cook for another 5-10 minutes.
5) Stir in cooked quinoa or rice and season with salt and pepper.
6) Fill the hollowed eggplants with the mixture.
7) Place the stuffed eggplants in a baking dish and bake for 30 minutes or until the eggplants are tender.
8) Garnish with fresh basil leaves before serving.

NUTRITIONAL INFORMATION (PER SERVING):
Calories: 300 kcal
Total Fat: 10 g
  - Monounsaturated Fat: 6 g
Total Carbohydrates: 47 g
  - Dietary Fiber: 13 g
Protein: 10 g
Sodium: 402 mg

HERB AND CHEESE POLENTA

A quick and comforting dish featuring polenta enriched with aromatic herbs and cheese.
HEART-HEALTHY

Preparation Time: 10 minutes
Cooking Time: 25 minutes
Total Time: 35 minutes
Serves: 4

INGREDIENTS:
- 1 cup polenta
- 4 cups water or vegetable broth
- 1/2 cup Parmesan cheese, grated
- 1 tbsp olive oil
- 1 tsp rosemary, finely chopped
- 1 tsp thyme, finely chopped
- Salt and pepper to taste

INSTRUCTIONS:
1) Bring water or vegetable broth to a boil in a medium saucepan.
2) Gradually add polenta, stirring constantly to prevent lumps.
3) Reduce heat to low and continue to stir until the polenta thickens, about 20-25 minutes.
4) Remove from heat and stir in olive oil, rosemary, thyme, and grated Parmesan cheese.
5) Season with salt and pepper to taste.

NUTRITIONAL INFORMATION (PER SERVING):
Calories: 250 kcal
Total Fat: 8 g
Monounsaturated Fat: 4 g
Total Carbohydrates: 35 g
Dietary Fiber: 1 g
Protein: 9 g
Sodium: 400 mg

CAULIFLOWER RICE WITH SUN-DRIED TOMATOES

A low-carb alternative to traditional rice, filled with the flavors of sun-dried tomatoes and Mediterranean spices.
LOW-CALORIES

Preparation Time: 10 minutes
Cooking Time: 15 minutes
Total Time: 25 minutes
Serves: 4

INGREDIENTS:
- 1 large cauliflower head, grated
- 1/2 cup sun-dried tomatoes, chopped (take a look at the snack section for the home-made "sun-dried" tomato recipe!)
- 1/4 cup pine nuts
- 2 tbsp olive oil
- 1/2 tsp paprika
- Salt and pepper to taste

INSTRUCTIONS:
1) In a large skillet, heat the olive oil over medium heat.
2) Add the grated cauliflower and cook for about 5-7 minutes until it softens.
3) Stir in the sun-dried tomatoes, pine nuts, paprika, salt, and pepper.
4) Cook for another 5-8 minutes, stirring occasionally.

Chef's Note:
Great as a side dish or combine with some roasted vegetables for a main course.

NUTRITIONAL INFORMATION (PER SERVING):
Calories: 200 kcal
Total Fat: 14 g
Monounsaturated Fat: 8 g
Total Carbohydrates: 16 g
Dietary Fiber: 5 g
Protein: 6 g
Sodium: 150 mg

VEGETARIAN MOUSSAKA

A time-honored dish from Greece, featuring layers of eggplant, potatoes, and a rich béchamel sauce, all seasoned with herbs and spices.
SPECIAL OCCASION

Preparation Time: 30 minutes
Cooking Time: 1 hour
Total Time: 1 hour 30 minutes
Serves: 4-6

INGREDIENTS:
- 2 large eggplants, sliced

- 2 large potatoes, sliced
- 4 cups béchamel sauce (homemade or store-bought)
- 2 tbsp olive oil
- 1 tsp dried oregano
- 1 tsp dried thyme
- Salt and pepper to taste

INSTRUCTIONS:
1. Preheat the oven to 350°F (175°C).
2. Lightly salt the sliced eggplants and let them sit for 30 minutes to remove bitterness. Rinse and pat dry.
3. Brush olive oil over the slices of eggplant and potato and season with oregano, thyme, salt, and pepper.
4. In a skillet, sauté the eggplant and potato slices until slightly tender.
5. In a baking dish, start by layering half of the potatoes at the bottom, followed by half of the eggplant slices.
6. Pour half of the béchamel sauce over the layered vegetables.
7. Repeat layers and top with the remaining béchamel sauce.
8. Bake for 40-45 minutes or until the top is golden and bubbly.

Chef's Note:
Serve warm, preferably with a side of fresh Greek salad or olives for an authentic Mediterranean meal.

NUTRITIONAL INFORMATION (PER SERVING):
Calories: 350 kcal
Total Fat: 14 g
Monounsaturated Fat: 9 g
Total Carbohydrates: 48 g
Dietary Fiber: 10 g
Protein: 12 g
Sodium: 550 mg

EGGPLANT ROLLATINI
Thin slices of eggplant rolled up with a flavorful filling, baked to perfection.
KID-FRIENDLY

Preparation Time: 25 minutes
Cooking Time: 35 minutes
Total Time: 60 minutes
Serves: 4

INGREDIENTS:
- 2 large eggplants, thinly sliced lengthwise
- 1 cup ricotta cheese (or use vegan alternative)
- 1 cup spinach, finely chopped
- 2 cloves garlic, minced
- 1 cup marinara sauce
- 2 tbsp olive oil
- Salt and pepper to taste

INSTRUCTIONS:

1) Preheat the oven to 400°F (200°C).
2) Brush the eggplant slices lightly with olive oil and bake for 10 minutes, turning halfway.
3) In a bowl, mix together ricotta cheese, spinach, garlic, salt, and pepper.
4) Spread a spoonful of the cheese mixture onto each eggplant slice, roll it up and place it in a baking dish.
5) Pour marinara sauce over the rolls.
6) Cover and bake for 25 minutes.

Chef's Note:
These rollatini make a great main dish and pair well with a Mediterranean couscous salad.

NUTRITIONAL INFORMATION (PER SERVING):
Calories: 300 kcal
Total Fat: 18 g
Monounsaturated Fat: 8 g
Total Carbohydrates: 28 g
Dietary Fiber: 9 g
Protein: 12 g
Sodium: 400 mg

GRILLED POLENTA
MEAL-PREP FRIENDLY

Preparation Time: 15 minutes (plus 1 hour for chilling polenta)
Cooking Time: 30 minutes
Total Time: 45 minutes (plus 1 hour for chilling polenta)
Serves: 4

INGREDIENTS:
- 1 cup coarse polenta (cornmeal)
- 4 cups vegetable broth or water
- 1/4 cup grated Parmesan cheese
- 2 tablespoons olive oil, plus extra for brushing
- Salt and pepper to taste

INSTRUCTIONS:
1. In a medium saucepan, bring the vegetable broth or water to a boil. Slowly whisk in the polenta, reducing heat to low.
2. Cook the polenta, stirring frequently, until it thickens and pulls away from the sides of the pan, approximately 25-30 minutes.
3. Stir in the grated Parmesan cheese, olive oil, salt, and pepper. Adjust seasoning to taste.
4. Pour the cooked polenta into a greased 8x8-inch baking dish, smoothing the top with a spatula. Allow it to cool, then place in the refrigerator for at least 1 hour to set.
5. Preheat the grill to medium-high heat.
6. Remove the chilled polenta from the refrigerator and turn it out onto a cutting board. Slice it into squares or triangles.
7. Lightly brush both sides of each polenta piece with olive oil.

8. Grill the polenta pieces for 3-4 minutes per side, or until they have nice grill marks.
9. Serve immediately as a side dish or as a base for other toppings like grilled vegetables or a flavorful sauce.

Chef's Note:
Grilled polenta is incredibly versatile. It's also incredibly easy to meal prep with leftover polenta! It can be enjoyed with a variety of toppings such as sautéed mushrooms, marinara sauce, roasted vegetables or grilled seafood. It also keep in the fridge for up to three days and freezes well for up to 6 months. For a dairy-free version, simply omit the Parmesan cheese and use a plant-based alternative.

NUTRITIONAL INFORMATION (PER SERVING):
Calories: 210 kcal
Total Fat: 9 g
Saturated Fat: 2 g
Total Carbohydrates: 28 g
Dietary Fiber: 2 g
Protein: 6 g
Sodium: 490 mg

FAVA BEAN PUREE WITH DILL

This simple yet flavorful Fava Bean Puree with Dill is a delightful side dish or appetizer, rich in protein and fiber. It's also perfect for spreading on whole-grain toast or using as a dip for vegetables.
VEGAN

Preparation Time: 15 minutes
Cooking Time: 20 minutes
Total Time: 35 minutes
Serves: 4

INGREDIENTS:
- 2 cups shelled fava beans (fresh or frozen)
- 3 cups water (for boiling)
- 2 garlic cloves, minced
- 2 tablespoons olive oil
- 1 lemon, juiced
- Salt and freshly ground black pepper, to taste
- 1/4 cup fresh dill, chopped
- 2 tablespoons tahini (optional)

INSTRUCTIONS:
1. In a medium pot, bring 3 cups of water to a boil. Add a pinch of salt and the shelled fava beans. Boil for 5-7 minutes until tender but not mushy. Drain and let cool for a few minutes.
2. If using fresh fava beans, remove the outer skin from each bean. This step is optional but results in a smoother puree.
3. In a food processor, combine the boiled fava beans, garlic, olive oil, and lemon juice. Blend until you achieve a smooth, creamy texture.

4. Transfer the puree to a bowl and season with salt and freshly ground black pepper to taste.
5. Stir in the chopped fresh dill. If you're using tahini, add it now and mix well.
6. Serve immediately as a side dish, or cover and refrigerate for up to 3 days. You can also use it as a spread on whole-grain toast or as a dip for vegetables.

Chef's Note:
Feel free to adjust the consistency by adding more olive oil or a splash of water. You can also add more garlic or lemon juice to suit your taste preferences.

NUTRITIONAL INFORMATION (PER SERVING):
Calories: 300 kcal
Total Fat: 12 g
   Monounsaturated Fat: 8 g
   Polyunsaturated Fat: 1 g
Total Carbohydrates: 36 g
   Dietary Fiber: 9 g
Protein: 13 g
Sodium: 250 mg

LENTIL~STUFFED ZUCCHINI BOATS

Halved zucchini filled with a hearty lentil and vegetable mix, baked to perfection.
MEAL-PREP FRIENDLY

Preparation Time: 20 minutes
Cooking Time: 30 minutes
Total Time: 50 minutes
Serves: 4

INGREDIENTS:
- 4 medium zucchinis, halved lengthwise
- 2 cups cooked lentils
- 1 small onion, chopped
- 2 cloves garlic, minced
- 1/4 cup sun-dried tomatoes, chopped (see recipe in Snacks and Dips for home-made version)
- 2 tbsp olive oil
- 1 tsp cumin
- Salt and pepper to taste

INSTRUCTIONS:
1) Preheat the oven to 375°F (190°C).
2) Scoop out the flesh of the zucchini halves to make boats.
3) In a skillet, heat olive oil over medium heat. Add onion and garlic and sauté until translucent.
4) Add lentils, the zucchini flesh, sun-dried tomatoes, cumin, salt, and pepper. Cook for 5 minutes.
5) Stuff the zucchini boats with the lentil mixture.
6) Place the stuffed zucchini in a baking dish and bake for 30 minutes or until zucchini is tender.

Chef's Note:

Serve with a side of tzatziki sauce for a creamy addition. Perfect for a double or triple batch that can be froze and reheated in less than 5 minutes (oven is better than the microwave to preserve the crunchiness)

NUTRITIONAL INFORMATION (PER SERVING):
Calories: 280 kcal
Total Fat: 8 g
Monounsaturated Fat: 5 g
Total Carbohydrates: 38 g
Dietary Fiber: 14 g
Protein: 14 g
Sodium: 100 mg

GEMISTA

Versatile and healthy vegetable medley.
MIX-AND-MATCH

Preparation Time: 30 minutes
Cooking Time: 1 hour
Total Time: 1 hour 30 minutes
Serves: 4-6

INGREDIENTS:
• 4 large tomatoes
• 4 green bell peppers
• 1 cup long-grain rice, uncooked
• 1 large onion, finely chopped
• 2 cloves garlic, minced
• 1 zucchini, grated
• 1 carrot, grated
• 1/4 cup pine nuts (optional)
• 1/4 cup fresh parsley, chopped
• 1/4 cup fresh mint, chopped
• 1/2 cup extra-virgin olive oil
• 1 1/2 cups vegetable broth or tomato juice
• Salt and pepper, to taste

INSTRUCTIONS:
1. Preheat the oven to 375°F (190°C). Core the tomatoes, keeping the pulp. Remove the tops of the bell peppers and discard the seeds.
2. Chop the tomato pulp and set aside.
3. In a pan, heat 2 tablespoons of olive oil and sauté onions and garlic until soft. Add the rice and sauté for another couple of minutes.
4. Add the chopped tomato pulp, grated zucchini, grated carrot, pine nuts, parsley, and mint to the pan. Season with salt and pepper.
5. Pour in 1/2 cup vegetable broth or tomato juice and simmer until the liquid is mostly absorbed. Remove from heat.
6. Fill the cored tomatoes and hollowed-out peppers with the rice mixture. Place them in a baking dish.
7. Pour the remaining vegetable broth or tomato juice around the stuffed vegetables in the dish. Drizzle remaining olive oil over the top.
8. Cover the baking dish with aluminum foil and bake for 45 minutes. Remove the foil and bake for an additional

15 minutes, or until the vegetables are soft and the tops slightly browned.

Chef's Note:
Gemista is versatile and keeps well. Feel free to:
1. Use other types of vegetables like eggplant or zucchini for stuffing.
2. Substitute quinoa for rice for added protein.
3. Include ground meat for a non-vegetarian version.
4. Top with crumbled feta before the final 15 minutes of baking for added flavor.
5. Serve with a dollop of Greek yogurt or a slice of crusty bread.

NUTRITIONAL INFORMATION (PER SERVING):
Calories: 320 kcal
Total Fat: 18 g
     Monounsaturated Fat: 13 g
Total Carbohydrates: 35 g
     Dietary Fiber: 6 g
Protein: 6 g
Sodium: 420 mg

RATATOUILLE

A classic French vegetable medley that's dense with flavour and tastes even better the next day.
MEAL-PREP FRIENDLY

Preparation Time: 20 minutes
Cooking Time: 40 minutes
Total Time: 60 minutes
Serves: 4

INGREDIENTS:
• 1 medium zucchini, sliced into rounds
• 1 medium yellow squash, sliced into rounds
• 1 medium eggplant, sliced into rounds
• 1 red bell pepper, sliced
• 1 green bell pepper, sliced
• 1 medium onion, sliced
• 3 cloves garlic, minced
• 1 can (14 oz) diced tomatoes
• 2 tablespoons olive oil
• 1 teaspoon dried thyme
• 1 teaspoon dried rosemary
• Salt and pepper, to taste
• 2 tablespoons fresh basil, chopped (for garnish)

INSTRUCTIONS:
1. Preheat the oven to 375°F (190°C).
2. In a large skillet, heat 1 tablespoon of olive oil over medium heat. Add garlic and onion, and sauté until translucent.
3. Add the canned tomatoes, thyme, and rosemary. Stir and let it simmer for about 5 minutes.
4. Pour this tomato mixture into the base of a large baking dish, spreading it out evenly.

5. Neatly arrange the sliced zucchini, yellow squash, eggplant, and bell peppers on top of the tomato mixture in the baking dish. Overlap them and alternate the vegetables for color variation.
6. Drizzle the remaining olive oil over the vegetables and season with salt and pepper.
7. Cover the baking dish with aluminum foil and bake for 35-40 minutes, or until the vegetables are tender.
8. Garnish with freshly chopped basil before serving.

Chef's Note:
1. For a more Italian flair, sprinkle some Parmesan cheese on top before baking.
2. If you like it spicy, add some red chili flakes to the tomato mixture.
3. For an autumnal twist, add some slices of butternut squash.
4. You can also add a few dollops of pesto for added flavor.
5. For a protein boost, serve with grilled chicken or tofu.

NUTRITIONAL INFORMATION (PER SERVING):
Calories: 400 kcal
Total Fat: 14 g
    Monounsaturated Fat: 10 g
Total Carbohydrates: 58 g
    Dietary Fiber: 14 g
Protein: 10 g
Sodium: 280 mg

SICILIAN EGGPLANT CAPONATA

A classic Sicilian dish featuring eggplant cooked with tomatoes, olives, and capers.
VEGAN

Preparation Time: 20 minutes
Cooking Time: 40 minutes
Total Time: 60 minutes
Serves: 4

INGREDIENTS:
- 2 medium eggplants, cubed
- 1 cup cherry tomatoes, halved
- 1/2 cup black olives, pitted and sliced
- 1/4 cup capers
- 1 onion, chopped
- 2 cloves garlic, minced
- 1/4 cup olive oil
- Salt and pepper to taste

INSTRUCTIONS:
1) In a large skillet, heat olive oil over medium heat.
2) Add the onions and garlic, sauté until translucent.
3) Add eggplant cubes, cook for about 10 minutes until they begin to soften.
4) Stir in cherry tomatoes, black olives, and capers.

5) Cover and simmer for 20-30 minutes until all vegetables are tender.
6) Season with salt and pepper to taste.

NUTRITIONAL INFORMATION (PER SERVING):
Calories: 220 kcal
Total Fat: 14 g
Monounsaturated Fat: 10 g
Total Carbohydrates: 24 g
Dietary Fiber: 10 g
Protein: 4 g
Sodium: 200 mg

GREEK GIGANTES BEANS WITH TOMATOES

VEGAN

Preparation Time: 15 minutes (plus overnight soaking)
Cooking Time: 1 hour 30 minutes
Total Time: 1 hour 45 minutes (plus overnight soaking)
Serves: 6

INGREDIENTS:
- 1 pound gigantes beans (or large lima beans), soaked overnight
- 1 large onion, finely chopped
- 4 cloves garlic, minced
- 1 can (28 oz) whole peeled tomatoes, crushed by hand
- 1/4 cup olive oil
- 1/2 teaspoon oregano
- 1/2 teaspoon paprika
- Salt and pepper, to taste
- 1/4 cup fresh parsley, finely chopped for garnish

INSTRUCTIONS:
1. Drain the soaked beans and place them in a large pot of water. Bring to a boil, then reduce heat and simmer for 40-50 minutes, or until beans are tender but not mushy. Drain and set aside.
2. Preheat the oven to 350°F (175°C).
3. In a large ovenproof skillet or Dutch oven, heat the olive oil over medium heat. Add the chopped onion and garlic and sauté until translucent, about 5 minutes.
4. Add the hand-crushed tomatoes, oregano, paprika, salt, and pepper. Stir to combine.
5. Add the boiled beans to the tomato mixture and stir gently to coat the beans with the sauce.
6. Cover the skillet or Dutch oven and place it in the preheated oven. Bake for 40 minutes, stirring once halfway through.
7. Remove the lid and continue to bake for an additional 10 minutes, or until the sauce has thickened.
8. Remove from oven, garnish with chopped parsley, and serve hot.

Chef's Note:

This dish is excellent when served with crusty bread or a simple green salad. It also pairs well with grilled or roasted meats for a hearty meal.

NUTRITIONAL INFORMATION (PER SERVING):

Calories: 280 kcal
Total Fat: 10 g
Saturated Fat: 1 g
Total Carbohydrates: 38 g
Dietary Fiber: 10 g
Protein: 11 g
Sodium: 80 mg

SPANISH ESPINACAS CON GARBANZOS (SPINACH WITH CHICKPEAS)

Delight in the warmth and richness of this classic Spanish dish that blends nutrient-packed spinach with hearty chickpeas.
ONE-POT MEAL

Preparation Time: 15 minutes
Cooking Time: 25 minutes
Total Time: 40 minutes
Serves: 4

INGREDIENTS:

- 2 tablespoons olive oil
- 1 onion, finely chopped
- 4 cloves garlic, minced
- 1 teaspoon smoked paprika
- 1 teaspoon ground cumin
- 1/4 teaspoon cayenne pepper (optional, for heat)
- 1 can (15 oz) chickpeas, drained and rinsed
- 1 can (14.5 oz) diced tomatoes, drained
- 10 oz fresh spinach, washed and roughly chopped
- Salt and pepper to taste

INSTRUCTIONS:

1. Heat olive oil in a large skillet over medium heat. Add the chopped onion and sauté until translucent, about 5 minutes.
2. Add the minced garlic, smoked paprika, ground cumin, and cayenne pepper (if using). Stir well and cook for another minute, allowing the spices to bloom.
3. Add the drained chickpeas and diced tomatoes to the skillet. Stir to combine with the onion and spices.
4. Cover the skillet and let the mixture simmer for 10 minutes on low heat.
5. Add the chopped spinach to the skillet in batches, stirring each time to wilt the spinach. Continue cooking for another 5 minutes until all the spinach is wilted and well combined with the chickpea mixture.
6. Season with salt and pepper to taste. Stir well to combine.
7. Serve warm, either as a main course or a side dish.

Chef's Note:

Feel free to add some lemon juice or a dash of sherry vinegar for an extra kick. This dish can also be served with a sprinkle of toasted almonds for added crunch.

NUTRITIONAL INFORMATION (PER SERVING):

Calories: 220 kcal
Total Fat: 8 g
Monounsaturated Fat: 5 g
Total Carbohydrates: 28 g
Dietary Fiber: 8 g
Protein: 9 g
Sodium: 430 mg

TUSCAN WHITE BEAN STEW WITH GARLIC BREAD

SPECIAL OCCASION

Preparation Time: 20 minutes
Cooking Time: 40 minutes
Total Time: 1 hour
Serves: 4

INGREDIENTS:

For the Stew:

- 2 tablespoons olive oil
- 1 large onion, diced
- 3 cloves garlic, minced
- 4 cups vegetable broth
- 2 cans (15 oz each) cannellini beans, drained and rinsed
- 1 can (14.5 oz) diced tomatoes
- 1 teaspoon dried thyme
- 1 teaspoon dried rosemary
- Salt and black pepper, to taste
- 4 cups kale, stems removed and leaves chopped

For the Garlic Bread:

- 1 baguette, sliced
- 4 tablespoons unsalted butter, melted
- 3 cloves garlic, minced
- 2 tablespoons parsley, finely chopped
- Salt to taste

INSTRUCTIONS:

For the Stew:

1. Heat the olive oil in a large pot over medium heat. Add the diced onion and cook until translucent, about 5 minutes.
2. Add the minced garlic and cook for another minute, or until fragrant.
3. Pour in the vegetable broth, cannellini beans, diced tomatoes, thyme, and rosemary. Stir to combine.
4. Bring the mixture to a boil, then reduce heat to low and simmer for 30 minutes.
5. Season with salt and black pepper to taste. Add the chopped kale and cook until wilted, about 5 minutes.

For the Garlic Bread:

1. Preheat the oven to 400°F (200°C).
2. In a small bowl, combine the melted butter, minced garlic, chopped parsley, and salt.
3. Brush the butter mixture onto the baguette slices and arrange them on a baking sheet.
4. Bake for 10 minutes, or until the bread is golden and crispy.

NUTRITIONAL INFORMATION (PER SERVING):
Calories: 530 kcal
Total Fat: 20 g
Saturated Fat: 8 g
Total Carbohydrates: 70 g
Dietary Fiber: 15 g
Protein: 20 g
Sodium: 850 mg

FALAFEL WITH TAHINI SAUCE

Beloved by children and adults is a great dinner with some whole wheat pita bread and a light cucumber and tomato salad, but also doubles as a snack. Make a double batch and freeze it or keep it in the fridge for up to a week. It also makes for a great meze (appetizer plate) with some olives, cheese, and whatever snacks you can conjure up from our extensive recipe section at the end of the book.

KID FRIENDLY

Preparation Time: 20 minutes (plus soaking time for chickpeas)
Cooking Time: 10 minutes
Total Time: 30 minutes
Serves: 4-6

INGREDIENTS:
- 1 cup dried chickpeas, soaked overnight
- 1/2 large onion, roughly chopped (about 1 cup)
- 2 tablespoons finely chopped fresh parsley
- 2 tablespoons finely chopped fresh cilantro
- 1 teaspoon salt
- 1/2-1 teaspoon dried hot red pepper
- 4 cloves of garlic
- 1 teaspoon cumin
- 1 teaspoon baking powder
- 4-6 tablespoons flour
- Soybean or vegetable oil for frying
- 1/2 cup tahini
- 2 tablespoons lemon juice
- 1 clove garlic, grated
- Salt to taste

INSTRUCTIONS:
1. Drain soaked chickpeas and pulse in a food processor until finely minced but not puréed.
2. Add onion, parsley, cilantro, salt, hot pepper, garlic, and cumin to the food processor. Pulse until well blended but still coarse.
3. Sprinkle in the baking powder and 4 tablespoons of the flour. Pulse briefly.
4. Heat oil in a deep pan to 375°F (190°C).

5. Form chickpea mixture into small balls and fry until golden, about 5 minutes.
6. For the tahini sauce, mix tahini, lemon juice, garlic, and salt. Add water to reach desired consistency.

Chef's Note:
Don't substitute dry chickpeas for canned chickpeas, they remain too chuncky and will make your falafels dry. Falafel can be served in pita bread with lettuce, tomato, and tahini sauce, or as part of a meze platter.
For a healthier version you can oven-bake or air-fry the falafel.

NUTRITIONAL INFORMATION (PER SERVING):
Calories: 350 kcal
Total Fat: 15 g
Monounsaturated Fat: 6 g
Total Carbohydrates: 45 g
Dietary Fiber: 8 g
Protein: 12 g
Sodium: 400 mg

BRAISED FENNEL WITH CHESTNUTS AND SHALLOTS / FINOCCHIO IN PADELLA CON CASTAGNE E SCALOGNI

An Italian winter favorite featuring fennel braised with chestnuts and shallots for a comforting side dish.
LOW-CALORIES

Preparation Time: 10 minutes
Cooking Time: 35 minutes
Total Time: 45 minutes
Serves: 4 servings

INGREDIENTS:
- 2 fennel bulbs, cut into wedges
- 1 cup chestnuts, cooked and peeled
- 3 shallots, thinly sliced
- 2 tablespoons olive oil
- 1 cup vegetable broth
- Salt and pepper to taste

INSTRUCTIONS:
1) Heat olive oil in a large skillet over medium heat. Add shallots and sauté until translucent.
2) Add fennel wedges and cook until they start to brown, about 5 minutes.
3) Stir in chestnuts and season with salt and pepper.
4) Add vegetable broth, cover, and simmer for about 25 minutes, or until the fennel is tender.
5) Remove the lid and let the liquid evaporate, about 5 more minutes.

Chef's Note:
This dish pairs well with roast meats or can stand alone as a hearty vegetarian meal.

NUTRITIONAL INFORMATION (PER SERVING):
Calories: 160 kcal
Total Fat: 8 g
Monounsaturated Fat: 6 g
Total Carbohydrates: 21 g
Dietary Fiber: 5 g
Protein: 2 g
Sodium: 310 mg

NORTH AFRICAN ROASTED CHICKPEA BOWL

A North African-inspired dish featuring spiced, roasted chickpeas served over grains or greens.
GLUTEN-FREE

Preparation Time: 15 minutes
Cooking Time: 25 minutes
Total Time: 40 minutes
Serves: 4

INGREDIENTS:
- 2 cans (15 oz each) chickpeas, drained and rinsed
- 2 tbsp olive oil
- 1 tsp cumin
- 1 tsp paprika
- 1/2 tsp cinnamon
- Salt and pepper to taste
- Optional: 4 cups cooked quinoa or greens for serving

INSTRUCTIONS:
1) Preheat the oven to 400°F (200°C).
2) In a large bowl, combine chickpeas, olive oil, cumin, paprika, cinnamon, salt, and pepper.
3) Spread the chickpeas on a baking sheet.
4) Roast for 20-25 minutes, stirring halfway through, until chickpeas are crispy.
5) Serve over cooked quinoa or greens.

Chef's Note:
Add some tahini sauce for a creamy texture and added flavor.

NUTRITIONAL INFORMATION (PER SERVING):
Calories: 260 kcal
Total Fat: 9 g
Monounsaturated Fat: 5 g
Total Carbohydrates: 36 g
Dietary Fiber: 9 g
Protein: 10 g
Sodium: 300 mg

SPAGHETTI AGLIO E OLIO

Indulge in the simplicity of this Italian classic where garlic, red pepper flakes, and olive oil marry perfectly to elevate simple spaghetti. A quick yet satisfying dish!
SUPER-QUICK!

Preparation Time: 10 minutes
Cooking Time: 10 minutes
Total Time: 20 minutes
Serves: 4

INGREDIENTS:
- 400g spaghetti
- 1/2 cup extra-virgin olive oil
- 6-8 garlic cloves, thinly sliced
- 1/2 teaspoon red pepper flakes, or to taste
- Salt, to taste
- Freshly ground black pepper, to taste
- 1/4 cup fresh parsley, finely chopped
- 1/2 cup grated Parmesan cheese (optional)

INSTRUCTIONS:
1. Boil a large pot of salted water. Add the spaghetti and cook until al dente, according to package instructions. Reserve about 1 cup of pasta cooking water and then drain the spaghetti.
2. While the pasta is cooking, heat the olive oil in a large skillet over low-medium heat. Add the thinly sliced garlic and cook gently until it becomes golden brown. Be cautious not to burn the garlic as it will turn bitter.
3. Add the red pepper flakes to the skillet and stir for about 30 seconds, allowing the flavors to meld into the oil.
4. Add the drained spaghetti to the skillet, tossing to combine with the garlic oil. If the pasta seems too dry, add a little of the reserved pasta cooking water.
5. Season with salt and freshly ground black pepper. Stir in the fresh parsley.
6. Divide the pasta among serving dishes. Optionally, sprinkle with grated Parmesan cheese before serving.

NUTRITIONAL INFORMATION (PER SERVING):
Calories: 550 kcal
Total Fat: 25 g
    Monounsaturated Fat: 18 g
Total Carbohydrates: 70 g
    Dietary Fiber: 3 g
Protein: 12 g
Sodium: 200 mg

FASOLAKIA

A classic Greek green bean stew cooked in tomato sauce and olive oil.
ONE-POT MEAL

Preparation Time: 15 minutes
Cooking Time: 40 minutes
Total Time: 55 minutes
Serves: 4

INGREDIENTS:
- 1 lb green beans, trimmed
- 1 can (14 oz) diced tomatoes

- 1 onion, chopped
- 2 cloves garlic, minced
- 1/4 cup olive oil
- 1 cup water
- Salt and pepper to taste

INSTRUCTIONS:
1) In a large pot, heat olive oil over medium heat. Add the onions and garlic and sauté until translucent.
2) Add green beans to the pot and sauté for a couple of minutes.
3) Pour in diced tomatoes, including the juice.
4) Add water and bring to a simmer.
5) Cover and cook for 35-40 minutes or until the beans are tender.
6) Season with salt and pepper to taste.

Chef's Note:
Fasolakia is a great one-pot meal that can be served hot or at room temperature, and it pairs well with crusty bread or brown rice.

NUTRITIONAL INFORMATION (PER SERVING):
Calories: 220 kcal
Total Fat: 14 g
Monounsaturated Fat: 10 g
Total Carbohydrates: 20 g
Dietary Fiber: 6 g
Protein: 4 g
Sodium: 300 mg

GRILLED ASPARAGUS AND LEMON BUTTER
SUPER-QUICK!

Preparation Time: 10 minutes
Cooking Time: 10 minutes
Total Time: 20 minutes
Serves: 4

INGREDIENTS:
For the Asparagus:
- 1 bunch of asparagus, ends trimmed
- 1 tablespoon olive oil
- Salt and black pepper, to taste
For the Lemon Butter:
- 1/2 cup unsalted butter, softened
- Zest of 1 lemon
- 1 tablespoon lemon juice
- Salt to taste
- A pinch of black pepper

INSTRUCTIONS:
For the Asparagus:
1. Preheat the grill to medium-high heat.
2. In a mixing bowl, toss the asparagus with olive oil, salt, and black pepper.

3. Place the asparagus spears on the grill, perpendicular to the grates to prevent them from falling through.
4. Grill for 5-7 minutes, turning occasionally, until tender and slightly charred.

For the Lemon Butter:
1. In a small bowl, combine the softened butter, lemon zest, lemon juice, salt, and a pinch of black pepper.
2. Mix until well incorporated.

To Serve:
1. Transfer the grilled asparagus to a serving platter.
2. Dollop the lemon butter over the asparagus while they are still warm so the butter melts into them.

Chef's Note:
The lemon butter adds a refreshing twist to the earthy asparagus, making this dish perfect for spring and summer meals. It pairs excellently with grilled fish or chicken. Enjoy!

NUTRITIONAL INFORMATION (PER SERVING):
Calories: 220 kcal
Total Fat: 21 g
Saturated Fat: 12 g
Total Carbohydrates: 5 g
Dietary Fiber: 2 g
Protein: 3 g
Sodium: 60 mg

TAJINE KHODHRA ~ MOROCCAN VEGETABLE TAJINE

A rich and flavorful vegetable stew spiced with traditional Moroccan herbs and spices, cooked in a tajine or slow-cooker.

SPECIAL OCCASION

Preparation Time: 20 minutes
Cooking Time: 45 minutes
Total Time: 65 minutes
Serves: 4-6

INGREDIENTS:
- 2 tablespoons olive oil
- 1 onion, chopped
- 3 garlic cloves, minced
- 2 carrots, sliced
- 1 zucchini, sliced
- 1 red bell pepper, chopped
- 1 can (15 oz) chickpeas, drained and rinsed
- 1 can (14 oz) diced tomatoes
- 2 teaspoons ground cumin
- 1 teaspoon ground coriander
- 1 teaspoon paprika
- Salt and pepper to taste
- 1/4 cup chopped fresh cilantro
- 1/4 cup chopped fresh parsley

INSTRUCTIONS:

1) Heat olive oil in a tajine or large, deep skillet over medium heat.
2) Add the onion and garlic, sautéing until translucent.
3) Add the carrots, zucchini, and red bell pepper, cooking until they start to soften.
4) Stir in the chickpeas, diced tomatoes, ground cumin, ground coriander, and paprika.
5) Cover and simmer for 30-40 minutes, until the vegetables are tender.
6) Season with salt and pepper, then garnish with fresh cilantro and parsley before serving.

NUTRITIONAL INFORMATION (PER SERVING):

Calories: 200 kcal
Total Fat: 7 g
Monounsaturated Fat: 5 g
Total Carbohydrates: 28 g
Dietary Fiber: 8 g
Protein: 7 g
Sodium: 200 mg

GREEK PITA POCKET WITH HUMMUS AND VEGGIES

A quick and easy meal perfect for lunch or a light dinner, filled with vibrant vegetables and creamy hummus.
SUPER-QUICK!

Preparation Time: 15 minutes
Cooking Time: 0 minutes
Total Time: 15 minutes
Serves: 4

INGREDIENTS:

- 4 whole-grain pita bread pockets
- 1 cup hummus
- 1 cucumber, thinly sliced
- 1 red bell pepper, thinly sliced
- 1 cup cherry tomatoes, halved
- 1/2 red onion, thinly sliced
- 1 cup baby spinach leaves
- 1/2 cup feta cheese, crumbled (optional)
- 1/4 cup Kalamata olives, pitted and sliced
- Salt and pepper, to taste
- 1 lemon, cut into wedges (for serving)

INSTRUCTIONS:

1. Cut the pita bread pockets in half to create two pockets from each piece of bread.
2. Carefully open each pita pocket to make room for the fillings.
3. Spread about 2 tablespoons of hummus inside each pita pocket, covering the inner surfaces.
4. Start layering the vegetables by first adding a few baby spinach leaves, followed by cucumber slices, red bell pepper slices, and a handful of cherry tomatoes.
5. Add the thinly sliced red onion, crumbled feta cheese (if using), and Kalamata olives to each pocket.
6. Season with a pinch of salt and pepper, to taste.
7. Serve immediately with a wedge of lemon on the side for squeezing over the pita pocket contents.

Chef's Note:

This Greek Pita Pocket is highly customizable. You can swap out or add ingredients based on what you have available or what you like. Other protein options can include grilled chicken, tofu, or even falafel.

NUTRITIONAL INFORMATION (PER SERVING):

Calories: 350 kcal
Total Fat: 12 g
   Monounsaturated Fat: 3 g
Total Carbohydrates: 50 g
   Dietary Fiber: 10 g
Protein: 12 g
Sodium: 450 mg

Salads

TABOULEH

Crunchy, refreshing and packed with nutrients.
Preparation Time: 20 minutes
Cooking Time: 0 minutes
Total Time: 20 minutes
Serves: 4

INGREDIENTS:

- 1 cup bulgur wheat
- 1 1/2 cups boiling water
- 1 1/2 cups fresh parsley, finely chopped
- 1 cup fresh mint leaves, finely chopped
- 2 medium tomatoes, finely diced
- 1 cucumber, finely diced
- 4 green onions, thinly sliced
- Juice of 2 lemons
- 1/4 cup extra-virgin olive oil
- Salt and pepper to taste

INSTRUCTIONS:

1. In a heatproof bowl, pour boiling water over bulgur wheat. Cover and let stand for about 20-30 minutes, or until the bulgur is tender.
2. Drain any excess water from the bulgur and fluff it with a fork.
3. In a large bowl, combine the soaked and drained bulgur with chopped parsley, mint, tomatoes, cucumber, and green onions.
4. In a small bowl, whisk together the lemon juice, olive oil, salt, and pepper.
5. Pour the dressing over the salad mixture and toss well to combine.
6. Refrigerate for at least one hour to allow the flavors to meld together. Serve chilled.

Chef's Note:

Tabouleh is excellent as a vegetarian dish but can easily be complemented with different proteins:

1. Grilled chicken strips would go well for a meaty addition.
2. For a seafood twist, consider adding grilled shrimp.
3. Tofu or tempeh can be used for a vegan protein option.
4. Falafel balls can be added for more Middle Eastern flair.
5. Sliced boiled eggs can also be a good protein option.

NUTRITIONAL INFORMATION (PER SERVING):

Calories: 240 kcal
Total Fat: 12 g
    Monounsaturated Fat: 8 g
Total Carbohydrates: 31 g
    Dietary Fiber: 8 g
Protein: 6 g
Sodium: 20 mg

MOROCCAN ORANGE AND OLIVE SALAD

A burst of citrus and olive flavors in this North African inspired salad. It's dairy-free and packed with Vitamin C.

Preparation Time: 15 minutes
Cooking Time: 0 minutes
Total Time: 15 minutes
Serves: 4

INGREDIENTS:

- 4 large oranges, peeled and sliced
- 1/2 cup black olives, pitted and halved
- 1/4 cup fresh parsley, chopped
- 2 tablespoons olive oil
- Salt and pepper to taste

INSTRUCTIONS:

1) Arrange the sliced oranges on a serving platter.
2) Scatter the black olives and parsley over the oranges.
3) Drizzle olive oil over the salad.
4) Season with salt and pepper to taste, and serve immediately.

Chef's Note:

For added sweetness, you can sprinkle some pomegranate seeds on top.

NUTRITIONAL INFORMATION (PER SERVING):

Calories: 150 kcal
Total Fat: 8 g
Monounsaturated Fat: 6 g
Total Carbohydrates: 20 g
Dietary Fiber: 4 g
Protein: 2 g
Sodium: 150 mg

SPANISH GAZPACHO SALAD

An innovative twist to traditional Gazpacho, this cold salad is refreshing and offers a blend of juicy vegetables. Originates from Spain and is so quick to prepare.

Preparation Time: 10 minutes
Cooking Time: 0 minutes
Total Time: 10 minutes
Serves: 4

INGREDIENTS:
- 4 ripe tomatoes, diced
- 1 cucumber, diced
- 1 bell pepper, diced
- 1/2 red onion, diced
- 2 cups tomato juice
- 1/4 cup olive oil
- 2 tablespoons red wine vinegar
- Salt and pepper to taste

INSTRUCTIONS:
1) Combine diced tomatoes, cucumber, bell pepper, and red onion in a large bowl.
2) In a separate bowl, mix together tomato juice, olive oil, and red wine vinegar.
3) Pour the liquid mixture over the diced vegetables.
4) Season with salt and pepper, and toss everything to combine.
5) Chill for at least 30 minutes before serving for flavors to meld.

NUTRITIONAL INFORMATION (PER SERVING):
Calories: 180 kcal
Total Fat: 14 g
Monounsaturated Fat: 10 g
Total Carbohydrates: 15 g
Dietary Fiber: 3 g
Protein: 2 g
Sodium: 50 mg

CLASSIC AVOCADO, TOMATO & MOZZARELLA SALAD

A classic Mediterranean combination of avocado, tomatoes, and mozzarella that provides a refreshing bite.
SUPER-QUICK!

Preparation Time: 10 minutes
Total Time: 10 minutes
Serves: 4 servings

INGREDIENTS:
- 2 ripe avocados, cubed
- 2 medium tomatoes, cubed
- 1 cup mozzarella balls
- 1 tablespoon olive oil
- Salt and pepper to taste

INSTRUCTIONS:
1) Combine avocados, tomatoes, and mozzarella balls in a salad bowl.
2) Drizzle with olive oil, and season with salt and pepper.
3) Toss gently to combine and serve immediately.

NUTRITIONAL INFORMATION (PER SERVING):
Calories: 190 kcal

Total Fat: 16 g
Carbohydrates: 9 g
Protein: 5 g
Sodium: 80 mg

TUNA NIÇOISE SALAD

A classic French salad that combines fresh vegetables, hearty tuna, and vibrant flavors for a balanced, nutritious meal.
DAIRY-FREE

Preparation Time: 20 minutes
Cooking Time: 10 minutes
Total Time: 30 minutes
Serves: 4

INGREDIENTS:
- 4 tuna steaks (4–6 oz each)
- 8 small potatoes, boiled and halved
- 4 hard-boiled eggs, quartered
- 1 cup green beans, blanched
- 1 cup cherry tomatoes, halved
- 1/2 cup Kalamata olives, pitted
- 1/4 cup capers
- 1 head romaine or butter lettuce, torn
- Salt and pepper, to taste

For the Dressing:
- 1/4 cup extra-virgin olive oil
- 2 tbsp red wine vinegar
- 1 tbsp Dijon mustard
- 1 garlic clove, minced
- Salt and pepper, to taste

INSTRUCTIONS:
1. Season the tuna steaks with salt and pepper.
2. Heat a grill pan or barbecue grill over medium-high heat. Grill the tuna steaks for about 2–3 minutes on each side or until cooked to your liking. Remove from heat and let rest.
3. In a large bowl, place the torn lettuce as the base.
4. Arrange the boiled potatoes, hard-boiled eggs, green beans, cherry tomatoes, olives, and capers on top of the lettuce.
5. Slice the grilled tuna into 1/2-inch thick slices and place on the salad.
6. In a small bowl, whisk together the olive oil, red wine vinegar, Dijon mustard, minced garlic, salt, and pepper to make the dressing.
7. Drizzle the dressing over the salad just before serving. Toss gently to combine if desired.

Chef's Note:
The beauty of a Niçoise salad is its versatility. You can substitute the green beans with asparagus, or use arugula instead of romaine lettuce for a peppery kick. Anchovies are also a traditional addition if you enjoy them.

NUTRITIONAL INFORMATION (PER SERVING):
  Calories: 450 kcal
  Total Fat: 20 g
      Monounsaturated Fat: 12 g
  Total Carbohydrates: 30 g
      Dietary Fiber: 6 g
  Protein: 35 g
  Sodium: 420 mg

INSALATA DI TONNO, UOVA E ACCIUGHE ~ TUNA, EGG & ANCHOVY SALAD

A Mediterranean favorite, featuring protein-rich tuna and eggs, balanced by the rich umami flavor of anchovies. It's perfect for picnincs and will keep for up to 4 days in the fridge. To avoid the greens to wilt add them fresh every time you serve it.

MEAL-PREP FRIENDLY

Preparation Time: 20 minutes
Cooking Time: 10 minutes
Total Time: 30 minutes
Serves: 4 servings

INGREDIENTS:
- 2 cans tuna in olive oil, drained
- 4 boiled eggs, sliced
- 6 anchovy fillets
- 2 cups mixed greens
- 1 tablespoon olive oil
- 1 tablespoon red wine vinegar
- Salt and pepper to taste

INSTRUCTIONS:
1) Arrange mixed greens on a large serving plate.
2) Top with tuna, boiled egg slices, and anchovy fillets.
3) In a small bowl, whisk together olive oil, red wine vinegar, salt, and pepper.
4) Drizzle the dressing over the salad and serve.

NUTRITIONAL INFORMATION (PER SERVING):
Calories: 270 kcal
Total Fat: 16 g
Carbohydrates: 3 g
Protein: 27 g
Sodium: 300 mg

GRILLED TUNA SALAD

This Grilled Tuna Salad brings together perfectly seared tuna steaks with a medley of fresh vegetables and a tangy vinaigrette, offering a healthy and satisfying meal.

HEART-HEALTHY

Preparation Time: 15 minutes
Cook Time: 10 minutes
Total Time: 25 minutes
Serves: 4
INGREDIENTS:
- 4 tuna steaks (4-6 oz each)
- Salt and pepper to season
- 2 tablespoons olive oil for grilling

For the Salad:
- 8 cups mixed salad greens (e.g., arugula, spinach, romaine)
- 1 cucumber, sliced
- 1 red bell pepper, sliced
- 1/4 red onion, thinly sliced
- 1/2 cup cherry tomatoes, halved
- 1/4 cup Kalamata olives, pitted and sliced

For the Dressing:
- Juice of 1 lemon
- 1/4 cup extra-virgin olive oil
- 2 cloves garlic, minced
- 1 teaspoon Dijon mustard
- Salt and freshly ground black pepper to taste

INSTRUCTIONS:
1. Preheat the grill to medium-high heat.
2. Season the tuna steaks with salt and pepper, and brush them lightly with olive oil.
3. Place the tuna steaks on the hot grill and cook for about 2-3 minutes per side, depending on the thickness of the steaks and your desired level of doneness.
4. Remove the tuna from the grill and let it rest for a few minutes before slicing.
5. In a large bowl, combine the mixed salad greens, cucumber, red bell pepper, red onion, cherry tomatoes, and Kalamata olives.
6. In a small bowl, whisk together the lemon juice, extra-virgin olive oil, minced garlic, and Dijon mustard. Season the dressing with salt and freshly ground black pepper to taste.
7. Pour the dressing over the salad and toss well to combine.
8. Divide the salad among four plates, and top each with slices of the grilled tuna.
9. Serve immediately, optionally garnished with extra lemon wedges or fresh herbs.

Chef's Note:
Serve this salad as a stand-alone dish or pair it with some whole-grain bread or quinoa for extra heartiness.

NUTRITIONAL INFORMATION (PER SERVING):
  Calories: 500 kcal
  Total Fat: 30g
  Total Carbohydrates: 12g
  Dietary Fiber: 3g
  Protein: 45g
  Sodium: 450mg

MEDITERRANEAN GRILLED OCTOPUS SALAD

This salad will transport you to coastal Greece in an explosion of flavors and textures.
SPECIAL OCCASION

Preparation Time: 30 minutes
Cooking Time: 40 minutes
Total Time: 1 hour 10 minutes
Serves: 4

INGREDIENTS:

- 1 large octopus (about 2–3 lbs), cleaned and tentacles separated
- 1 lemon, halved
- 4 garlic cloves, crushed
- 2 bay leaves
- 1 teaspoon black peppercorns
- 4 cups water

For the Salad:

- 2 cups arugula
- 1 cup cherry tomatoes, halved
- 1 cucumber, sliced
- 1 red onion, thinly sliced
- 1/2 cup Kalamata olives, pitted
- 1/4 cup parsley leaves, roughly chopped
- Salt and pepper, to taste

For the Dressing:

- 1/4 cup extra-virgin olive oil
- 2 tablespoons red wine vinegar
- 1 teaspoon dried oregano
- 1 garlic clove, minced
- Salt and pepper, to taste

INSTRUCTIONS:

1. In a large pot, combine water, lemon halves, crushed garlic, bay leaves, and peppercorns. Bring to a boil.
2. Add the octopus to the boiling water and cook for about 30–40 minutes, or until tender. Remove from heat and let it cool in the cooking liquid.
3. Once cool, cut the octopus tentacles into bite-sized pieces.
4. Preheat a grill or grill pan over medium-high heat. Grill the octopus pieces for about 3–4 minutes per side, until they get a nice char. Remove from grill and set aside.
5. In a large salad bowl, combine arugula, cherry tomatoes, cucumber, red onion, olives, and parsley.
6. Place the grilled octopus on top of the vegetables.
7. In a small bowl, whisk together the olive oil, red wine vinegar, oregano, minced garlic, salt, and pepper to make the dressing.
8. Drizzle the dressing over the salad, tossing gently to combine. Season with additional salt and pepper if needed.

Chef's Note:
If you prefer other seafood, this salad also pairs well with grilled squid or shrimp. Additionally, consider adding feta cheese for a creamy texture and enhanced flavor.

NUTRITIONAL INFORMATION (PER SERVING):

Calories: 360 kcal
Total Fat: 14 g
    Monounsaturated Fat: 9 g
Total Carbohydrates: 16 g
    Dietary Fiber: 3 g
Protein: 40 g
Sodium: 520 mg

MOROCCAN CHICKPEA SALAD

Savor the vibrant flavors of this Moroccan Chickpea Salad that combines the earthiness of chickpeas with exotic spices and colorful vegetables. A perfect side dish or a wholesome meal on its own.
SUPER-QUICK!

Preparation Time: 15 minutes
Cooking Time: 0 minutes (if using canned chickpeas)
Total Time: 15 minutes
Serves: 4-6

INGREDIENTS:

- 2 cans (15 oz each) chickpeas, drained and rinsed
- 1 medium red bell pepper, finely chopped
- 1 medium cucumber, diced
- 1 small red onion, finely chopped
- 1 cup cherry tomatoes, halved
- 1/4 cup fresh parsley, finely chopped
- 1/4 cup fresh mint, finely chopped
- 1/4 cup fresh cilantro, finely chopped
- 1 lemon, juiced
- 3 tablespoons extra-virgin olive oil
- 1 teaspoon ground cumin
- 1/2 teaspoon paprika
- Salt and pepper to taste

INSTRUCTIONS:

1. In a large bowl, combine the drained chickpeas, chopped bell pepper, diced cucumber, chopped red onion, and halved cherry tomatoes.
2. In a separate bowl, prepare the dressing by whisking together lemon juice, extra-virgin olive oil, ground cumin, paprika, salt, and pepper.
3. Pour the dressing over the salad and mix well to coat all the ingredients.
4. Add the freshly chopped parsley, mint, and cilantro to the salad. Toss until the herbs are evenly distributed.
5. Allow the salad to sit for at least 10-15 minutes for the flavors to meld together.
6. Serve chilled or at room temperature. Garnish with additional herbs if desired.

Chef's Note:

If you have time, you can use dried chickpeas soaked overnight and then boiled until tender for a more authentic texture. This salad also works well as a filling for pita bread or as a side to grilled meats.

NUTRITIONAL INFORMATION (PER SERVING):

Calories: 220 kcal
Total Fat: 9 g
Monounsaturated Fat: 6 g
Total Carbohydrates: 28 g
Dietary Fiber: 7 g
Protein: 7 g
Sodium: 200 mg

CHICKPEA AND TOMATO SALAD WITH FETA

Easy to make and high in protein and fiber, this Chickpea and Tomato Salad with Feta is perfect for a light lunch or as a flavorful side dish.
SUPER-QUICK!

Preparation Time: 15 minutes
Cooking Time: 0 minutes
Total Time: 15 minutes
Serves: 4

INGREDIENTS:

- 1 can (15 oz) chickpeas, drained and rinsed
- 2 cups cherry tomatoes, halved
- 1 medium red onion, finely diced
- 1 cucumber, diced
- 1/2 cup feta cheese, crumbled
- 2 tablespoons olive oil
- Juice of 1 lemon
- 1 teaspoon dried oregano
- Salt and pepper, to taste
- Fresh basil or parsley, for garnish (optional)

INSTRUCTIONS:

1. In a large mixing bowl, combine the drained chickpeas, cherry tomatoes, red onion, and cucumber.
2. In a separate smaller bowl, whisk together the olive oil, lemon juice, dried oregano, salt, and pepper.
3. Pour the dressing over the chickpea mixture and toss to combine thoroughly.
4. Add the crumbled feta cheese to the salad and gently mix.
5. If you're using fresh basil or parsley, chop it finely and sprinkle over the salad for garnish.
6. Serve immediately or let it chill in the fridge for about 30 minutes to allow the flavors to meld together.

Chef's Note:

This salad makes a great standalone meal, but you can also use it as a side dish for grilled meats or fish. If you'd like to make it a more substantial meal, add grilled chicken or shrimp.

NUTRITIONAL INFORMATION (PER SERVING):

Calories: 250 kcal
Total Fat: 12 g
Monounsaturated Fat: 6 g
Total Carbohydrates: 25 g
Dietary Fiber: 6 g
Protein: 10 g
Sodium: 400 mg

HORTA ~ GREEK WILD GREENS SALAD

Embrace the simplicity of Greek village cuisine with this nutritious and earthy blend of mixed greens.
SUPER-QUICK!

Preparation Time: 10 minutes
Cooking Time: 5 minutes
Total Time: 15 minutes
Serves: 4

INGREDIENTS:

- 4 cups mixed wild greens (dandelion, spinach, chard)
- 3 cloves garlic, minced
- 2 tbsp olive oil
- Juice of 1 lemon
- Salt to taste

INSTRUCTIONS:

1) Wash and roughly chop the wild greens.
2) Steam the greens for about 3-4 minutes until wilted but still vibrant.
3) In a bowl, combine the steamed greens, minced garlic, olive oil, and lemon juice.
4) Toss well and season with salt before serving.

Chef's Note:

Great as a side dish with grilled fish or meat. Optionally, you can add some chopped olives for extra flavor.

NUTRITIONAL INFORMATION (PER SERVING):

Calories: 80 kcal
Total Fat: 7 g
Monounsaturated Fat: 5 g
Total Carbohydrates: 5 g
Dietary Fiber: 2 g
Protein: 1 g
Sodium: 200 mg

INSALATA CAPRESE ~ ITALIAN TOMATO AND MOZZARELLA SALAD

Transport your taste buds to the Amalfi coast with this timeless Italian classic featuring fresh mozzarella and ripe tomatoes.
SUPER-QUICK!

Preparation Time: 10 minutes
Cooking Time: 0 minutes
Total Time: 10 minutes
Serves: 4

INGREDIENTS:
- 4 large ripe tomatoes, sliced
- 200g fresh mozzarella cheese, sliced
- 1 bunch fresh basil leaves
- 3 tbsp extra-virgin olive oil
- Balsamic glaze for drizzling (optional)
- Salt and pepper to taste

INSTRUCTIONS:
1) On a serving platter, alternate slices of tomato, mozzarella, and basil leaves.
2) Drizzle the olive oil evenly over the layers.
3) Season with salt and pepper.
4) Optional: Drizzle a little balsamic glaze for added richness and tanginess.

Chef's Note:
To make it extra special, use heirloom tomatoes and buffalo mozzarella. Serve as a main in a larger portion or as a side dish to grilled meats.

NUTRITIONAL INFORMATION (PER SERVING):
Calories: 250 kcal
Total Fat: 20 g
Monounsaturated Fat: 12 g
Total Carbohydrates: 7 g
Dietary Fiber: 2 g
Protein: 10 g
Sodium: 300 mg

SICILIAN EGGPLANT AND FIG SALAD

A harmonious blend of savory and sweet, featuring the robust flavors of Sicily.

VEGAN

Preparation Time: 10 minutes
Cooking Time: 0 minutes
Total Time: 10 minutes
Serves: 4

INGREDIENTS:
- 2 medium eggplants, diced
- 6 fresh figs, quartered
- 1/4 cup capers
- 1/4 cup pine nuts, toasted
- 1/4 cup extra-virgin olive oil
- Juice of 1 lemon
- Salt and pepper to taste

INSTRUCTIONS:

1) In a large salad bowl, combine the diced eggplants, quartered figs, and capers.
2) Add the toasted pine nuts to the mixture.
3) Drizzle the olive oil and lemon juice over the salad.
4) Toss all ingredients gently to mix well.
5) Season with salt and pepper according to your preference.

NUTRITIONAL INFORMATION (PER SERVING):
Calories: 270 kcal
Total Fat: 18 g
Monounsaturated Fat: 13 g
Total Carbohydrates: 25 g
Dietary Fiber: 7 g
Protein: 3 g
Sodium: 200 mg

3-WAYS LEBANESE FATTOUSH

Experience the vibrant flavors of Lebanese cuisine with this versatile and colorful salad that can be customized to match the seasonality of fresh produce.

MIX-AND-MATCH

Preparation Time: 20 minutes
Cooking Time: 5 minutes (to toast pita)
Total Time: 25 minutes
Serves: 4

INGREDIENTS:
- 2 cups mixed greens (lettuce, spinach, arugula)
- 1 cup cherry tomatoes, halved
- 1 cucumber, diced
- 1/2 red onion, thinly sliced
- 1/4 cup radish slices
- 1/4 cup mint leaves, chopped
- 1/4 cup parsley leaves, chopped
- 1 large or 2 small pita bread, toasted and broken into pieces
- 1/4 cup olive oil
- Juice of 1 lemon
- 1 clove garlic, minced
- 1 tsp sumac
- Salt and pepper to taste

INSTRUCTIONS:
1) In a large bowl, combine the mixed greens, cherry tomatoes, cucumber, red onion, radish slices, mint leaves, and parsley.
2) Toast pita bread in a preheated oven at 375°F (190°C) for 5-7 minutes until crisp. Break into small pieces.
3) Prepare the dressing by whisking together olive oil, lemon juice, garlic, sumac, salt, and pepper.
4) Add the toasted pita to the salad and drizzle the dressing over it. Toss well to combine.
5) Serve immediately to enjoy the crunch of the pita.

Variations:

- Summer Fattoush

Replace cherry tomatoes with heirloom tomatoes
Use basil instead of mint
Add slices of fresh peaches for a fruity twist

- Fall Fattoush

Substitute mixed greens with kale or Swiss chard
Use roasted butternut squash cubes instead of cucumber
Add pomegranate seeds for extra crunch and color

- Winter Fattoush

Replace radishes with slices of roasted beets
Use endive or radicchio instead of lettuce
Add segments of blood oranges or grapefruits for a citrusy burst.

Chef's Note:

This Fattoush recipe can be adapted to your own tastes and the ingredients available in different seasons. It's a versatile dish that's perfect for using up any extra vegetables you may have.

NUTRITIONAL INFORMATION (PER SERVING):

Calories: 210 kcal
Total Fat: 15 g
Monounsaturated Fat: 11 g
Total Carbohydrates: 17 g
Dietary Fiber: 3 g
Protein: 3 g
Sodium: 150 mg

ITALIAN WHITE BEAN SALAD

A rustic and fulfilling salad straight from the Italian countryside, combining creamy beans with tangy vinaigrette.
MEAL-PREP FRIENDLY

Preparation Time: 15 minutes
Cooking Time: 0 minutes (if using canned beans)
Total Time: 15 minutes
Serves: 4

INGREDIENTS:

- 2 cans (15 oz each) white beans (such as cannellini or navy beans), drained and rinsed
- 1 cup cherry tomatoes, halved
- 1/2 red onion, thinly sliced
- 1/4 cup fresh basil, chopped
- 1/4 cup fresh parsley, chopped
- 2 garlic cloves, minced
- 1/4 cup extra-virgin olive oil
- 3 tablespoons red wine vinegar
- Salt and pepper to taste
- Grated zest of 1 lemon (optional for added flavor)

INSTRUCTIONS:

1) In a large mixing bowl, combine the drained and rinsed white beans, halved cherry tomatoes, and thinly sliced red onion.
2) Add the chopped basil and parsley to the mixture.
3) In a separate smaller bowl or jar, combine the minced garlic, extra-virgin olive oil, red wine vinegar, salt, pepper, and lemon zest (if using). Whisk or shake until well combined.
4) Pour the vinaigrette over the bean mixture and toss gently to coat.
5) Adjust seasoning with additional salt and pepper, if necessary.
6) Allow the salad to marinate for at least 30 minutes before serving for best flavor, or serve immediately if needed.

Chef's Note:

This salad pairs wonderfully with crusty Italian bread or as a side to grilled meats. If you prepare it a day in advance and refrigerate, the flavors will meld even more, making it perfect for meal-prep. Add some grated Parmesan cheese on top before serving for an extra touch of Italy!

NUTRITIONAL INFORMATION (PER SERVING):

Calories: 340 kcal
Total Fat: 14 g
Monounsaturated Fat: 10 g
Total Carbohydrates: 40 g
Dietary Fiber: 10 g
Protein: 14 g
Sodium: 300 mg

GREEK SALAD WITH GRILLED CHICKEN

A protein-rich Mediterranean meal that perfectly combines the crispness of Greek salad with the savoriness of grilled chicken.
MIX-AND-MATCH

Preparation Time: 15 minutes
Cooking Time: 12 minutes
Total Time: 27 minutes
Serves: 4

INGREDIENTS:

- 2 boneless, skinless chicken breasts
- 1 large cucumber, diced
- 4 medium tomatoes, diced
- 1 red onion, thinly sliced
- 1/2 cup Kalamata olives, pitted
- 1/2 cup feta cheese, crumbled
- 1/4 cup extra-virgin olive oil
- Juice of 1 lemon
- 2 tbsp fresh oregano, chopped
- Salt and pepper, to taste

INSTRUCTIONS:

1. Preheat the grill hot to a medium-high heat, roughly around 400°F (204°C).
2. Lightly season both sides of the chicken breasts with salt, pepper, and a splash of olive oil. Do this a few hours in advance or overnight if you can. You can grill the chicken in advance or use chicken from another leftover grilled chicken such as Mediterranean Herb-Grilled Chicken for this recipes. You may also used leftover grilled beef or lamb. This recipe goes great with all sorts of proteins including falafel or tofu for vegetarians.
3. Place the chicken on the grill and cook for 6 minutes on each side, or until the internal temperature reaches 165°F (74°C). Then remove from the grill and set aside to rest.
4. Dice the cucumber and tomatoes, thinly slice the red onion, and chop the olives.
5. In a large bowl, combine cucumber, tomatoes, red onion, olives, and crumbled feta.
6. In a separate bowl, whisk together olive oil, lemon juice, chopped oregano, salt, and pepper.
7. Add the dressing to the salad ingredients and mix well.
8. Thinly slice the rested grilled chicken.
9. Place the sliced chicken on top of the salad and serve immediately.

Chef's Note:

This salad without the chicken can serve as a refreshing side dish for various meals. You can also make it your own by trying the following variations:

1. Replace chicken with grilled shrimp for a seafood twist.
2. Use grilled halloumi cheese instead of feta for a unique flavor.
3. Add some toasted walnuts for a crunchy texture.
4. Mix in some avocado slices for added creaminess.
5. For a vegetarian version, swap the chicken with grilled tofu or tempeh.

NUTRITIONAL INFORMATION (PER SERVING):

Calories: 350 kcal
Total Fat: 20 g
    Monounsaturated Fat: 13 g
Total Carbohydrates: 15 g
    Dietary Fiber: 4 g
Protein: 28 g
Sodium: 450 mg

WATERMELON, FETA, AND MINT SALAD

Enjoy this refreshing and light salad that captures the essence of summer. The combination of sweet watermelon, tangy feta, and fresh mint is perfect for a hot day.

SUPER-QUICK!

Preparation Time: 15 minutes
Total Time: 15 minutes
Serves: 4

INGREDIENTS:

- 4 cups watermelon, cubed
- 1 cup feta cheese, crumbled
- 1/2 cup fresh mint leaves, finely chopped
- 1 tablespoon extra-virgin olive oil
- 1 tablespoon fresh lime juice
- Salt and pepper to taste

INSTRUCTIONS:

1. In a large bowl, combine the watermelon cubes and crumbled feta cheese.
2. In a separate bowl, whisk together the olive oil and lime juice. Season with a pinch of salt and pepper to taste.
3. Drizzle the olive oil and lime juice dressing over the watermelon and feta mixture. Toss gently to combine.
4. Sprinkle the finely chopped mint leaves over the salad, and give it another gentle toss.
5. Serve immediately or chill in the fridge for up to 2 hours before serving. The flavors meld beautifully as it chills.

Chef's Note:

You can also add some thinly sliced red onion or cucumber for extra crunch and flavor. This salad is excellent as a side dish for grilled meats or as a standalone light meal.

NUTRITIONAL INFORMATION (PER SERVING):

Calories: 250 kcal
Total Fat: 12 g
Monounsaturated Fat: 6 g
Total Carbohydrates: 30 g
Dietary Fiber: 2 g
Protein: 8 g
Sodium: 320 mg

Soups

TARATOR – COLD GREEK YOGURT SOUP

A cooling and refreshing soup that's perfect for hot summer days, straight from the Greek isles.
SUPER-QUICK!

Preparation Time: 10 minutes
Cooking Time: 0 minutes
Total Time: 10 minutes
Serves: 4

INGREDIENTS:
- 3 cups Greek yogurt
- 1 large cucumber, peeled and diced
- 2 cloves garlic, minced
- 2 tablespoons dill, finely chopped
- 1 tablespoon olive oil
- 1 tablespoon white vinegar
- Salt and pepper to taste
- 1 cup cold water (optional for thinner consistency)

INSTRUCTIONS:
1. In a large bowl, mix Greek yogurt, diced cucumber, minced garlic, and chopped dill.
2. Add olive oil and white vinegar to the yogurt mixture and stir well.
3. Season with salt and pepper to your liking.
4. If you prefer a thinner consistency, add cold water and mix until well incorporated.
5. Chill the soup in the refrigerator for at least 30 minutes before serving.

Chef's Note:
This soup is best consumed fresh but can be stored in the refrigerator for up to 24 hours. A drizzle of extra virgin olive oil just before serving can add an additional layer of flavor.

NUTRITIONAL INFORMATION (PER SERVING):
Calories: 180 kcal
Total Fat: 8 g
Monounsaturated Fat: 4 g
Total Carbohydrates: 12 g
Dietary Fiber: 0 g
Protein: 16 g
Sodium: 50 mg

ITALIAN RIBOLLITA

A hearty Tuscan soup that's perfect for cold days, filled with beans, vegetables, and bread. Make a large batch and freeze it in portion, you'll always have a comforting soup just 5 minutes of microwave away.
MEAL-PREP FRIENDLY

Preparation Time: 15 minutes
Cooking Time: 40 minutes
Total Time: 55 minutes
Serves: 6

INGREDIENTS:
- 1/4 cup olive oil
- 1 onion, chopped
- 3 carrots, diced
- 3 celery stalks, diced
- 4 cloves garlic, minced
- 1 can (14 oz) cannellini beans, drained and rinsed or 1 cup pre-cooked cannellini
- 1 can (14 oz) diced tomatoes
- 4 cups vegetable broth
- 1 loaf stale Italian bread, torn into pieces
- 2 cups chopped kale
- Salt and pepper to taste
- Parmesan cheese for garnish (optional)

INSTRUCTIONS:
1) Heat the olive oil in a large pot over medium heat. Add the chopped onion, carrots, celery, and garlic. Cook until softened, about 10 minutes.
2) Add the cannellini beans, diced tomatoes, and vegetable broth. Bring to a boil.
3) Reduce heat and add the torn bread and chopped kale. Simmer for about 30 minutes.
4) Season with salt and pepper to taste

NUTRITIONAL INFORMATION (PER SERVING):
Calories: 300 kcal
Total Fat: 10 g
Monounsaturated Fat: 6 g
Total Carbohydrates: 42 g
Dietary Fiber: 8 g
Protein: 10 g
Sodium: 800 mg

ALGERIAN HARIRA

A nutritious and comforting soup, offering a taste of Algeria.
VEGAN

Preparation Time: 20 minutes
Cooking Time: 45 minutes
Total Time: 65 minutes
Serves: 6

INGREDIENTS:
- 2 tablespoons olive oil
- 1 onion, chopped
- 2 cloves garlic, minced

- 1 can (14 oz) chickpeas, drained and rinsed
- 1 can (14 oz) lentils, drained and rinsed
- 1 can (14 oz) diced tomatoes
- 6 cups vegetable broth
- 1 teaspoon ground cumin
- 1 teaspoon ground coriander
- 1/2 teaspoon ground cinnamon
- 1/4 cup fresh cilantro, chopped
- 1/4 cup fresh parsley, chopped
- Salt and pepper to taste
- Lemon wedges for serving

INSTRUCTIONS:
1) Heat the olive oil in a large pot over medium heat. Add the chopped onion and minced garlic. Sauté until the onion becomes translucent.
2) Add chickpeas, lentils, and diced tomatoes to the pot. Stir to combine.
3) Pour in the vegetable broth and add cumin, coriander, and cinnamon. Bring to a boil.
4) Reduce heat to low and simmer for about 30 minutes, stirring occasionally.
5) Stir in chopped cilantro and parsley. Season with salt and pepper to taste.
6) Serve hot with lemon wedges on the side.

NUTRITIONAL INFORMATION (PER SERVING):
Calories: 220 kcal
Total Fat: 6 g
Monounsaturated Fat: 4 g
Total Carbohydrates: 32 g
Dietary Fiber: 9 g
Protein: 10 g
Sodium: 900 mg

TURKISH RED LENTIL SOUP

Indulge in this hearty Turkish red lentil soup that brings warmth and nutritious goodness.
VEGAN

Preparation Time: 10 minutes
Cooking Time: 25 minutes
Total Time: 35 minutes
Serves: 4

INGREDIENTS:
- 1 cup red lentils
- 1 large onion, diced
- 1 carrot, diced
- 1 potato, diced
- 4 cups vegetable broth
- 1 tsp cumin
- 1 tsp paprika
- Salt and pepper to taste
- Olive oil for sautéing

INSTRUCTIONS:
1) In a pot, heat a splash of olive oil and sauté the onions, carrot, and potato for 5 minutes.
2) Add the red lentils, vegetable broth, cumin, and paprika.
3) Bring to a boil, then lower heat and simmer for 20 minutes or until lentils and vegetables are soft.
4) Use an immersion blender to purée the soup to your preferred texture.
5) Season with salt and pepper before serving.

NUTRITIONAL INFORMATION (PER SERVING):
Calories: 240 kcal
Total Fat: 4 g
Monounsaturated Fat: 2 g
Total Carbohydrates: 42 g
Dietary Fiber: 11 g
Protein: 12 g
Sodium: 700 mg

SPANISH GAZPACHO SOUP

Refresh yourself with this chilled Spanish gazpacho, a perfect summer appetizer.
SUPER-QUICK!

Preparation Time: 15 minutes
Cooking Time: 0 minutes
Total Time: 15 minutes
Serves: 4

INGREDIENTS:
- 4 ripe tomatoes, chopped
- 1 cucumber, peeled and chopped
- 1 bell pepper, chopped
- 1 small red onion, chopped
- 2 cloves garlic
- 3 cups tomato juice
- 2 tbsp olive oil
- 1 tbsp red wine vinegar
- Salt and pepper to taste

INSTRUCTIONS:
1) Combine all the chopped vegetables in a blender.
2) Add the tomato juice, olive oil, and red wine vinegar.
3) Blend until smooth or leave a bit chunky, as per your preference.
4) Chill the gazpacho in the fridge for at least 2 hours before serving.
5) Season with salt and pepper, and serve chilled.

NUTRITIONAL INFORMATION (PER SERVING):
Calories: 150 kcal
Total Fat: 7 g
Monounsaturated Fat: 5 g
Total Carbohydrates: 22 g
Dietary Fiber: 4 g
Protein: 3 g

Sodium: 620 mg

CHILLED MELON SOUP

VEGAN

Preparation Time: 15 minutes
Chilling Time: 2 hours
Total Time: 2 hours 15 minutes
Serves: 4

INGREDIENTS:

- 4 cups cantaloupe or honeydew melon, cubed
- 1 cup coconut milk or almond milk
- 2 tablespoons fresh lime juice
- 1 tablespoon honey or agave syrup (optional)
- Mint leaves for garnish
- A pinch of salt

INSTRUCTIONS:

1. In a blender, combine the melon cubes, coconut or almond milk, lime juice, and a pinch of salt. If you want your soup a bit sweeter, add honey or agave syrup.
2. Blend the mixture until smooth and creamy. Taste and adjust seasoning or sweetness if necessary.
3. Transfer the blended mixture into a large bowl or pitcher, and cover it tightly with plastic wrap or a lid.
4. Chill the soup in the refrigerator for at least 2 hours to allow the flavors to meld together.
5. When you're ready to serve, pour the chilled melon soup into individual bowls or glasses, and garnish with fresh mint leaves.

Chef's Note:

For a more complex flavor, you can add a bit of ginger or lemongrass to the blend. This soup is versatile and works well with various types of melon; feel free to use watermelon or a mix of your favorite melons.

NUTRITIONAL INFORMATION (PER SERVING):

Calories: 120 kcal
Total Fat: 4 g
Saturated Fat: 3 g
Total Carbohydrates: 20 g
Dietary Fiber: 1 g
Protein: 1 g
Sodium: 45 mg

CRETAN TOMATO RICE SOUP

A simple and rustic soup originating from the island of Crete, combining ripe tomatoes and arborio rice for a hearty meal.

GLUTEN-FREE

Preparation Time: 10 minutes
Cooking Time: 30 minutes
Total Time: 40 minutes
Serves: 4

INGREDIENTS:

- 4 ripe tomatoes, diced
- 1/2 cup arborio rice
- 1 onion, finely chopped
- 2 cloves garlic, minced
- 4 cups vegetable broth
- 1/4 cup extra-virgin olive oil
- 1 teaspoon dried oregano
- Salt and pepper to taste
- Fresh basil leaves for garnish

INSTRUCTIONS:

1) In a large pot, heat olive oil over medium heat. Add chopped onion and garlic, sautéing until translucent.
2) Add diced tomatoes and cook for 5 minutes, until they start to break down.
3) Pour in vegetable broth and bring to a simmer.
4) Add arborio rice and dried oregano to the pot.
5) Cover and simmer for about 20-25 minutes, or until rice is tender.
6) Season with salt and pepper to taste.
7) Garnish with fresh basil leaves before serving.

NUTRITIONAL INFORMATION (PER SERVING):

Calories: 230 kcal
Total Fat: 14 g
Monounsaturated Fat: 10 g
Total Carbohydrates: 25 g
Dietary Fiber: 3 g
Protein: 4 g
Sodium: 800 mg

ITALIAN MINESTRONE SOUP

Experience the bounty of Italian vegetables in this wholesome, heart-healthy Minestrone Soup.

HEART-HEALTHY

Preparation Time: 20 minutes
Cooking Time: 40 minutes
Total Time: 60 minutes
Serves: 6

INGREDIENTS:

- 4 cups vegetable broth
- 1 can (14 oz) diced tomatoes
- 1 onion, diced
- 2 carrots, diced
- 1 zucchini, diced
- 2 potatoes, diced
- 1 cup kidney beans, canned or boiled
- 2 cloves garlic, minced
- 1 tsp dried oregano
- Salt and pepper to taste
- Olive oil for sautéing

- Optional: 1 cup small pasta like macaroni or ditalini

INSTRUCTIONS:
1) In a large pot, heat olive oil and sauté onion and garlic until translucent.
2) Add carrots, zucchini, and potatoes, sautéing for an additional 5 minutes.
3) Pour in the vegetable broth, diced tomatoes, and oregano.
4) Bring to a boil and then lower the heat to simmer for 25-30 minutes, or until vegetables are soft.
5) Add the kidney beans and optional pasta. Cook for another 10 minutes.
6) Season with salt and pepper to taste before serving.

Chef's Note:
This soup is perfect for meal prep and tastes even better the next day.

NUTRITIONAL INFORMATION (PER SERVING):
Calories: 260 kcal
Total Fat: 3 g
Monounsaturated Fat: 1 g
Total Carbohydrates: 42 g
Dietary Fiber: 8 g
Protein: 8 g
Sodium: 650 mg

SPANISH SOPA DE AJO ~ GARLIC SOUP

A soul-warming Spanish classic infused with garlic, paprika, and a hint of saffron.
SPECIAL OCCASION

Preparation Time: 10 minutes
Cooking Time: 25 minutes
Total Time: 35 minutes
Serves: 4

INGREDIENTS:
- 1/4 cup olive oil
- 8 cloves garlic, thinly sliced
- 4 slices stale bread, torn into pieces
- 1 teaspoon paprika
- Pinch of saffron (optional)
- 6 cups chicken or vegetable broth
- 2 eggs (optional)
- Salt and pepper to taste

INSTRUCTIONS:
1) Heat olive oil in a large pot over medium heat. Add garlic slices and cook until lightly golden.
2) Add torn bread pieces and paprika, stirring to coat in the flavored oil.
3) If using saffron, add it to the pot for a luxurious touch.
4) Pour in the chicken or vegetable broth and bring to a simmer.
5) Season with salt and pepper to taste.

6) If using eggs, crack them into the soup and poach for about 4 minutes or until whites are set but yolks remain runny.
7) Serve hot.

Chef's Note:
This soup pairs well with a glass of Spanish red wine. If you have leftovers, you can store them in the refrigerator for up to 2 days.

NUTRITIONAL INFORMATION (PER SERVING):
Calories: 220 kcal
Total Fat: 14 g
Monounsaturated Fat: 10 g
Total Carbohydrates: 15 g
Dietary Fiber: 2 g
Protein: 8 g
Sodium: 900 mg

PROVENCAL FISH SOUP

A fragrant and rich fish soup from the southern coast of France, flavored with fennel and saffron.
SPECIAL OCCASION

Preparation Time: 20 minutes
Cooking Time: 40 minutes
Total Time: 60 minutes
Serves: 4

INGREDIENTS:
- 1 lb mixed white fish (like cod, snapper), diced
- 1 onion, chopped
- 1 fennel bulb, thinly sliced
- 2 cloves garlic, minced
- 1 can (14 oz) diced tomatoes
- 4 cups fish or vegetable broth
- 1/4 teaspoon saffron threads
- 1 tablespoon olive oil
- Salt and pepper to taste

INSTRUCTIONS:
1) Heat olive oil in a large pot over medium heat. Add chopped onion, fennel, and garlic. Cook until softened.
2) Add the diced tomatoes, including their juice, to the pot.
3) Stir in saffron threads and fish or vegetable broth. Bring to a simmer.
4) Add diced fish to the pot, and simmer for another 10-15 minutes, until fish is cooked through.
5) Season with salt and pepper to taste.
6) Serve hot.

NUTRITIONAL INFORMATION (PER SERVING):
Calories: 240 kcal
Total Fat: 8 g
Monounsaturated Fat: 5 g
Total Carbohydrates: 12 g

Dietary Fiber: 3 g
Protein: 28 g
Sodium: 800 mg

GREEK LEMON CHICKEN SOUP (AVGOLEMONO)

A creamy, citrusy soup that brings the flavors of Greece right to your table.
GLUTEN-FREE

Preparation Time: 10 minutes
Cooking Time: 25 minutes
Total Time: 35 minutes
Serves: 4

INGREDIENTS:

- 4 cups chicken broth
- 2 chicken breasts, cooked and shredded
- 1/3 cup rice
- 2 lemons, juiced
- 2 eggs
- Salt and pepper to taste

INSTRUCTIONS:

1) In a pot, bring the chicken broth to a boil.
2) Add orzo or rice, simmer until tender (orzo 10 minutes, rice 20 minutes).
3) In a separate bowl, whisk lemon juice and eggs together.
4) Slowly add a cup of the hot broth to the lemon-egg mixture while whisking to temper the eggs.
5) Stir the tempered lemon-egg mixture back into the pot.
6) Add shredded chicken and cook for another 5 minutes.
7) Season with salt and pepper before serving.

Chef's Note:

Serve with a slice of lemon and a sprinkle of fresh parsley for added flavor.

NUTRITIONAL INFORMATION (PER SERVING):

Calories: 200 kcal
Total Fat: 5 g
Monounsaturated Fat: 2 g
Total Carbohydrates: 20 g
Dietary Fiber: 1 g
Protein: 20 g
Sodium: 750 mg

ZUPPA DI CANNELLINI, ORZO E POMODORI ~ CANNELLINI BEAN, BARLEY, AND TOMATO SOUP

A hearty Mediterranean soup featuring cannellini beans, barley, and tomatoes for a filling meal.
LOW-CALORIES

Preparation Time: 10 minutes
Cooking Time: 35 minutes
Total Time: 45 minutes
Serves: 4-6 servings

INGREDIENTS:

- 1 cup canned cannellini beans, drained and rinsed
- 1/2 cup pearl barley
- 1 can (14.5 oz) diced tomatoes
- 1 medium onion, diced
- 2 cloves garlic, minced
- 4 cups vegetable broth
- 2 tablespoons olive oil
- Salt and pepper to taste
- Fresh basil for garnish

INSTRUCTIONS:

1) In a large pot, heat the olive oil over medium heat. Add onion and garlic, sautéing until translucent.
2) Add barley to the pot and sauté for 2 minutes.
3) Add tomatoes and vegetable broth. Bring to a boil.
4) Lower heat, add cannellini beans, and simmer for 30 minutes or until barley is cooked.
5) Season with salt and pepper.
6) Garnish with fresh basil before serving.

NUTRITIONAL INFORMATION (PER SERVING):

Calories: 180 kcal
Total Fat: 4 g
Carbohydrates: 30 g
Protein: 8 g
Sodium: 540 mg

TUSCAN BEAN SOUP WITH KALE AND SAUSAGE

Warm and delicious, everything you want for a chilly evening.
GLUTEN-FREE

Preparation Time: 15 minutes
Cooking Time: 35 minutes
Total Time: 50 minutes
Serves: 6

INGREDIENTS:

- 1 tablespoon olive oil
- 1 medium onion, diced
- 3 cloves garlic, minced
- 1 pound Italian sausage, casings removed
- 4 cups chicken broth
- 2 cans (15 oz each) cannellini beans, drained and rinsed
- 1 bunch kale, stems removed and leaves torn into pieces
- 1 teaspoon dried oregano
- 1/2 teaspoon dried thyme

- Salt and pepper, to taste
- Optional: grated Parmesan cheese for garnish

INSTRUCTIONS:
1. Heat olive oil in a large pot over medium heat. Add the diced onion and minced garlic, sautéing until the onion is translucent, about 5 minutes.
2. Add the sausage to the pot and break it up with a wooden spoon. Cook until the sausage is browned, about 7-8 minutes.
3. Pour in the chicken broth and bring the mixture to a simmer.
4. Add the drained cannellini beans, torn kale leaves, dried oregano, and dried thyme to the pot.
5. Stir well and continue to simmer for about 15-20 minutes, or until the kale is tender.
6. Season with salt and pepper to taste. Serve hot, optionally garnished with grated Parmesan cheese.

Chef's Note:
You can easily make this soup vegetarian by omitting the sausage and using vegetable broth instead of chicken broth. Feel free to add other vegetables like carrots or potatoes for more complexity.

NUTRITIONAL INFORMATION (PER SERVING):
Calories: 390 kcal
Total Fat: 20 g
   Monounsaturated Fat: 8 g
Total Carbohydrates: 30 g
   Dietary Fiber: 7 g
Protein: 22 g
Sodium: 920 mg

CANNELLINI BEAN AND ESCAROLE SOUP
A hearty and nutritious soup to keep in the freezer and whip out anytime you feel like you want to eat a warm hug.
ONE-POT MEAL

Preparation Time: 15 minutes
Cooking Time: 40 minutes
Total Time: 55 minutes
Serves: 4

INGREDIENTS:
- 1 can (15 oz) cannellini beans, drained and rinsed
- 1 head of escarole, chopped
- 1 medium onion, finely chopped
- 3 cloves garlic, minced
- 1 quart vegetable or chicken broth
- 1 tablespoon extra-virgin olive oil
- Salt and pepper to taste
- 1/2 teaspoon red pepper flakes (optional)
- Grated Parmesan cheese for garnish

INSTRUCTIONS:

1. In a large pot, heat the olive oil over medium heat. Add the chopped onion and garlic, sautéing until the onion becomes translucent.
2. Add the chopped escarole to the pot, stirring until it begins to wilt.
3. Pour in the vegetable or chicken broth, and bring the mixture to a gentle boil.
4. Reduce the heat to low and add the drained cannellini beans. If using red pepper flakes, add them at this point.
5. Let the soup simmer for about 30 minutes, allowing the flavors to meld together.
6. Season with salt and pepper to taste.
7. Serve hot, garnished with grated Parmesan cheese.

Chef's Note:
Feel free to add some diced carrots or celery for additional flavor and nutrients. This soup pairs well with a crusty bread and a glass of dry white wine.

NUTRITIONAL INFORMATION (PER SERVING):
Calories: 420 kcal
Total Fat: 8 g
Monounsaturated Fat: 4 g
Total Carbohydrates: 62 g
Dietary Fiber: 15 g
Protein: 20 g
Sodium: 780 mg

ROASTED RED PEPPER AND TOMATO SOUP ~ SHORBAT TAMATUM BIL FILFIL HAMRA
A Middle Eastern-inspired soup featuring roasted red peppers and tomatoes, perfect for a comforting vegan meal.
VEGAN

Preparation Time: 15 minutes
Cooking Time: 30 minutes
Total Time: 45 minutes
Serves: 4 servings

INGREDIENTS:
- 3 large red peppers, roasted and peeled
- 4 large tomatoes, diced
- 1 onion, diced
- 3 cloves garlic, minced
- 4 cups vegetable broth
- 2 tablespoons olive oil
- Salt and pepper to taste

INSTRUCTIONS:
1) In a pot, heat olive oil over medium heat. Add the onion and garlic and sauté until translucent.
2) Add the diced tomatoes and roasted red peppers to the pot.
3) Pour in vegetable broth and bring to a simmer.
4) Using an immersion blender, puree the soup until smooth.

5) Season with salt and pepper, and serve hot.

NUTRITIONAL INFORMATION (PER SERVING):
Calories: 160 kcal
Total Fat: 7 g
Carbohydrates: 21 g
Protein: 4 g
Sodium: 500 mg

CHESTNUT AND MUSHROOM SOUP

A hearty winter soup, both filling and healthy. Takes a bit of work, but is well worth the effort.
SPECIAL OCCASION

Preparation Time: 30 minutes
Cooking Time: 45 minutes
Total Time: 1 hour 15 minutes
Serves: 6-8

INGREDIENTS:
- 1 pound chestnuts, shelled and peeled
- 2 tablespoons olive oil
- 1 medium onion, finely chopped
- 4 cloves garlic, minced
- 1 pound mixed mushrooms (shiitake, cremini, portobello), sliced
- 1 cup dry white wine
- 6 cups vegetable or chicken broth
- 2 bay leaves
- 1 teaspoon fresh thyme leaves
- Salt and black pepper to taste
- 1 cup heavy cream (optional)
- Chopped parsley for garnish

INSTRUCTIONS:
1. Boil the chestnuts in water for 20-25 minutes until tender. Drain and chop them into small pieces.
2. In a large pot, heat olive oil over medium heat. Add the onions and garlic, sautéing until they become translucent.
3. Stir in the sliced mushrooms and sauté for another 5-7 minutes until they release their moisture.
4. Pour in the white wine and let it reduce for a couple of minutes.
5. Add the broth, bay leaves, and fresh thyme to the pot. Bring the mixture to a simmer.
6. Continue to simmer the soup for about 30-45 minutes or until flavors meld together and the soup has slightly thickened.
7. Stir in the optional heavy cream, if using. Season with salt and black pepper.
8. Serve hot, garnished with chopped parsley.

Chef's Note:
For a more luxurious texture, you can blend a portion of the soup and mix it back into the pot. This soup keeps well in the refrigerator for up to 3 days and can also be frozen for later use.

NUTRITIONAL INFORMATION (PER SERVING):
Calories: 280 kcal
Total Fat: 10 g
Monounsaturated Fat: 6 g
Total Carbohydrates: 35 g
Dietary Fiber: 4 g
Protein: 8 g
Sodium: 800 mg

MEDITERRANEAN ZUCCHINI AND ALMOND SOUP

A creamy zucchini soup thickened with almonds, offering a unique twist on traditional vegetable soups.
DAIRY-FREE

Preparation Time: 10 minutes
Cooking Time: 25 minutes
Total Time: 35 minutes
Serves: 4

INGREDIENTS:
- 2 tablespoons olive oil
- 1 onion, chopped
- 2 garlic cloves, minced
- 4 medium zucchinis, sliced
- 1/4 cup almonds, crushed
- 4 cups vegetable broth
- Salt and pepper to taste
- A sprig of fresh basil for garnish

INSTRUCTIONS:
- Heat olive oil in a pot over medium heat.
- Add the onion and garlic, sautéing until softened.
- Add the sliced zucchinis and almonds to the pot.
- Pour in the vegetable broth and bring to a boil.
- Reduce heat and simmer for 20 minutes.
- Use an immersion blender to puree the soup until smooth.
- Season with salt and pepper.
- Garnish with a sprig of fresh basil before serving.

NUTRITIONAL INFORMATION (PER SERVING):
Calories: 180 kcal
Total Fat: 10 g
Total Carbohydrates: 20 g
Dietary Fiber: 4 g
Protein: 5 g
Sodium: 750 mg

HARIRA BEL LAHM ~ HARIRA WITH LAMB SOUP

A light version of the traditional Moroccan soup, featuring lean lamb and lentils.
GLUTEN-FREE

Preparation Time: 15 minutes
Cooking Time: 45 minutes
Total Time: 1 hour
Serves: 6

INGREDIENTS:

- 200g lean lamb, diced
- 1 cup lentils, soaked for 1 hour
- 1 onion, chopped
- 2 tomatoes, diced
- 1 tbsp olive oil
- 1 tsp cinnamon
- 1 tsp cumin
- 1 tsp paprika
- 6 cups vegetable stock
- Salt and pepper to taste
- Fresh cilantro, chopped for garnish

INSTRUCTIONS:

1) Heat olive oil in a large pot and brown the lamb pieces (ideally you want to marinate the lamb for a few hours in just salt and pepper first).
2) Add onions, cooking until translucent.
3) Add spices, lentils, and diced tomatoes, stirring well to incorporate.
4) Pour in vegetable stock and bring to a simmer. Cook until lamb and lentils are tender, around 35-40 minutes.
5) Season with salt and pepper, garnish with fresh cilantro, and serve hot.

- **NUTRITIONAL INFORMATION (PER SERVING):**
- Calories: 210 kcal
- Total Fat: 5 g
- Total Carbohydrates: 20 g
- Protein: 18 g
- Sodium: 350 mg

FAKES (GREEK LENTIL SOUP)

A hearty and nutritious Mediterranean classic that's rich in protein and fiber.
MIX-AND-MATCH

Preparation Time: 10 minutes
Cooking Time: 45 minutes

Total Time: 55 minutes
Serves: 4

INGREDIENTS:
- 1 cup green lentils, rinsed
- 1 large onion, diced
- 2 cloves garlic, minced
- 1 medium carrot, diced
- 1 bay leaf
- 1 teaspoon dried oregano
- 1/4 cup extra-virgin olive oil
- 4 cups vegetable broth (or 2 if using already cooked lentils)
- Juice of 1 lemon
- Salt and pepper, to taste

INSTRUCTIONS:
1. Rinse the lentils under cold running water.
2. In a pot, heat the olive oil over medium heat. Add the diced onion, garlic, and carrot, sautéing until soft.
3. Add the rinsed lentils to the pot along with the bay leaf, dried oregano, salt, and pepper. Add potatoes here is using (see notes). Stir to combine.
4. Add the vegetable broth to the pot and bring it to a boil.
5. Once boiling, reduce the heat to low, cover, and let it simmer for about 40 minutes or until lentils are tender. If you are using already cooked lentils, 15 minutes will suffice and you can reduce the broth to 2 cups.
6. Once the lentils are cooked, remove the bay leaf and stir in the lemon juice.
7. Taste for seasoning, adding more salt, pepper, or lemon juice as needed.
8. Ladle the soup into bowls and serve hot.

Chef's Note:
This soup is perfect as a standalone meal or as a starter for a more elaborate dinner. For variations, you can:
1. Add a dollop of Greek yogurt or a sprinkle of feta cheese on top before serving.
2. Stir in some spinach or kale for added greens. Add just 5 minutes before finishing to cook the soup.
3. Add diced potatoes for a more hearty texture when adding lentils.
4. Use chicken broth instead of vegetable broth for a different flavor profile.
5. Garnish with fresh parsley or dill for extra color and taste.

NUTRITIONAL INFORMATION (PER SERVING):
Calories: 260 kcal
Total Fat: 14 g
    Monounsaturated Fat: 10 g
Total Carbohydrates: 25 g
    Dietary Fiber: 11 g
Protein: 11 g
Sodium: 700 mg

Desserts

LOKUM ~ TURKISH DELIGHT

Chewy, sweet, and fragrant, this classic Turkish sweet is a treat for the senses.

DAIRY-FREE

Preparation Time: 20 minutes
Cooking Time: 60 minutes
Total Time: 80 minutes
Serves: 24 pieces

INGREDIENTS:

- 2 cups granulated sugar
- 1 cup water
- 1 tsp lemon juice
- 1 cup cornstarch
- 1 tsp rosewater
- Food coloring (optional)
- Powdered sugar for dusting

INSTRUCTIONS:

1) In a saucepan, combine sugar, 1/2 cup water, and lemon juice. Boil until it reaches 240°F (115°C) on a sugar thermometer.
2) In another saucepan, dissolve cornstarch in 1/2 cup water and heat until thickened.
3) Slowly mix the sugar syrup into the cornstarch mixture. Cook on low heat, stirring constantly, for about 50 minutes.
4) Add rosewater and optional food coloring. Stir until well combined.
5) Pour mixture into a greased 8x8-inch pan and let cool.
6) Once set, cut into squares and dust with powdered sugar.

Chef's Note:

For a different flavor, you can replace rosewater with orange blossom water.

NUTRITIONAL INFORMATION (PER SERVING):

Calories: 90 kcal
Total Fat: 0 g
Total Carbohydrates: 22 g
Dietary Fiber: 0 g
Protein: 0 g
Sodium: 5 mg

TRADITIONAL TIRAMISU

An iconic Italian dessert featuring layers of coffee-soaked ladyfingers and a creamy mascarpone mixture, light yet decadent.

SPECIAL OCCASION

Preparation Time: 30 minutes
Chilling Time: 4-6 hours
Total Time: 4-6 hours 30 minutes
Serves: 8

INGREDIENTS:

- 6 large egg yolks
- 3/4 cup granulated sugar
- 2/3 cup milk
- 1 1/4 cups mascarpone cheese
- 1 1/2 cups brewed espresso, cooled
- 1 teaspoon vanilla extract
- 1 pack of ladyfingers (approximately 24)
- 1 tablespoon unsweetened cocoa powder for dusting
- Optional: Dark chocolate shavings for garnish

INSTRUCTIONS:

1) In a heatproof bowl, whisk together the egg yolks and sugar until well blended.
2) Place the bowl over a pot of simmering water (double boiler) and add the milk. Cook, whisking constantly, until the mixture thickens. Remove from heat and let cool.
3) In a separate bowl, fold the mascarpone cheese into the egg yolk mixture until smooth.
4) In a small bowl, combine the brewed espresso and vanilla extract.
5) Quickly dip each ladyfinger into the coffee mixture, making sure not to soak them. Arrange a layer of dipped ladyfingers at the bottom of a serving dish.
6) Spread half of the mascarpone mixture over the ladyfingers.
7) Add another layer of dipped ladyfingers.
8) Spread the remaining mascarpone mixture over the ladyfingers.
9) Cover and chill in the refrigerator for at least 4-6 hours to allow the flavors to meld together.
10) Before serving, dust the top with cocoa powder and optionally garnish with dark chocolate shavings.

Chef's Note:

You can also add a splash of coffee liqueur like Ameretto or Marsala wine to the espresso mixture for an extra kick. The dish can be stored in the refrigerator for up to 2 days.

NUTRITIONAL INFORMATION (PER SERVING):

Calories: 300 kcal
Total Fat: 20 g
Monounsaturated Fat: 10 g
Total Carbohydrates: 28 g
Dietary Fiber: 0 g
Protein: 6 g
Sodium: 80 mg

IMQARET ~ MALTESE DATE PASTRIES

Fragrant with spices and filled with dates, these pastries are a Maltese delicacy.

SPECIAL OCCASION

Preparation Time: 30 minutes
Cooking Time: 20 minutes
Total Time: 50 minutes
Serves: 12

INGREDIENTS:
- 2 cups all-purpose flour
- 1/4 cup olive oil
- 1/4 cup water
- 1 cup pitted dates
- 1 tsp ground cinnamon
- 1/2 tsp ground cloves
- 1 tbsp orange zest
- Oil for frying

INSTRUCTIONS:
1) Make dough by combining flour, olive oil, and water. Knead until smooth.
2) Cook dates, cinnamon, cloves, and orange zest over low heat until it forms a paste.
3) Roll out the dough and cut into rectangles. Place a spoonful of date mixture in the center.
4) Fold dough over filling and seal edges. Cut into small rectangles.
5) Deep fry until golden brown.

Chef's Note:
Serve warm, optionally with a sprinkle of powdered sugar.

NUTRITIONAL INFORMATION (PER SERVING):
Calories: 180 kcal
Total Fat: 6 g
Monounsaturated Fat: 3 g
Total Carbohydrates: 30 g
Dietary Fiber: 2 g
Protein: 2 g
Sodium: 10 mg

MOROCCAN ORANGE CAKE

A moist, fragrant oil cake made with fresh oranges and a hint of cinnamon.

HEART-HEALTHY

Preparation Time: 20 minutes
Cooking Time: 35 minutes
Total Time: 55 minutes
Serves: 8

INGREDIENTS:
- 3 oranges
- 3/4 cup olive oil
- 1 cup granulated sugar
- 2 cups all-purpose flour
- 1 tsp baking powder
- 1/2 tsp cinnamon
- 1/4 cup slivered almonds for garnish

INSTRUCTIONS:
1) Preheat oven to 350°F (175°C). Grease a 9-inch round cake pan.
2) Zest and juice 2 oranges. Slice the remaining orange thinly for decoration.
3) Mix olive oil, orange juice, zest, and sugar in a bowl.
4) Combine flour, baking powder, and cinnamon. Mix into the wet ingredients until smooth.
5) Pour into prepared pan and decorate with orange slices and almonds.
6) Bake for 35-40 minutes or until a toothpick comes out clean.

NUTRITIONAL INFORMATION (PER SERVING):
Calories: 350 kcal
Total Fat: 15 g
Monounsaturated Fat: 10 g
Total Carbohydrates: 50 g
Dietary Fiber: 2 g
Protein: 3 g
Sodium: 50 mg

CREMA CATALANA ~ CATALAN CREAM

A Spanish classic, similar to crème brûlée but infused with citrus and cinnamon flavors.

SPECIAL OCCASION

Preparation Time: 10 minutes
Cooking Time: 20 minutes
Chilling Time: 2 hours
Total Time: 2 hours 30 minutes
Serves: 4

INGREDIENTS:
- 2 cups whole milk
- Zest of 1 orange
- 1 cinnamon stick
- 4 egg yolks
- 1/2 cup granulated sugar
- 1 tablespoon cornstarch
- Extra sugar for caramelizing

INSTRUCTIONS:
1) Heat milk, orange zest, and cinnamon stick in a saucepan until it nearly reaches a boil. Remove from heat.
2) In a separate bowl, whisk egg yolks, sugar, and cornstarch until smooth.
3) Gradually add the hot milk to the egg yolk mixture while whisking continuously.

4) Return the mixture to the saucepan and cook over low heat, stirring constantly, until it thickens.
5) Remove the cinnamon stick and orange zest, and pour the custard into individual ramekins.
6) Chill for at least 2 hours to set.
7) Just before serving, sprinkle a thin layer of sugar on top and caramelize using a kitchen torch.

NUTRITIONAL INFORMATION (PER SERVING):
Calories: 250 kcal
Total Fat: 8 g
Monounsaturated Fat: 3 g
Total Carbohydrates: 35 g
Dietary Fiber: 0 g
Protein: 5 g
Sodium: 100 mg

TORTA DI CAROTE E CARDAMOMO ~ SWEET CARROT AND CARDAMOM TORTE

A fusion dessert that brings together the earthy sweetness of carrots and the aromatic spice of cardamom, making it a unique yet traditional dish that can be enjoyed year-round.
SPECIAL OCCASION

Preparation Time: 20 minutes
Cooking Time: 40-45 minutes
Total Time: 60-65 minutes
Serves: 8

INGREDIENTS:
- 2 cups grated carrots
- 1 1/2 cups all-purpose flour
- 1 1/2 teaspoons baking powder
- 1 teaspoon ground cardamom
- 1/2 teaspoon salt
- 1 cup granulated sugar
- 3 large eggs
- 1/2 cup olive oil
- 1 teaspoon vanilla extract
- Optional: 1/2 cup chopped walnuts or almonds
- Optional: Icing sugar for dusting

INSTRUCTIONS:
1) Preheat your oven to 350°F (175°C). Grease and line a 9-inch round cake pan.
2) In a medium-sized bowl, mix together the all-purpose flour, baking powder, ground cardamom, and salt. Set aside.
3) In a separate large bowl, whisk together the sugar and eggs until pale and fluffy.
4) Gradually add the olive oil and vanilla extract to the egg mixture while whisking.
5) Fold in the dry ingredients into the wet mixture until just combined.
6) Add the grated carrots and optional nuts to the batter and mix until evenly distributed.

7) Pour the batter into the prepared cake pan and smooth the top with a spatula.
8) Bake for 40-45 minutes or until a toothpick inserted into the center comes out clean.
9) Remove from the oven and let cool in the pan for 10 minutes. Then transfer to a wire rack to cool completely.
10) Optional: Dust the top of the cake with icing sugar before serving.

Chef's Note:
For an added touch, you can serve this cake with a dollop of Greek yogurt flavored with a sprinkle of cardamom and a drizzle of honey.

NUTRITIONAL INFORMATION (PER SERVING):
Calories: 330 kcal
Total Fat: 16 g
Monounsaturated Fat: 10 g
Total Carbohydrates: 42 g
Dietary Fiber: 2 g
Protein: 5 g
Sodium: 240 mg

FRUIT, GRANOLA, AND YOGURT PARFAITS

This Mediterranean-inspired dessert parfait combines the natural sweetness of fresh fruits with crunchy granola and creamy yogurt for a light yet fulfilling treat.
SUPER-QUICK!

Preparation Time: 10 minutes
Total Time: 10 minutes
Serves: 2

INGREDIENTS:
1) 1 cup low-fat Greek yogurt (or a dairy-free alternative like coconut yogurt)
2) 1 cup mixed fresh fruit (e.g., berries, apple slices, or peach chunks)
3) 1/2 cup granola (preferably homemade or low sugar)
4) Optional: drizzle of honey or a natural sweetener like stevia for added sweetness
5) Optional: pinch of cinnamon or cardamom for added flavor

INSTRUCTIONS:
1) Take two glasses or jars and start by adding a layer of yogurt at the bottom.
2) Add a layer of mixed fruit on top of the yogurt.
3) Sprinkle a layer of granola over the fruit.
4) Repeat the layers until the glass or jar is filled.
5) Optional: Drizzle a small amount of honey or natural sweetener over the top layer.
6) Optional: Add a pinch of cinnamon or cardamom for added flavor.
7) Serve immediately, or cover and refrigerate for up to 2 hours before serving.

Chef's Note:
You can prepare these parfaits a day ahead and keep them in the fridge for a quick and easy dessert or breakfast option. Feel free to swap out the fruits according to the season or your personal preference.

Variations:
Use tropical fruits like mango and pineapple for a summer vibe.
Add a layer of chia pudding for added nutrition.
Mix in some dark chocolate chips or cacao nibs for a touch of decadence.

NUTRITIONAL INFORMATION (PER SERVING):
Calories: 200 kcal
Total Fat: 3 g
Monounsaturated Fat: 1 g
Total Carbohydrates: 35 g
Dietary Fiber: 4 g
Protein: 10 g
Sodium: 50 mg

MEDITERRANEAN COLD RICE PUDDING WITH RAISINS

A delicate pudding infused with cinnamon and nutmeg, that's perfect for light seet treat and even better as a breakfast choice. Just do it the night before and you'll have it ready in the morning, or better yet prepare individual portion to keep in the fridge for the whole week

GLUTEN-FREE

Preparation Time: 10 minutes
Cooking Time: 25 minutes
Chilling Time: 2 hours
Total Time: 2 hours 35 minutes
Serves: 6

INGREDIENTS:
- 1 cup Arborio rice or short-grain rice
- 4 cups whole milk
- 1/2 cup granulated sugar
- 1 teaspoon vanilla extract
- 1 teaspoon ground cinnamon
- 1/4 teaspoon ground nutmeg
- 1/2 cup raisins
- Optional: Zest of 1 lemon or orange

INSTRUCTIONS:
1. Rinse the rice in cold water until the water runs clear. Drain well.
2. In a large saucepan, combine the rinsed rice and milk. Cook over medium heat, stirring frequently to avoid sticking, until the mixture begins to simmer.
3. Lower the heat to maintain a gentle simmer and cook, stirring occasionally, for 18-20 minutes, or until the rice is tender and the mixture thickens.

4. Add the granulated sugar, vanilla extract, ground cinnamon, and ground nutmeg to the rice mixture. Stir until the sugar dissolves.
5. Stir in the raisins and optional citrus zest, then remove from heat.
6. Allow the pudding to cool to room temperature before transferring it to a serving dish or individual bowls.
7. Cover and refrigerate for at least 2 hours, allowing the flavors to meld and the pudding to thicken further.

Chef's Note:
For a different taste profile, you can substitute the raisins with dried cranberries or chopped dried apricots. A sprinkle of toasted almonds or walnuts can add a delightful crunch to the dish.

NUTRITIONAL INFORMATION (PER SERVING):
Calories: 270 kcal
Total Fat: 5 g
Monounsaturated Fat: 2 g
Total Carbohydrates: 50 g
Dietary Fiber: 1 g
Protein: 7 g
Sodium: 80 mg

MEDITERRANEAN FRESH FRUIT MEDLEY WITH MINT

A vibrant, refreshing fruit salad that captures the essence of the Mediterranean with a burst of minty freshness. This is a free dessert, you can choose it as lunch or dinner for those days when you'd rather eat something sweet.

VEGAN

Preparation Time: 10 minutes
Total Time: 10 minutes
Serves: 4

INGREDIENTS:
- 1 cup watermelon cubes
- 1 cup cantaloupe cubes
- 1 cup honeydew melon cubes
- 1 orange, segmented
- 1 cup strawberries, halved
- 1/2 cup blueberries
- 1/2 cup pomegranate arils
- Juice of 1 lemon
- 2 tablespoons fresh mint leaves, finely chopped
- 1 tablespoon honey or agave syrup (optional)

INSTRUCTIONS:
1. Prepare all the fruits by washing, peeling, and cutting them into bite-sized pieces or segments.
2. In a large mixing bowl, combine the watermelon, cantaloupe, honeydew melon, orange segments, strawberries, blueberries, and pomegranate arils.

3. In a separate small bowl, mix together the lemon juice and chopped mint leaves. If you prefer a sweeter salad, add honey or agave syrup to the lemon-mint mixture.
4. Drizzle the lemon-mint mixture over the fruit in the large bowl.
5. Gently toss everything to combine, making sure the fruits are well-coated with the lemon-mint mixture.
6. Serve immediately or let it chill in the refrigerator for about 30 minutes before serving to allow the flavors to meld.

Chef's Note:

This fruit medley is incredibly flexible. Feel free to use other seasonal fruits or add a touch of Mediterranean herbs like basil for a different twist.

NUTRITIONAL INFORMATION (PER SERVING):

Calories: 90 kcal
Total Fat: 0.5 g
    Monounsaturated Fat: 0 g
    Polyunsaturated Fat: 0 g
Total Carbohydrates: 22 g
    Dietary Fiber: 3 g
Protein: 1 g
Sodium: 10 mg

LEBANESE ATAYEF ~ STUFFED PANCAKES

Delicate, stuffed semolina pancakes often enjoyed during Ramadan in Lebanon. Why don't you try them for a breakfast your kids will love?
KID-FRIENDLY

Preparation Time: 20 minutes
Cooking Time: 15 minutes
Total Time: 35 minutes
Serves: 10

INGREDIENTS:

- 1 cup all-purpose flour
- 1/2 cup semolina
- 1 tsp baking powder
- 1 1/2 cups water
- 1/2 tsp yeast
- For the filling:
- 1 cup walnuts, chopped
- 1/4 cup sugar
- 1 tsp cinnamon

INSTRUCTIONS:

1) Mix flour, semolina, baking powder, water, and yeast to form a smooth batter. Let it rest for an hour.
2) Heat a non-stick skillet over medium heat.
3) Pour small rounds of batter onto the skillet. Cook until bubbles form but do not flip.
4) Mix the filling ingredients in a separate bowl.
5) Place a small amount of filling in the center of each pancake and fold in half, pressing the edges to seal.

6) Serve as is, or fry until crispy.

NUTRITIONAL INFORMATION (PER SERVING):

Calories: 180 kcal
Total Fat: 9 g
Monounsaturated Fat: 3 g
Total Carbohydrates: 21 g
Dietary Fiber: 2 g
Protein: 4 g
Sodium: 35 mg

ITALIAN FIG & ALMOND CAKE

An Italian treat showcasing the rich, sweet flavors of figs, complemented by crunchy almonds.
GLUTEN-FREE

Preparation Time: 20 minutes
Cooking Time: 45 minutes
Total Time: 1 hour 5 minutes
Serves: 8

INGREDIENTS:

- 1 1/2 cups almond flour
- 1/2 cup coconut flour
- 1 teaspoon baking powder
- 1/2 cup olive oil
- 1/2 cup honey
- 3 large eggs
- 1 teaspoon vanilla extract
- 1 cup dried figs, chopped
- 1/2 cup sliced almonds

INSTRUCTIONS:

1) Preheat oven to 350°F (175°C). Grease a 9-inch round cake pan.
2) In a bowl, combine almond flour, coconut flour, and baking powder.
3) In another bowl, mix olive oil, honey, eggs, and vanilla extract.
4) Combine wet and dry ingredients. Add chopped figs.
5) Pour batter into prepared cake pan.
6) Sprinkle sliced almonds on top.
7) Bake for 45 minutes or until a toothpick comes out clean.
8) Let cool before serving.

NUTRITIONAL INFORMATION (PER SERVING):

Calories: 360 kcal
Total Fat: 24 g
Monounsaturated Fat: 10 g
Total Carbohydrates: 31 g
Dietary Fiber: 5 g
Protein: 8 g
Sodium: 85 mg

MOROCCAN MINT TEA GRANITA

A refreshing granita made from classic Moroccan mint tea, perfect for hot summer days.
HEART-HEALTHY

Preparation Time: 10 minutes
Freezing Time: 3 hours
Total Time: 3 hours 10 minutes
Serves: 4

INGREDIENTS:
- 4 cups water
- 2 tablespoons green tea leaves
- 1 bunch fresh mint leaves
- 1/2 cup sugar

INSTRUCTIONS:
1) Boil water and steep green tea and mint leaves for 5 minutes.
2) Strain and add sugar, stirring until dissolved.
3) Pour into a shallow dish and freeze for 1 hour.
4) Scrape with a fork and freeze again.
5) Repeat the scraping and freezing process every 30 minutes until fully frozen.
6) Serve in chilled glasses.

Chef's Note:
For added zest, you can sprinkle a little lemon juice over the granita before serving.

NUTRITIONAL INFORMATION (PER SERVING):
Calories: 120 kcal
Total Fat: 0 g
Total Carbohydrates: 30 g
Dietary Fiber: 0 g
Protein: 0 g
Sodium: 5 mg

KARITHOPITA ~ GREEK WALNUT CAKE

A spiced Greek walnut cake soaked in honey syrup, perfect for any occasion.
SPECIAL OCCASION

Preparation Time: 20 minutes
Cooking Time: 40 minutes
Total Time: 1 hour
Serves: 12

INGREDIENTS:
- 2 cups chopped walnuts
- 1 cup sugar
- 1 cup flour
- 1 teaspoon baking powder
- 1 teaspoon ground cinnamon
- 1/2 teaspoon ground cloves
- 4 eggs
- 1/2 cup olive oil
- 1 cup honey
- 1/2 cup water

INSTRUCTIONS:
1) Preheat oven to 350°F (175°C). Grease a 9x13-inch baking pan.
2) In a bowl, combine walnuts, sugar, flour, baking powder, cinnamon, and cloves.
3) In another bowl, whisk together eggs and olive oil.
4) Combine wet and dry ingredients and pour into prepared pan.
5) Bake for 40 minutes or until a toothpick comes out clean.
6) While the cake is baking, prepare syrup by simmering honey and water for 10 minutes.
7) Pour hot syrup over the baked cake while both are still warm.
8) Allow to cool and soak up the syrup before serving.

Chef's Note:
This cake is best enjoyed after it has soaked in the syrup for several hours or overnight.

NUTRITIONAL INFORMATION (PER SERVING):
Calories: 420 kcal
Total Fat: 24 g
Monounsaturated Fat: 7 g
Total Carbohydrates: 48 g
Dietary Fiber: 2 g
Protein: 6 g
Sodium: 55 mg

LEBANESE NIGHTS (LAYALI LUBNAN)

A semolina pudding topped with whipped cream and crushed pistachios.
KID-FRIENDLY

Preparation Time: 20 minutes
Cooking Time: 10 minutes
Total Time: 30 minutes
Serves: 6

INGREDIENTS:
- 1 cup semolina
- 4 cups whole milk
- 1/2 cup sugar
- 1 teaspoon orange blossom water
- Whipped cream
- Crushed pistachios for garnish

INSTRUCTIONS:
1) Combine semolina, milk, and sugar in a saucepan.
2) Cook over medium heat, stirring constantly until thickened.
3) Remove from heat and add orange blossom water.
4) Pour into a serving dish and let it cool.

5) Top with whipped cream and garnish with crushed pistachios.

NUTRITIONAL INFORMATION (PER SERVING):
Calories: 250 kcal
Total Fat: 8 g
Total Carbohydrates: 36 g
Dietary Fiber: 1 g
Protein: 7 g
Sodium: 80 mg

TURKISH APRICOT DELIGHT

A quick and easy Turkish dessert made with dried apricots and nuts.
SUPER-QUICK!

Preparation Time: 15 minutes
Total Time: 15 minutes
Serves: 4

INGREDIENTS:
- 20 dried apricots
- 1 cup hot water
- 20 almonds or pistachios
- 1/4 cup coconut flakes for garnish

INSTRUCTIONS:
1) Soak dried apricots in hot water for 10 minutes until they become plump.
2) Drain and make a small slit in each apricot.
3) Insert an almond or pistachio into each slit.
4) Roll the stuffed apricots in coconut flakes.

NUTRITIONAL INFORMATION (PER SERVING):
Calories: 180 kcal
Total Fat: 5 g
Total Carbohydrates: 35 g
Dietary Fiber: 4 g
Protein: 3 g
Sodium: 10 mg

CLASSIC BAKLAVA

Indulge in this timeless Middle Eastern dessert layered with flaky phyllo dough, finely chopped nuts, and sweetened with aromatic syrup. A piece of classic baklava makes any occasion special.
MEAL-PREP FRIENDLY

Preparation Time: 30 minutes
Cooking Time: 45 minutes
Total Time: 1 hour 15 minutes
Serves: 12-16

INGREDIENTS:
- 1 package (16 oz) phyllo dough, thawed
- 2 cups mixed nuts (such as walnuts, almonds, and pistachios), finely chopped
- 1 cup unsalted butter, melted
- 1 teaspoon ground cinnamon
- 1 cup granulated sugar
- 1 cup water
- 1/2 cup honey
- 1 teaspoon vanilla extract
- 1/2 teaspoon lemon juice

INSTRUCTIONS:
1. **Preheat the Oven:** Preheat your oven to 350°F (175°C). Grease a 9x13-inch baking pan with melted butter.
2. **Prepare Nut Mixture:** In a bowl, combine the finely chopped nuts and ground cinnamon. Set aside.
3. **Assemble the Layers:** Place one sheet of phyllo dough into the greased pan. Brush generously with melted butter. Repeat the process, layering and buttering each sheet, until you have about 8 sheets layered.
4. **Add Nut Mixture:** Sprinkle a portion of the nut mixture evenly over the phyllo layers.
5. **Continue Layering:** Add another layer of phyllo and butter, followed by more nuts. Continue this pattern until all the nuts are used, finishing with a layer of phyllo.
6. **Slice:** With a sharp knife, carefully cut the assembled layers into squares or diamond shapes.
7. **Bake:** Place the pan in the preheated oven and bake for 45 minutes or until the baklava is golden brown and crisp.
8. **Prepare Syrup:** While the baklava is baking, prepare the syrup. In a saucepan, combine sugar, water, and lemon juice. Bring to a boil, then reduce to a simmer. Add honey and vanilla extract, stirring until fully incorporated. Remove from heat and let cool.
9. **Pour Syrup:** As soon as the baklava is out of the oven, evenly pour the cooled syrup over the hot baklava.
10. **Let Sit:** Allow the baklava to soak up the syrup for several hours or overnight for best results.
11. **Serve:** Serve the baklava garnished with additional chopped nuts if desired.

Chef's Note:
Make sure to keep the phyllo dough covered with a damp cloth while assembling the baklava, as it dries out quickly. Baklava can be stored at room temperature for 1-2 weeks if kept in an airtight container; otherwise, it may dry out more quickly. For a longer shelf life, you can refrigerate it for up to 3 weeks, although the texture may become less crispy. If you wish to store baklava for an extended period, it can be frozen for up to 3 months in an airtight container, separated by sheets of parchment paper. When you're ready to eat it, you can either thaw it at room temperature or briefly heat it in the oven to restore its crispiness. Keep in mind that heavily syruped baklava may have a shorter shelf life.

NUTRITIONAL INFORMATION (PER SERVING):
Calories: 370 kcal
Total Fat: 24 g

Monounsaturated Fat: 12 g
Total Carbohydrates: 36 g
Protein: 5 g
Sodium: 110 mg

WALNUT BAKLAVA ROLLS

Deliciously layered rolls of phyllo dough, filled with walnuts and spices, and sweetened with a honey syrup.

KID-FRIENDLY

Preparation Time: 30 minutes
Cooking Time: 40 minutes
Total Time: 1 hour 10 minutes
Serves: 12

INGREDIENTS:

- 1 package phyllo dough, thawed
- 2 cups walnuts, finely chopped
- 1 teaspoon ground cinnamon
- 1 cup melted butter
- 1 cup honey
- 1/2 cup water
- 1 teaspoon vanilla extract

INSTRUCTIONS:

1) Preheat oven to 350°F (175°C).
2) In a bowl, combine chopped walnuts and cinnamon.
3) Lay one sheet of phyllo dough flat and brush with melted butter.
4) Sprinkle a layer of walnut mixture on top.
5) Roll the phyllo sheet tightly.
6) Repeat with remaining sheets.
7) Place the rolls seam side down in a greased baking pan.
8) Bake for 40 minutes or until golden brown.
9) While baking, prepare syrup by combining honey, water, and vanilla in a saucepan. Boil for 10 minutes.
10) Pour hot syrup over the baked rolls.

NUTRITIONAL INFORMATION (PER SERVING):

Calories: 270 kcal
Total Fat: 24 g
Monounsaturated Fat: 7 g
Total Carbohydrates: 38 g
Dietary Fiber: 2 g
Protein: 5 g
Sodium: 150 mg

Dietary Fiber: 2 g

TORTA DI FRUTTA STAGIONALE ~ SEASONAL ITALIAN FRUIT CAKE

A rustic Italian cake that is low in fat and highlights the natural sweetness and nutrients of seasonal fruits.

HEART-HEALTHY

Preparation Time: 15 minutes
Cooking Time: 45 minutes
Total Time: 1 hour
Serves: 8

INGREDIENTS:

- 1 cup seasonal fruits (berries, apple slices, pear slices)
- 1 cup whole-wheat flour
- 1/2 cup sugar
- 1/4 cup olive oil
- 2 large eggs
- 1 tsp baking powder
- Zest of 1 lemon
- 1 tsp vanilla extract
- A pinch of salt

INSTRUCTIONS:

1) Preheat your oven to 350°F (175°C). Lightly grease a cake pan.
2) In a bowl, whisk together olive oil and sugar until well combined.
3) Add the eggs one at a time, beating after each addition.
4) Stir in lemon zest and vanilla extract.
5) In another bowl, combine whole-wheat flour, baking powder, and salt.
6) Gently fold the dry ingredients into the wet mixture.
7) Add in the seasonal fruits and fold until evenly distributed.
8) Pour the batter into the prepared cake pan.
9) Bake for 45 minutes or until a toothpick inserted comes out clean.
10) Allow to cool before serving.

Chef's Note:

This cake is excellent when served with a dollop of low-fat yogurt or a light dusting of powdered sugar. You can swap out fruits depending on the season—peaches in summer or apples in fall, for instance.

NUTRITIONAL INFORMATION (PER SERVING):

Calories: 160 kcal
Total Fat: 6 g
Monounsaturated Fat: 3 g
Total Carbohydrates: 24 g
Dietary Fiber: 2 g
Protein: 4 g
Sodium: 80 mg

FRESH FIG AND RICOTTA TART

A decadent, yet healthy dessert that is a great choice for a lovely
brunch or a sophisticated dinner
SPECIAL OCCASION

Preparation Time: 40 minutes
Cooking Time: 30 minutes
Total Time: 1 hour 10 minutes
Serves: 8

INGREDIENTS:

- 1 1/2 cups whole wheat flour
- 1/2 teaspoon salt
- 1/2 cup unsalted butter, chilled and cubed
- 4-6 tablespoons ice-cold water
- 1 cup ricotta cheese
- 1/4 cup honey
- 1 teaspoon vanilla extract
- 1 egg
- Zest of 1 lemon
- 8-10 fresh figs, halved or quartered depending on size
- 1 tablespoon extra-virgin olive oil or melted butter for brushing
- Additional honey for drizzling (optional)

INSTRUCTIONS:

1) Prepare the Pie Crust: In a food processor, combine whole wheat flour,
   salt, and chilled butter. Pulse until mixture resembles coarse crumbs.
   Add ice-cold water, one tablespoon at a time, pulsing until the dough
   starts to come together. Turn the dough onto a floured surface and
   knead lightly. Form into a disc, wrap in plastic wrap, and refrigerate
   for at least 20 minutes.

2) Preheat your oven to 375°F (190°C). Roll out the chilled dough on a
   floured surface to fit your tart pan. Place the rolled-out dough into
   the tart pan, gently pressing it into the edges. Trim off any excess
   dough.

3) Make the Ricotta Filling: In a medium bowl, mix together the ricotta,
   honey, vanilla extract, egg, and lemon zest until well combined.

4) Pour the ricotta mixture into the pie crust, using a spatula to spread
   it evenly.

5) Artfully arrange the fresh figs on top of the ricotta mixture.

6) Brush the edges of the pie crust and the tops of the figs with extra
   virgin olive oil or melted butter.

7) Bake for 30 minutes in the preheated oven, or until the crust turns
   golden and the filling is set.

8) Allow to cool for a few minutes before serving. Optionally, you can
   drizzle additional honey over the top for extra sweetness.

Chef's Note:

If you're unable to find fresh figs, use fig jam. When figs are in
season, you can try the amazing fig jam recipes in the Snacks and
Spreads section.

NUTRITIONAL INFORMATION (PER SERVING):

Calories: 295 kcal
Total Fat: 16 g
Monounsaturated Fat: 6 g
Total Carbohydrates: 32 g
Dietary Fiber: 3 g
Protein: 8 g
Sodium: 190 mg

Snacks and Dips

ZA'ATAR SPICED PITA CHIPS

Crispy pita chips seasoned with the fragrant za'atar spice blend, perfect for dipping or snacking.

KID FRIENDLY

Preparation Time: 10 minutes
Cooking Time: 10 minutes
Total Time: 20 minutes
Serves: 4

INGREDIENTS:

- 4 pita bread rounds
- 4 tablespoons olive oil
- 2 tablespoons za'atar spice blend
- Salt to taste

INSTRUCTIONS:

1) Preheat the oven to 375°F (190°C).
2) Cut each pita bread into 8 triangles.
3) Arrange the pita triangles on a baking sheet.
4) Drizzle with olive oil and sprinkle za'atar and salt evenly over them.
5) Bake for 10 minutes or until the chips are golden and crispy.

NUTRITIONAL INFORMATION (PER SERVING):

Calories: 250 kcal
Total Fat: 12 g
Total Carbohydrates: 30 g
Dietary Fiber: 1 g
Protein: 6 g
Sodium: 300 mg

MARINATED OLIVES AND FETA

A simple yet flavorful mix of olives and feta cheese marinated in olive oil and herbs.

MEAL-PREP FRIENDLY

Preparation Time: 10 minutes
Marinating Time: 1 hour
Total Time: 1 hour 10 minutes
Serves: 4

INGREDIENTS:

- 1 cup mixed olives
- 1 cup feta cheese, cubed
- 1/4 cup olive oil
- Zest of 1 lemon
- 1 teaspoon dried oregano
- 1/2 teaspoon crushed red pepper flakes

INSTRUCTIONS:

1) In a bowl, combine olives, feta cheese, olive oil, lemon zest, oregano, and red pepper flakes.
2) Mix well to ensure everything is evenly coated.
3) Cover and let it marinate in the refrigerator for at least 1 hour.

Chef's Note:

Easy to prepare and can be stored in the fridge for up to a week.

NUTRITIONAL INFORMATION (PER SERVING):

Calories: 250 kcal
Total Fat: 22 g
Total Carbohydrates: 4 g
Dietary Fiber: 1 g
Protein: 8 g
Sodium: 700 mg

GREEK YOGURT TZATZIKI

A light and refreshing cucumber yogurt dip, perfect for vegetables or grilled meats.

GLUTEN-FREE

Preparation Time: 15 minutes
Cooking Time: 0 minutes
Total Time: 15 minutes
Serves: 4

INGREDIENTS:

- 1 cup Greek yogurt
- 1 small cucumber, finely grated and pressed to reduce liquid
- 2 cloves garlic, minced
- Juice of 1/2 lemon
- 1 tablespoon fresh dill, chopped
- Salt and pepper to taste

INSTRUCTIONS:

1) In a bowl, mix together Greek yogurt, grated cucumber, minced garlic, and lemon juice.
2) Stir in chopped dill and season with salt and pepper.
3) Chill for at least 1 hour before serving to let flavors meld.

Chef's Note:

Tzatziki can be used as a dip for vegetables, a sauce for grilled meats, or a spread for sandwiches.

NUTRITIONAL INFORMATION (PER SERVING):

Calories: 50 kcal
Total Fat: 1 g

Monounsaturated Fat: 0 g
Total Carbohydrates: 4 g
Dietary Fiber: 0 g
Protein: 6 g
Sodium: 25 mg

Saturated Fat: 1 g
Total Carbohydrates: 10 g
Dietary Fiber: 5 g
Protein: 3 g
Sodium: 10 mg

BABA GANOUSH

VEGAN

Preparation Time: 15 minutes
Cooking Time: 45 minutes
Total Time: 1 hour
Serves: 6

INGREDIENTS:

- 2 medium eggplants
- 3 cloves garlic, peeled
- 1/4 cup tahini
- 3 tablespoons lemon juice
- 2 tablespoons olive oil, plus more for drizzling
- 1/2 teaspoon ground cumin
- Salt and pepper to taste
- Fresh parsley, for garnish
- Paprika, for garnish

INSTRUCTIONS:

1. Preheat your oven to 400°F (200°C). Line a baking sheet with parchment paper or aluminum foil.
2. Pierce the eggplants all over with a fork to allow steam to escape during roasting.
3. Place the pierced eggplants on the prepared baking sheet and roast for 40-45 minutes, turning them halfway through, until the skin is charred and the flesh is soft.
4. Remove the eggplants from the oven and allow them to cool for about 10 minutes. Once cooled, cut them open and scoop out the flesh, discarding the skin.
5. In a food processor, combine the roasted eggplant flesh, garlic, tahini, lemon juice, olive oil, and ground cumin. Process until smooth.
6. Season with salt and pepper to taste. If the mixture is too thick, add a little water to reach your desired consistency.
7. Transfer the baba ganoush to a serving bowl, and garnish with a drizzle of olive oil, a sprinkle of paprika, and fresh parsley.

Chef's Note:

Baba Ganoush can be served with pita bread, vegetable sticks, or as part of a Mediterranean mezze platter. For a smokier flavor, you can grill the eggplants instead of roasting them. Feel free to adjust the amount of garlic, lemon, and tahini to suit your taste.

NUTRITIONAL INFORMATION (PER SERVING):

Calories: 120 kcal
Total Fat: 9 g

PORTUGUESE SARDINE PATE

SUPER-QUICK!

Preparation Time: 15 minutes
Cooking Time: 0 minutes
Total Time: 15 minutes
Serves: 4

INGREDIENTS:

- 1 can (4.4 oz) sardines in olive oil, drained
- 4 oz cream cheese, softened
- 1 clove garlic, minced
- 1 tablespoon lemon juice
- 2 tablespoons chopped fresh parsley
- Salt and black pepper, to taste
- 1 teaspoon paprika, for garnish
- Olive oil, for drizzling
- Fresh parsley leaves, for garnish

INSTRUCTIONS:

1. Drain the sardines and place them in a food processor.
2. Add the softened cream cheese, minced garlic, lemon juice, and chopped parsley to the food processor.
3. Blend until smooth, scraping down the sides as needed. If the mixture is too thick, add a small drizzle of olive oil to reach the desired consistency.
4. Season with salt and black pepper to taste.
5. Transfer the pate to a serving bowl. Garnish with a sprinkle of paprika, a drizzle of olive oil, and a few parsley leaves.
6. Serve chilled with toasted baguette slices or crackers.

Chef's Note:

For a lighter version, you can substitute the cream cheese with Greek yogurt. To make it spicier, consider adding a dash of hot sauce or a pinch of red pepper flakes.

NUTRITIONAL INFORMATION (PER SERVING):

Calories: 160 kcal
Total Fat: 14 g
Saturated Fat: 5 g
Total Carbohydrates: 1 g
Dietary Fiber: 0 g
Protein: 8 g
Sodium: 180 mg

PICKLED TURNIPS

Always a great addition to a plate of meze or to a falafel pita with tzatziki.

MEAL-PREP FRIENDLY

Preparation Time: 15 minutes
Cooking Time: 0 minutes
Pickling Time: 3-7 days
Total Time: 3-7 days
Serves: Makes 1 quart jar

INGREDIENTS:

- 3-4 medium turnips, peeled and sliced into 1/4-inch thick sticks
- 1 small beet, peeled and sliced into 1/4-inch thick sticks (for color)
- 3-4 cloves garlic, peeled
- 1 1/2 cups distilled white vinegar
- 1 1/2 cups water
- 2 tablespoons kosher salt
- 1 teaspoon sugar (optional)
- 1/2 teaspoon coriander seeds (optional)
- 1/2 teaspoon mustard seeds (optional)

INSTRUCTIONS:

1. Sterilize a quart-sized glass jar and lid by boiling them in water for 10 minutes. Allow them to dry completely.
2. Pack the sliced turnips, beet sticks, and garlic cloves tightly into the sterilized jar.
3. In a separate bowl, mix together the distilled white vinegar, water, kosher salt, and sugar if using. Stir until the salt is completely dissolved.
4. If you're using coriander seeds and mustard seeds, add them to the liquid mixture.
5. Pour the liquid mixture into the jar, making sure to cover the turnips and beet sticks completely.
6. Seal the jar tightly and shake it to distribute the flavors.
7. Store the jar in a cool, dark place for at least 3 days and up to 7 days to allow the turnips to pickle. Once opened, store in the refrigerator.

Chef's Note:

These pickled turnips are a great addition to Mediterranean dishes, sandwiches, and salads. For a different flavor profile, you can experiment with adding other spices like peppercorns, cinnamon sticks, or bay leaves. They will keep in the fridge for up to 2 weeks. If you want to keep them longer, you'll have to can them.

NUTRITIONAL INFORMATION (PER SERVING):

Calories: 15 kcal
Total Fat: 0 g
    Monounsaturated Fat: 0 g
Total Carbohydrates: 3 g
    Dietary Fiber: 1 g
Protein: 0 g
Sodium: 870 mg

TURKISH MUHAMMARA DIP

A rich and spicy red pepper and walnut dip with a hint of pomegranate.
VEGAN

Preparation Time: 10 minutes
Total Time: 10 minutes
Serves: 4

INGREDIENTS:

- 2 red bell peppers, roasted and peeled
- 1 cup walnuts
- 1 garlic clove
- 2 tablespoons pomegranate molasses
- 1 tablespoon olive oil
- Salt and red pepper flakes to taste

INSTRUCTIONS:

1) In a blender or food processor, combine the roasted red peppers, walnuts, and garlic.
2) Add pomegranate molasses and olive oil, then blend until smooth.
3) Season with salt and red pepper flakes.
4) Serve chilled with pita bread or vegetable sticks.

NUTRITIONAL INFORMATION (PER SERVING):

Calories: 200 kcal
Total Fat: 18 g
Total Carbohydrates: 10 g
Dietary Fiber: 2 g
Protein: 4 g
Sodium: 50 mg

10-MINUTE GREEK HUMMUS VARIATIONS

A quick and easy hummus recipe that's perfect for a healthy snack, served with vegetable sticks or pita bread.
SUPER-QUICK!

Preparation Time: 10 minutes
Cooking Time: 0 minutes
Total Time: 10 minutes
Serves: 4

INGREDIENTS:

- 1 can (15 oz) chickpeas, drained and rinsed
- Juice of 1 lemon
- 2 tablespoons tahini
- 2 cloves garlic, minced
- 1/4 cup olive oil
- Salt and pepper to taste

INSTRUCTIONS:

1) In a food processor, combine the chickpeas, lemon juice, tahini, and minced garlic.
2) Process until smooth, then gradually add the olive oil while the machine is running.
3) Season with salt and pepper to taste.
4) Serve immediately with vegetable sticks or pita bread, or store in an airtight container in the fridge for up to 4 days.

Variations:

Roasted Red Pepper Hummus: Add 1/4 cup of roasted red peppers to the food processor along with the other ingredients for a colorful and slightly sweet twist.

Spinach and Feta Hummus: Add 1/4 cup cooked, drained, and chopped spinach and 2 tablespoons of crumbled feta cheese for a Greek-inspired variant.

Sun-Dried Tomato and Basil: Add 1/4 cup of sun-dried tomatoes and 1 tablespoon of fresh basil leaves for an Italian flair.

NUTRITIONAL INFORMATION (PER SERVING):

Calories: 220 kcal
Total Fat: 15 g
Monounsaturated Fat: 10 g
Total Carbohydrates: 18 g
Dietary Fiber: 4 g
Protein: 6 g
Sodium: 200 mg

ITALIAN BAKED OLIVES

A flavorful snack of mixed olives seasoned with herbs and spices, baked to perfection. Can be prepared in advance and stored for up to a week in the fridge.

MEAL-PREP FRIENDLY

Preparation Time: 5 minutes
Cooking Time: 20 minutes
Total Time: 25 minutes
Serves: 4

INGREDIENTS:

- 2 cups mixed olives (Kalamata, Castelvetrano, Gaeta, etc.)
- 2 tablespoons olive oil
- 1 teaspoon dried oregano
- 1 teaspoon dried thyme
- Zest of 1 lemon

INSTRUCTIONS:

1) Preheat the oven to 375°F (190°C).
2) In a mixing bowl, combine olives, olive oil, oregano, thyme, and lemon zest.
3) Spread the olive mixture on a baking sheet.
4) Bake for 20 minutes, stirring halfway through.
5) Serve warm or at room temperature.

NUTRITIONAL INFORMATION (PER SERVING):

Calories: 200 kcal
Total Fat: 20 g
Monounsaturated Fat: 15 g
Total Carbohydrates: 4 g
Dietary Fiber: 1 g
Protein: 1 g
Sodium: 800 mg

TUNISIAN HARISSA~SPICED POPCORN

A North African twist on a classic snack, featuring the bold flavors of harissa.

KID FRIENDLY

Preparation Time: 5 minutes
Cooking Time: 5 minutes
Total Time: 10 minutes
Serves: 4

INGREDIENTS:

- 1/2 cup popcorn kernels
- 1/4 cup vegetable oil
- 1 tablespoon harissa paste
- Salt to taste

INGREDIENTS:

1) Heat the vegetable oil in a large pot over medium heat.
2) Add three popcorn kernels to the oil. Once they pop, remove the pot from heat and take out the popped kernels.
3) Add the remaining popcorn kernels to the pot and cover it.
4) Place the pot back on the heat. Shake occasionally until the popping slows down.
5) Remove from heat and let sit until the popping stops completely.
6) Stir in harissa paste and salt to taste. Toss until well combined.

NUTRITIONAL INFORMATION (PER SERVING):

Calories: 110 kcal
Total Fat: 7 g
Monounsaturated Fat: 1 g
Total Carbohydrates: 10 g
Dietary Fiber: 2 g
Protein: 1 g
Sodium: 200 mg

MOROCCAN SPICED CHICKPEAS

Crispy oven-baked chickpeas with a touch of Moroccan spices.

GLUTEN-FREE

Preparation Time: 10 minutes
Cooking Time: 40 minutes
Total Time: 50 minutes
Serves: 4

INGREDIENTS:

- 2 cans (15 oz each) chickpeas, drained and rinsed
- 2 tablespoons olive oil
- 1 teaspoon paprika
- 1 teaspoon cumin
- 1/2 teaspoon cinnamon
- Salt to taste

INSTRUCTIONS:

1) Preheat your oven to 400°F (200°C).
2) Pat the chickpeas dry with a towel and spread them out on a baking sheet.
3) Drizzle olive oil and sprinkle the spices over the chickpeas.
4) Toss to evenly coat the chickpeas with the oil and spices.
5) Roast for 40 minutes, stirring halfway, or until crispy.
6) Let them cool before serving.

Chef's Note:
These chickpeas are great as a standalone snack or as a crunchy salad topping.

NUTRITIONAL INFORMATION (PER SERVING):
Calories: 210 kcal
Total Fat: 8 g
Total Carbohydrates: 28 g
Dietary Fiber: 8 g
Protein: 10 g
Sodium: 400 mg

HOME-MADE "SUN-DRIED" TOMATOES

A rich and flavorful way to preserve and enjoy the natural sweetness of tomatoes, intensified by slow drying.
MEAL-PREP FRIENDLY

Preparation Time: 10 minutes
Cooking Time: 6-12 hours (varies with method)
Total Time: 6-12 hours and 10 minutes
Serves: 4

INGREDIENTS:
- 10-12 ripe Roma tomatoes
- 1 teaspoon salt
- 2 teaspoons olive oil (optional)

INSTRUCTIONS:

1) Wash the tomatoes and slice them in half lengthwise. Remove seeds and excess moisture with a small spoon.
2) Lay the tomatoes cut-side up on a cooling rack placed on top of a baking sheet. This allows air to circulate all around the tomatoes.
3) Sprinkle salt over the tomatoes.
4) **Oven Drying Method:** Preheat your oven to the lowest setting, usually between 150-200°F (65-95°C). Place the prepared tomatoes in the oven and bake for 6-8 hours or until they are dried but still pliable.
5) **Food Dehydrator Method:** Place the prepared tomatoes in a single layer in your food dehydrator. Follow the manufacturer's instructions for drying tomatoes or vegetables, usually 6-12 hours at 135°F (57°C).
6) Once dried, let the tomatoes cool completely. They can be stored in a jar with olive oil or vacuum-sealed for longer shelf life.

Chef's Note:
If stored in olive oil, consider adding additional flavors like minced garlic, rosemary, or chili flakes. Ensure tomatoes are fully submerged in oil.

NUTRITIONAL INFORMATION (PER SERVING):
Calories: 35 kcal
Total Fat: 1 g
Monounsaturated Fat: 0.5 g
Total Carbohydrates: 7 g
Dietary Fiber: 2 g
Protein: 1 g
Sodium: 600 mg

ROASTED STUFFED FIGS

A delightful Mediterranean-inspired snack where the sweetness of figs meets the savory punch of blue cheese and prosciutto.
SPECIAL OCCASION

Preparation Time: 15 minutes
Cooking Time: 10 minutes
Total Time: 25 minutes
Serves: 4 (serving size: 2 figs)

INGREDIENTS:
- 8 fresh figs
- 1/2 cup blue cheese or gorgonzola, crumbled
- 8 slices prosciutto or thin ham
- Honey, for drizzling
- Fresh thyme, for garnish

INSTRUCTIONS:

1) Preheat the oven to 375°F (190°C).
2) Using a sharp knife, make an X cut on the top of each fig, going about halfway down but being careful not to slice through the fig.
3) Gently press the sides of the fig to open up the X cut a bit.
4) Stuff each fig with a generous amount of blue cheese.
5) Wrap each stuffed fig with a slice of prosciutto or ham.
6) Place the wrapped figs on a baking sheet.
7) Roast in the preheated oven for 10 minutes or until the prosciutto is crispy and the figs are tender.
8) Remove from the oven and drizzle with honey. Garnish with fresh thyme leaves.
9) Serve warm.

NUTRITIONAL INFORMATION (PER SERVING):
Calories: 180 kcal
Total Fat: 9 g
Monounsaturated Fat: 4 g
Total Carbohydrates: 22 g
Dietary Fiber: 3 g
Protein: 6 g
Sodium: 520 mg

PROVENÇAL TAPENADE CROSTINI

Enjoy the flavors of Southern France with this olive and caper spread served on toasted baguette slices.

SUPER-QUICK!

Preparation Time: 10 minutes
Cooking Time: 5 minutes
Total Time: 15 minutes
Serves: 6

INGREDIENTS:

- 1 cup pitted black olives (like Kalamata or Niçoise)
- 2 tablespoons capers
- 1 clove garlic
- 1/4 cup extra-virgin olive oil
- 1 French baguette, sliced and toasted

INSTRUCTIONS:

1) Combine olives, capers, and garlic in a food processor.
2) Pulse while gradually adding the olive oil until a coarse paste forms.
3) Spread the tapenade on toasted baguette slices.
4) Serve immediately or store the tapenade in an airtight container for future use.

NUTRITIONAL INFORMATION (PER SERVING):

Calories: 180 kcal
Total Fat: 14 g
Total Carbohydrates: 12 g
Dietary Fiber: 2 g
Protein: 3 g
Sodium: 420 mg

DOLMA ~ TURKISH STUFFED GRAPE LEAVES

Enjoy these little packets of flavor filled with rice and pine nuts, a classic Turkish delight.

GLUTEN-FREE

Preparation Time: 30 minutes
Cooking Time: 40 minutes
Total Time: 70 minutes
Serves: 6

INGREDIENTS:

- 1 jar of grape leaves, drained
- 1 cup cooked rice
- 1/4 cup pine nuts
- 2 tablespoons olive oil
- 1 lemon, juiced
- Salt and pepper to taste

INSTRUCTIONS:

1) Mix cooked rice, pine nuts, olive oil, and lemon juice. Season with salt and pepper.
2) Place a grape leaf on a flat surface, vein side up.
3) Place a teaspoon of the rice mixture in the center of the leaf.
4) Fold in the sides and roll up tightly.
5) Repeat with remaining leaves and filling.
6) Place the rolled leaves in a pot, seam-side down.
7) Cover with water and simmer for 40 minutes.
8) Serve warm or cold.

NUTRITIONAL INFORMATION (PER SERVING):

Calories: 160 kcal
Total Fat: 8 g
Total Carbohydrates: 20 g
Dietary Fiber: 2 g
Protein: 4 g
Sodium: 500 mg

PESTO

A classic Italian sauce made with fresh basil and pine nuts, perfect for pasta, sandwiches, or as a dip.

MIX-AND-MATCH

Preparation Time: 10 minutes
Cooking Time: 0 minutes
Total Time: 10 minutes
Serves: 4

INGREDIENTS:

- 2 cups fresh basil leaves
- 1/4 cup pine nuts
- 1 garlic clove
- 1/2 cup olive oil
- Salt and pepper to taste

INSTRUCTIONS:

1) Combine the basil leaves, pine nuts, and garlic in a food processor.
2) With the machine running, slowly add the olive oil until well combined.
3) Season with salt and pepper to taste.
4) Use immediately or store in an airtight container in the fridge.

Chef's Note:

Try substituting arugula for basil and walnuts for pine nuts for a pesto with a kick that combines wonderfully with fresh and aged goat cheese.

You can also try adding roasted pepper to the basil pesto and substituting almonds for pine nuts for a heart-healthy version (you can cut the oil to a ¼ cup in this case)

NUTRITIONAL INFORMATION (PER SERVING):

Calories: 180 kcal
Total Fat: 20 g
Monounsaturated Fat: 15 g
Total Carbohydrates: 1 g
Dietary Fiber: 0 g
Protein: 1 g
Sodium: 5 mg

HERBED GOAT CHEESE DIP

Indulge in this creamy, flavorful Herbed Goat Cheese Dip, perfect for spreading on crackers or using as a dip for vegetables. The blend of fresh herbs elevates this simple dish into an appetizer worthy of any occasion.

SUPER-QUICK!

Preparation Time: 10 minutes
Cooking Time: 0 minutes
Total Time: 10 minutes
Serves: 6-8

INGREDIENTS:

- 8 oz goat cheese, softened
- 1/2 cup sour cream
- 2 tablespoons extra-virgin olive oil
- 2 cloves garlic, minced
- 1 tablespoon fresh chives, finely chopped
- 1 tablespoon fresh parsley, finely chopped
- 1 tablespoon fresh basil, finely chopped
- 1 teaspoon lemon zest
- Salt and pepper to taste
- Assorted crackers and vegetables for serving

INSTRUCTIONS:

1. In a medium mixing bowl, combine the softened goat cheese, sour cream, and extra-virgin olive oil. Use a hand mixer or a whisk to blend until smooth.
2. Add in the minced garlic, fresh chives, parsley, basil, and lemon zest.
3. Season with salt and pepper to taste, and mix until all the ingredients are well incorporated.
4. Transfer the dip to a serving bowl, and garnish with a drizzle of olive oil and a sprinkle of additional fresh herbs, if desired.
5. Serve immediately with assorted crackers and vegetables, or refrigerate for later use. The flavors will meld together better if allowed to sit for at least an hour before serving.

Chef's Note:
Feel free to get creative with your herbs—dill, mint, or tarragon also work well in this recipe. For a spicier kick, consider adding a small amount of red pepper flakes.

NUTRITIONAL INFORMATION (PER SERVING):

Calories: 160 kcal
Total Fat: 14 g
Monounsaturated Fat: 6 g
Total Carbohydrates: 3 g
Dietary Fiber: 0 g
Protein: 6 g
Sodium: 210 mg

SMOKED MACKEREL AND CAPER SPREAD

Experience the smoky, briny flavors of the sea with this easy-to-make Smoked Mackerel and Caper Spread. Perfect for appetizers or a quick snack!

SUPER-QUICK!

Preparation Time: 15 minutes
Total Time: 15 minutes
Serves: 4

INGREDIENTS:

- 1 lb smoked mackerel fillets, skin removed and flaked
- 1/4 cup capers, drained and roughly chopped
- 1/4 cup cream cheese, softened
- 1/4 cup Greek yogurt
- 1 tablespoon lemon juice
- 1 tablespoon fresh dill, finely chopped
- Salt and pepper to taste
- Whole-grain bread or crackers for serving

INSTRUCTIONS:

1. In a medium mixing bowl, combine the flaked smoked mackerel, chopped capers, softened cream cheese, and Greek yogurt.
2. Add the lemon juice and fresh dill to the mixture.
3. Using a fork or a hand mixer, blend all the ingredients until well combined but still a bit chunky for texture. If the spread is too thick, you can add a bit more Greek yogurt to reach your desired consistency.
4. Season with salt and pepper to taste.
5. Transfer the spread to a serving bowl and garnish with a sprinkle of extra dill or a few capers if desired.
6. Serve immediately with whole-grain bread or crackers, or refrigerate for later use. If storing, cover the bowl with plastic wrap and consume within 2-3 days.

Chef's Note:
This spread pairs exceptionally well with thinly sliced cucumbers or radishes. It can also be used as a filling for wraps or sandwiches for a quick and nutritious lunch option.

NUTRITIONAL INFORMATION (PER SERVING):

Calories: 240 kcal
Total Fat: 14 g
Monounsaturated Fat: 4 g
Total Carbohydrates: 5 g
Dietary Fiber: 0 g
Protein: 25 g
Sodium: 380 mg

FIG JAM

Perfect for morning toasts or gourmet cheese pairings. Dive into nature's luxury with every jar.
MEAL-PREP FRIENDLY

Preparation Time: 20 minutes
Cooking Time: 40 minutes
Total Time: 1 hour
Serves: About 3 cups

INGREDIENTS:

- 2 pounds fresh figs, stems removed and chopped
- 1 1/2 cups granulated sugar
- Juice of 1 lemon
- 1 teaspoon vanilla extract (optional)
- 1/2 teaspoon ground cinnamon (optional)

INSTRUCTIONS:

1. In a large, heavy-bottomed saucepan, combine chopped figs, granulated sugar, and lemon juice. Stir to mix well.
2. Place the saucepan over medium heat. Bring the mixture to a simmer, stirring occasionally to make sure the sugar is dissolved.
3. Once the sugar has dissolved and the mixture is simmering, reduce the heat to low. Continue to cook, stirring frequently, until the mixture thickens, approximately 30-40 minutes. If you're using vanilla extract and cinnamon, add them halfway through the cooking time.
4. To test the jam's consistency, place a spoonful of the jam on a cold plate and let it sit for a minute. Run your finger through the jam; it should wrinkle and hold its shape. If not, continue cooking for another 5-10 minutes and test again.
5. Once the jam has reached the desired consistency, remove it from heat. If you prefer a smoother texture, use an immersion blender to puree the jam to your liking.
6. Transfer the hot jam into sterilized jars, leaving about 1/2-inch headspace. Seal the jars while they're still hot and allow them to cool to room temperature. Store in the refrigerator for up to 3 weeks, or follow proper canning procedures for longer storage.

Chef's Note:

You can replace the lemon juice with orange juice for a different flavor profile. For a more exotic twist, consider adding a touch of cardamom or nutmeg.

NUTRITIONAL INFORMATION (PER SERVING):

Calories: 44 kcal
Total Fat: 0.07 g
Total Carbohydrates: 11.27 g
Dietary Fiber: 0.63 g
Protein: 0.13 g
Sodium: 0.19 mg

Have you cooked your way through this book already?
Don't worry, I got some free extra heart-healthy recipes for you!

Click on the link or scan the QR Code to get your bonus!

https://bit.ly/48mcmdb

28-Days Meal Plan

I f you already tried the recipes, you have certainly found out for yourself that the Mediterranean diet is not only delicious, but extremely easy to master.
I have built for you a 28-days meal plan, with an easy meal prep for each week to ease you into your new lifestyle.
This meal plan is built to help you get accustomed to cooking with whole foods and making it easier with a carefully constructed meal prep which will make daily cooking a breeze. This meal plan's aim is also to familiarize yourself with certain kinds of preparations so widely used in Mediterranean cooking such as grilling, making paella and risotto, stewing, and so on. Week after week it will get easier to master this sort of recipe and you'll become a Mediterranean chef in no time!
To compile this meal plan I have followed these rules, which I strongly encourage you to follow to build your own meal plan once you have mastered the cooking basics and diet fundamentals of the Mediterranean diet.
The calories are indicative for a single serving of each recipe.

Balancing Nutrition:
- Aim to balance nutrition over several days, not just within each meal.
- You may not include every food group in each meal, but aim for overall nutritional harmony throughout the day and week.

Breakfast:
- Opt for a breakfast rich in protein and fiber to stay full for longer.
- Include fruits and a protein source like yogurt or eggs. For a savory twist, replace fruits with vegetables.

Lunch and Dinner:
- Always include vegetables or beans, olive oil, and a protein source such as cheese, fish, or nut butter.
- Supplement meals with a small portion of carbs like bread or rice.
- When including meat, chicken, or fish, add extra vegetables.
- Choose whole-grain breads devoid of additives, sugars, and unhealthy fats.
- Once a week, you can make a meze (appetizers) plate including up to three snacks

Snacks:
- Opt for seasonal fruits.
- Avoid starch-heavy snacks like crackers or breadsticks.
- Supplement starchy snacks with proteins like nuts, yogurt, or cheese.

Creating a Weekly Menu:
1. **Make a Template:**
   - Build a template based on weekly nutrition needs.
   - Aim for a caloric range between 1,700 to 2,200 calories per day depending on your needs. You should discuss this with your healthcare provider, if possible
   - Weekly plan should have 2 fish meals, at least 2 bean meals, 2-3 pasta or rice meals, 1 chicken meal, and 1 red meat meal.
2. **Choose Recipes:**
   - Factor in taste, schedule, and nutritional needs.
   - Opt for seasonal ingredients and common ingredients to save time and money.
   - Balance familiar recipes with new ones.
3. **Incorporate Leftovers:**
   - Vegetable casseroles and savory pies are good candidates for repurposing.
   - Aim to use leftovers within 2-3 days.
4. **Include Make-Ahead Recipes:**
   - Casseroles, savory pies, and roasted dishes can be made in advance.
   - Try to plan for recipes during the week for which you can use the same meal-prepped ingredients. For example, plan for Moroccan chickpea stew, Lebanese Chickpea soup, Roasted Chickpea snack for which you can soak and cook in advance 3 cups of chickpeas.

General Rules:
- Each meal plan serving corresponds to the single serving size in the recipe.
- All fruits should be medium-sized, unless otherwise specified.
- Optional 5 fluid ounces (150ml) of red wine adds 120 calories. Compensate by reducing half a serving of grain and fat.
- Snack recipes can replace a main meal if it fits within your plan.
- Ideally, the largest meal should be lunch.
- Drink at least 50 fluid ounces (1.5l) of water per day.
- Aim to drink at least 8 fluid ounces (240ml) of herbal tea daily, such as chamomile, thyme, or mountain tea.

WEEK 1

Please plan for leftovers as they are incorporated in the plan. The recipes that should be doubled for leftovers are indicated in **bold**.

Vegetables & Herbs:
1. **Chop Onions and Garlic**: Used in Lentil Soup, Minestrone, Chicken Cacciatore, and Paella.
2. **Slice Bell Peppers and Tomatoes**: Used in Greek Salad, Gazpacho, and Chicken Souvlaki Salad.
3. **Cube Cucumbers**: Used in Greek Salad and as a snack with Tzatziki.
4. **Chop Spinach**: For Spanakopita and Smoothies.
5. **Slice Zucchini and Eggplant**: For Ratatouille and Moussaka.
6. **Chop Fresh Herbs (Parsley, Basil, Rosemary)**: For garnishing and adding flavor to various dishes.

Proteins:
1. **Grill Chicken**: For Greek Salad and Chicken Souvlaki.
2. **Cook Lentils**: For Lentil Soup and Lentil Stuffed Bell Peppers.
3. **Prep Seafood**: For Creamy Seafood Risotto and Paella. (If using frozen seafood, consider thawing in the fridge overnight before the day you'll cook.)
4. **Make Falafel**: Can be made and stored in the fridge for a couple of days.

Snacks:
1. **Pre-cut Fruits**: Slice oranges, apples, and melon for quick snacks.
2. **Assemble Caprese Skewers**: Cherry tomatoes and mini mozzarella balls on skewers, you can prepare ahead, when you are making the Insalata Caprese.
3. **Make Hummus and Tzatziki**: Can be stored in an airtight container for up to a week.

Other Preparations:
1. **Make Whole-Grain Pancake Batter**: Store in an airtight container for up to two days.
2. **Prepare Greek Yogurt Parfait the Night Before**
3. **Prepare Overnight Oats the Night Before.**
4. **Make Frittata**: Can be sliced and stored for a few days in the fridge.
5. **Bake Spanakopita**: Can be reheated easily for breakfast or snacks.
6. **Prepare Beef Kofta a Day Ahead.**

Leftovers:
These can be portioned into individual servings and stored in the fridge for easy reheating: **Minestrone, Lentil Soup, Paella, Ratatouille, and Risotto.**

DAY 1

Breakfast:
1. Greek Yogurt Parfait with Honey and Walnuts (300 calories)
2. Spanakopita (Spinach Pie) (VEG) (250 calories)

Lunch:
1. Greek Salad with Grilled Chicken (450 calories)
2. Lentil Soup (Fakes) with potatoes (VEG) (350 calories)

Snack:
1. Fresh Orange Slices (VEG) (80 calories)
2. Kalamata Olives (VEG) (100 calories)

Dinner:
1. 15-Minute Greek Grilled Sardines with Steamed Asparagus (500 calories)
2. Gemista (Stuffed Tomatoes and Peppers) (VEG) (400 calories)

Total Daily Calories: 1,600 ~ 1,750

DAY 2

Breakfast:
1. Ricotta with Fresh Berries (VEG) (250 calories)
2. Frittata with Tomatoes and Basil (290 calories)

Lunch:
1. Italian Minestrone Soup (VEG) (260 calories) — Prepare extra for Day 5
2. Chicken Cacciatore over Cauliflower Rice (450 calories)

Snack:
1. Apple slices with Pecorino Cheese (VEG) (150 calories)
2. Marinated Artichokes (VEG) (90 calories)

Dinner:
1. Creamy Seafood Risotto (550 calories) — Prepare extra for Day 6
2. Insalata Caprese (VEG) (400 calories)

Total Daily Calories: 1,550 - 1,740

DAY 3

Breakfast:
1. Mediterranean Overnight Oats (VEG) (320 calories)
2. Leftover Frittata with Tomatoes and Basil (290 calories)

Lunch:
1. Leftover Lentil Soup (Fakes) (VEG) (350 calories)
2. Saffron Seafood Paella with Scallops (320 calories)

Snack:
1. Fresh Figs (VEG) (100 calories)

2. A handful of Almonds (VEG) (160 calories)

Dinner:
1. **Lentil Stuffed Bell Peppers** (VEG) (420 calories)
2. Tabouleh Salad with Grilled Chicken (500 calories)

Total Daily Calories: 1,650 - 1,850

DAY 4

Breakfast:
1. Fresh Fig and Yogurt (VEG) (240 calories)
2. Shakshuka (make it Cheesy or Green) (280 calories)

Lunch:
1. Falafel with Tzatziki and Side Salad (VEG) (520 calories)
2. Grilled Beef Kofta with Grilled Vegetables (600 calories)

Snack:
1. Sliced Cucumber with Hummus (VEG) (130 calories)
2. Melon Slices (VEG) (90 calories)

Dinner:
1. **Moussaka** (600 calories)
2. Leftover Gemista (Stuffed Tomatoes and Peppers) (VEG) (400 calories)

Total Daily Calories: 1,810 - 1,920

DAY 5

Breakfast:
1. Whole-grain Pancakes with Fresh Strawberries (VEG) (340 calories)
2. Greek Yogurt Parfait with Honey-Granola and Fresh Berries (VEG) (300 calories)

Lunch:
1. Leftover Italian Minestrone Soup (VEG) (360 calories)
2. Grilled Tuna Salad (500 calories)

Snack:
1. Sliced Apple with Walnuts (VEG) (140 calories)
2. Cherry Tomatoes with Mozzarella (Caprese Skewers) (VEG) (120 calories)

Dinner:
1. Leftover Lentil Stuffed Bell Peppers (VEG) (420 calories)
2. Rosemary Lamb Chops with Roasted Vegetables (550 calories)

Total Daily Calories: 1,760 - 1,890

DAY 6

Breakfast:
1. Smoothie with Spinach, Banana, and Almond Milk (VEG) (260 calories)
2. Pa Amb Tomaquet with Extra Avocado (VEG) (280 calories)

Lunch:
1. Meze Plate: Hummus, Tzatziki, Olives, Cucumbers, and Whole-grain Pita (VEG) (550 calories)
2. Chicken Souvlaki with Greek Salad (600 calories)

Snack:
1. Fresh Figs (VEG) (100 calories)
2. Apricots with Ricotta Cheese (VEG) (110 calories)

Dinner:
1. Leftover Creamy Seafood Risotto (550 calories)
2. **Ratatouille** (VEG) (400 calories)

Total Daily Calories: 1,850 - 1,940

DAY 7

Breakfast:
1. Oatmeal with Cinnamon and Sliced Almonds (VEG) (290 calories)
2. Leftover Whole-grain Pancakes with Fresh Strawberries (VEG) (340 calories)

Lunch:
1. Leftover Saffron Seafood Paella with Scallops (550 calories)
2. Italian White Bean Salad (VEG) (380 calories)

Snack:
1. Sliced Pear with Goat Cheese (VEG) (130 calories)
2. Dried Figs and Walnuts (VEG) (160 calories)

Dinner:
1. Leftover Moussaka (600 calories)
2. Leftover Ratatouille (VEG) (520 calories)

Dessert:
1. Walnut Baklava Rolls (one piece) (270 calories)

Total Daily Calories: 1,780 - 2,010

WEEK 2

Vegetables & Herbs:
1. **Chop Onions and Garlic**: For Gazpacho, Ribollita, Chickpea and Tomato Salad, Lentil-Stuffed Zucchini Boats and Seafood Paella.
2. **Slice Asparagus**: For Shrimp and Asparagus Risotto and Mediterranean Pan-Seared Salmon with Asparagus.
3. **Dice Tomatoes**: For Gazpacho, Chickpea and Tomato Salad, and Seafood Paella.
4. **Chop Spinach**: For Scrambled Eggs and Spanakopita.
5. **Chop Fresh Herbs (Basil, Parsley, Mint)**: For Spanakopita, Tabbouleh, and Spaghetti Aglio e Olio.

Proteins:
1. **Cook Chickpeas**: For Avocado and Chickpea Toast, Chickpea and Tomato Salad and Falafel.
2. **Cook Lentils**: For Lentil and Mushroom Stuffed Tomatoes and Lentil-Stuffed Zucchini Boats.
3. **Marinate Chicken**: For Chicken Shawarma and Grilled Chicken with Tabbouleh Salad.
4. **Prep Seafood**: For Seafood Paella. Buy fresh, clean, and freeze mix ahead of time.

Snacks:
1. **Slice Fruits**: Sliced pear, kiwi, mango, and watermelon for snacks.
2. **Prepare Pickled Turnips**: For Falafel meal.
3. **Make Tahini Sauce**: Can be stored for up to a week.

Other Preparations:
1. **Cook Whole-Grain Bread**: For Whole-Grain French Toast and toast with avocado.
2. **Make Fresh Fig and Ricotta Tart**: For the dessert of the week.
3. **Make Gazpacho**: Can be stored in the fridge for 2-3 days.
4. **Make Chia Seed Pudding**: Prepare individual portions for easy access.
5. **Make Italian Ribollita**: Can be stored in the fridge for up to 3 days.
6. **Prepare Bifteki Patties**: they'll keep up to two days in the fridge (otherwise freeze cooked)
7. **Prepare Falafel**: Store in an airtight container in the fridge.
8. **Cook Tabbouleh Salad**: Keeps well for 2 days in the fridge.

Leftovers:
These can be portioned into individual servings and stored in the fridge for easy reheating:
Ribollita, Gazpacho, Eggplant Parmesan, Lentil-Stuffed Zucchini Boats, and Lentil and Mushroom Stuffed Tomatoes:

DAY 8

Breakfast:
1. Scrambled Eggs with Spinach and Feta (260 calories)
2. Chia Seed Pudding with Almond Milk and Berries (VEG) (280 calories)

Lunch:
1. **Italian Ribollita** (VEG) (300 calories) — Prepare extra for Day 10
2. Grilled Swordfish with Grilled Vegetables (520 calories)

Snack:
1. Sliced Apple with Hazelnuts (VEG) (160 calories)
2. Marinated Olives and Feta Cheese (VEG) (150 calories)

Dinner:
1. **Eggplant Parmesan** (VEG) (500 calories) — Prepare extra for Day 11
2. Chicken Skillet-Style Shawarma with Tahini Sauce and Side Salad (550 calories)

<u>Total Daily Calories: 1,700 - 1,810</u>

DAY 9

Breakfast:
1. Mango and Yogurt Smoothie (VEG) (270 calories)
2. Whole-Grain Toast with Avocado and Tomato Slices (VEG) (300 calories)

Lunch:
1. **Gazpacho** (VEG) (340 calories) — Prepare extra for Day 12
2. Shrimp and Asparagus Risotto (480 calories)

Snack:
1. Fresh Peach Slices (VEG) (90 calories)
2. Sliced Cucumber with Cottage Cheese (VEG) (110 calories)

Dinner:
1. Tagine of Lamb with Apricots (550 calories)
2. **Lentil-Stuffed Zucchini Boats** (VEG) (450 calories) — Prepare extra for Day 12

<u>Total Daily Calories: 1,680 - 1,790</u>

DAY 10

Breakfast:
1. Overnight Muesli with Fresh Berries (VEG) (290 calories)
2. Leftover Scrambled Eggs with Spinach and Feta (260 calories)

Lunch:
1. Leftover Italian Bean Soup (Minestra di Fagioli) (VEG) (360 calories)
2. Greek Pita Pocket with Hummus and Veggies (VEG) (420 calories)

Snack:
1. Grapes with Almonds (VEG) (150 calories)
2. Cherry Tomatoes with Feta Cubes (VEG) (120 calories)

Dinner:
1. Meze Plate: Baba Ganoush, Tabouleh, and Dolma (VEG) (580 calories)
2. Bifteki with Roasted Vegetables (600 calories)

Total Daily Calories: 1,750 - 1,870

DAY 11

Breakfast:
1. Cottage Cheese with Pineapple Slices (VEG) (260 calories)
2. Whole-Grain Oatmeal with Chopped Nuts and Honey (VEG) (290 calories)

Lunch:
1. Tuna Nicoise Salad (520 calories)
2. Leftover Eggplant Parmesan (VEG) (500 calories)

Snack:
1. Sliced Carrots and Bell Peppers with Guacamole (VEG) (140 calories)
2. Fresh Orange Wedges (VEG) (80 calories)

Dinner:
1. Mediterranean Grilled Octopus Salad (540 calories)
2. Lentil and Mushroom Stuffed Tomatoes (VEG) (460 calories) — Prepare extra for Day 13

Total Daily Calories: 1,730 - 1,850

DAY 12

Breakfast:
1. Whole-Grain French Toast with Sliced Bananas (VEG) (310 calories)
2. Smoothie with Blueberries, Spinach, and Almond Butter (VEG) (270 calories)

Lunch:
1. Leftover Gazpacho (VEG) (340 calories)
2. Chickpea and Tomato Salad with Feta (VEG) (400 calories)

Snack:
1. Sliced Pear with Walnuts (VEG) (160 calories)
2. Fresh Grapes (VEG) (90 calories)

Dinner:
1. Leftover Zucchini Boats (VEG) (450 calories)
2. Classic Seafood Paella (550 calories)

Total Daily Calories: 1,750 - 1,850

DAY 13

Breakfast:
1. Greek Yogurt with Fresh Strawberries and a Drizzle of Honey (VEG) (260 calories)
2. Mediterranean Avocado and Chickpea Toast (VEG) (300 calories)

Lunch:
1. Spanakopita with Side Salad (VEG) (500 calories)
2. Leftover Lentil and Mushroom Stuffed Tomatoes (VEG) (460 calories)

Snack:
1. Dried Apricots and Pistachios (VEG) (140 calories)
2. Watermelon Slices (VEG) (80 calories)

Dinner:
1. Grilled Chicken with Tabbouleh Salad (540 calories)
2. Spaghetti Aglio e Olio with Sautéed Spinach (VEG) (500 calories)

Total Daily Calories: 1,780 - 1,900

DAY 14

Breakfast:
1. Mediterranean Scrambled Tofu with Spinach and Mushrooms (VEG) (270 calories)
2. Overnight Muesli with Fresh Berries (VEG) (290 calories)

Lunch:
1. Falafel with Tahini Sauce and Pickled Turnips (VEG) (420 calories)
2. Mediiterranean Pan-Seared Salmon with Asparagus (500 calories)

Snack:
1. Sliced Kiwi and Mango (VEG) (120 calories)
2. Celery Sticks with Almond Butter (VEG) (150 calories)

Dinner:
1. Risotto with Porcini Mushrooms (VEG) (480 calories)
2. Lamb Kebabs with Grilled Vegetables (550 calories)

Dessert:
1. Fresh Fig and Ricotta Tart (one slice) (250 calories)

Total Daily Calories: 1,840 - 2,060

Week 3

Proteins:
1. **Chicken:** Marinate for Moroccan Chicken Couscous and Lemon and Oregano Grilled Chicken on Day 26.
2. **Turkey:** Prepare stuffing for Mediterranean Turkey Stuffed Peppers on Day 28.

Vegetables:
1. **Tomatoes:** Dice for the soups and salads across multiple days.
2. **Zucchini:** Slice for Mediterranean Zucchini and Potato Omelette on Day 23.
3. **Bell Peppers:** Slice for salads and prepare for stuffed peppers on Day 28.
4. **Asparagus:** Prepare for Day 27's Poached Eggs with Asparagus Spears.
5. **Portobello Mushrooms:** Clean and prepare for Lentil-Stuffed Portobello Mushrooms on Day 25 and 26.
6. **Escarole:** Wash and chop for Cannellini Bean and Escarole Soup on Day 22 and 24.
7. **Assorted Veggies:** Chop cucumber, lettuce, carrots, and other salad veggies for the week's salads.

Grains and Legumes:
1. **Rice:** Cook rice for Cretan Tomato Rice Soup for Days 23 and 25.
2. **Beans:** Soak and cook Cannellini beans for the soup on Day 22 and 24, and Fava beans for Day 26.
3. **Quinoa:** Prepare for Mediterranean Quinoa Porridge on Day 25.
4. **Whole-Grain Bread:** Slice and toast for days where whole-grain toast is part of the menu.

Dairy and Eggs:
1. **Feta:** Crumble for Watermelon Salad on Day 22 and other recipes that require it.
2. **Greek Yogurt:** Portion for snacks.
3. **Ricotta:** Portion for Herbed Goat Cheese Dip on Day 24 and Ricotta with Fresh Herbs on Day 25.
4. **Mozzarella:** Cube or slice for various recipes.

Snacks and Fruits:
1. **Fresh Fruits:** Slice or cube melons, mango, and other fruits for snacks and salads.
2. **Olives:** Marinate olives for Day 22.
3. **Labneh:** Prepare Labneh with Za'atar for Day 23.
4. **Hummus:** Prepare and portion for snacks on Day 27 and 28.

Sauces and Others:
1. **Dressings and Vinaigrettes:** Prepare lemon vinaigrette for Sheet Pan Chicken on Day 25 and olive relish for Grilled Sea Bass on Day 25.
2. **Garlic and Lemon Marinade:** Prepare for Grilled Calamari on Day 22.

Day 15

Breakfast:
1. Mediterranean Spinach and Feta Omelette (VEG) (300 calories)
2. Mediterranean Overnight Oats with Apricots and Almonds (VEG) (270 calories)

Lunch:
1. Sicilian Eggplant Caponata with Whole-Grain Bread (VEG) (400 calories)
2. Harira bel Lahm (310 calories)

Snack:
1. Sliced Cantaloupe (VEG) (60 calories)
2. Harissa Spice Pop-Corn (VEG) (90 calories)

Dinner:
1. **Zucchini Lasagna** (VEG) (520 calories) — Prepare extra for Day 17
2. Turkish Lamb Kebabs with Mediterranean Quinoa Salad (610 calories)

Total Daily Calories: 1,670 - 1,830

Day 16

Breakfast:
1. Greek Yogurt Parfait with Honey and Walnuts (VEG) (290 calories)
2. Watermelon Smoothie (VEG) (220 calories)

Lunch:
1. Lebanese Fattoush Salad (VEG) (390 calories)
2. Grilled Trout with Mediterranean Relish (500 calories)

Snack:
1. Fresh Figs (VEG) (100 calories)
2. Goat Cheese with Olive Tapenade (150 calories)

Dinner:
1. **Spanish Espinacas con Garbanzos (Spinach with Chickpeas)** (VEG) (540 calories) — Prepare extra for Day 18
2. Moussaka (610 calories)

Total Daily Calories: 1,640 - 1,870

Day 17

Breakfast:
1. Fresh Berry Salad with Cottage Cheese (VEG) (270 calories)
2. Cold Rice Pudding with Raisins (VEG) (260 calories)

Lunch:
1. Leftover Zucchini Lasagna (VEG) (520 calories)
2. Tuscan Bean Soup with Kale and Sausage (500 calories)

Snack:
1. Cherry Tomatoes with Basil (VEG) (50 calories)
2. Pomegranate Seeds (VEG) (80 calories)

Dinner:
1. Moroccan Vegetable Couscous (VEG) (520 calories)
2. Chicken Souvlaki with Greek Salad (580 calories)

Total Daily Calories: 1,630 - 1,720

DAY 18

Breakfast:
1. Whole-Grain Toast with Ricotta and Fig Jam (VEG) (280 calories)
2. Chilled Melon Soup (VEG) (240 calories)

Lunch:
1. Leftover Espinacas con Garbanzos (Spinach with Chickpeas) (VEG) (540 calories)
2. Italian Minestrone Soup with Ciabatta (450 calories)

Snack:
1. Apricots with Almond Paste (VEG) (130 calories)
2. Fresh Blueberries (VEG) (70 calories)

Dinner:
1. Bucatini with Tomato, Basil, and Mozzarella (VEG) (530 calories)
2. Turkish Kofta with Baba Ganoush (600 calories)

Total Daily Calories: 1,690 - 1,820

DAY 19

Breakfast:
1. Cucumber and Yogurt Smoothie (VEG) (220 calories)
2. Green Shakshuka (300 calories)

Lunch:
1. Greek Gigantes Beans with Tomatoes (VEG) (480 calories)
2. Grilled Calamari with Lemon and Herbs (520 calories)

Snack:
1. Sliced Apple with Cinnamon (VEG) (100 calories)
2. Olives and Pickles (VEG) (90 calories)

Dinner:
1. Ratatouille with Grilled Polenta (VEG) (550 calories)
   — Prepare extra for Day 21
2. North African Spiced Chicken Stew (590 calories)

Total Daily Calories: 1,710 - 1,850

DAY 20

Breakfast:
1. Oatmeal with Fresh Pears and Honey (VEG) (290 calories)
2. Orange and Pineapple Smoothie (VEG) (250 calories)

Lunch:
1. Tabouleh Salad (VEG) (380 calories)
2. Portuguese Sardine Pate on Whole-Grain Toast (430 calories)

Snack:
1. Sliced Banana with Nutmeg (VEG) (90 calories)
2. Fresh Grapes (VEG) (70 calories)

Dinner:
1. Tuscan White Bean Stew with Garlic Bread (VEG) (510 calories)
2. Grilled Swordfish with Grilled Asparagus and Lemon Butter (550 calories)

Dessert:
1. Baklava (One Serving) (250 calories)

Total Daily Calories: 1,720 - 1,880

DAY 21

Breakfast:
1. Mediterranean Barley Porridge with Dried Fruits (VEG) (300 calories)
2. Mediterranean Fresh Fruit Medley with Mint (VEG) (240 calories)

Lunch:
1. Insalata Caprese with Ciabatta (VEG) (410 calories)
2. Classic Seafood Paella (530 calories)

Snack:
1. Moroccan Spiced Chickpeas (VEG) (130 calories)
2. Fresh Nectarine Slices (VEG) (70 calories)

Dinner:
1. Leftover Ratatouille with Grilled Polenta (VEG) (550 calories)
2. Osso Buco with Sautéed Spinach (590 calories)

Total Daily Calories: 1,740 - 1,880

WEEK 4

Proteins:
1. **Marinade Chicken:**
2. **Turkish Beef Kofta:** Prepare and store uncooked kofta for Day 24.
3. **Greek Lamb Souvlaki:** Marinate lamb for Day 27 dinner.

Vegetables:
1. **Moroccan Chickpea Salad:** Wash and cut vegetables (Day 27).
2. **Stuffed Tomatoes with Rice and Herbs:** Hollow out tomatoes and prepare herbs for stuffing (Day 25 and Day 26).
3. **Eggplant Involtini:** Slice and salt eggplant for draining (Day 24 and Day 27).
4. **Asparagus and Pea Risotto:** Wash and cut asparagus and peas (Day 25).
5. **Vegan Moussaka:** Prepare the layers separately (Day 22 and Day 23).

Grains and Legumes:
1. **Cannellini Bean and Escarole Soup:** Cook a large batch of cannellini beans (Day 22 and Day 24).
2. **Lentil and Spinach Soup:** Precook lentils (Day 23 and Day 25).
3. **Stuffed Tomatoes with Rice and Herbs:** Cook enough rice for stuffing (Day 25 and Day 26).
4. **Paella with Chicken and Rabbit:** Precook rice (Day 24).
5. **Portuguese Fish Stew:** Prepare and store separately the potatoes and rice (Day 23 and Day 26).

Dairy and Eggs:
1. **Herbed Ricotta:** Mix ricotta with herbs for snack (Day 25).
2. **Tzatziki:** Mix yogurt with cucumber and herbs (Day 27).
3. **Fresh Goat Cheese with Thyme:** Mix goat cheese with thyme (Day 26).

Snacks and Fruits:
1. **Hummus:** Prepare a batch of hummus (Day 27).
2. **Marinated Olives:** Prepare a batch (Day 22).
3. **Labneh with Za'atar:** Mix and store (Day 23).
4. **Fruits:** Slice and store fruits like mango, grapes, and nectarines.

Sauces and Others:
1. **Pomegranate Sauce:** Prepare for Turkish Beef Kofta (Day 24).
2. **Lemon and Olive Relish:** Prepare for grilled sea bass (Day 25).
3. **Marinade for Lemon and Oregano Grilled Chicken:** Prepare and store (Day 26).

DAY 22

Breakfast:
1. Watermelon, Feta, and Mint Salad (VEG) (250 calories)
2. Scrambled Eggs with Fresh Dill and Feta (280 calories)

Lunch:
1. **Cannellini Bean and Escarole Soup** (VEG) (420 calories) — Prepare extra for Day 24
2. Grilled Calamari with Garlic and Lemon (500 calories)

Snack:
1. Fresh Plums (VEG) (60 calories)
2. Marinated Olives (VEG) (100 calories)

Dinner:
1. **Vegetarian Moussaka** (VEG) (470 calories) — Prepare extra for Day 23
2. Moroccan Chicken Couscous (550 calories)

Total Daily Calories: 1,500 - 1,580

DAY 23

Breakfast:
1. Mediterranean Pistachio and Oat Porridge (VEG) (270 calories)
2. Mediterranean Zucchini and Potato Omelette (260 calories)

Lunch:
1. **Cretan Tomato Rice Soup** (VEG) (390 calories) — Prepare extra for Day 25
2. Swordfish a la Siciliana (490 calories)

Snack:
1. Fresh Mango Slices (VEG) (70 calories)
2. Labneh with Za'atar (120 calories)

Dinner:
1. Leftover Vegetarian Moussaka (VEG) (470 calories)
2. **Portuguese Fish Stew** (500 calories) — Prepare extra for Day 26

Total Daily Calories: 1,490 - 1,540

DAY 24

Breakfast:
1. Fresh Fig and Ricotta Whole-Wheat Toast (VEG) (270 calories)
2. Smoked Mackerel and Caper Spread on Whole-Grain Bread (240 calories)

Lunch:
1. Leftover Cannellini Bean and Escarole Soup (VEG) (420 calories)

2. Paella with Chicken and Rabbit (540 calories)

Snack:
1. Fresh Nectarine (VEG) (60 calories)
2. Herbed Goat Cheese Dip (110 calories)

Dinner:
1. **Eggplant Rollatini** (VEG) (440 calories) — Prepare extra for Day 27
2. Turkish Beef Kofta with Pomegranate Sauce (510 calories)

<u>Total Daily Calories: 1,490 - 1,590</u>

DAY 25

Breakfast:
1. Mediterranean Quinoa Porridge with Fresh Berries and Nuts (VEG) (290 calories)
2. Scrambled Tofu with Spinach and Tomatoes (VEG) (270 calories)

Lunch:
1. Leftover Cretan Tomato Rice Soup (VEG) (390 calories)
2. Sheet Pan Chicken with roasted spring vegetables and lemon vinaigrette (510 calories)

Snack:
1. Fresh Grapes (VEG) (80 calories)
2. Ricotta with Fresh Herbs (110 calories)

Dinner:
1. **Lentil-Stuffed Portobello Mushroom** (VEG) (470 calories) — Prepare extra for Day 26
2. Grilled Sea Bass with Olive Relish (560 calories)

<u>Total Daily Calories: 1,520 - 1,640</u>

DAY 26

Breakfast:
1. Fresh Pineapple and Mint Salad (VEG) (250 calories)
2. Sardine and Avocado Toast (270 calories)

Lunch:
1. Fava Bean Puree with Dill and Whole Wheat Bread(VEG) (400 calories)
2. Leftover Portuguese Fish Stew (490 calories)

Snack:
1. Dried Apricots (VEG) (70 calories)
2. Fresh Goat Cheese with Thyme (130 calories)

Dinner:

1. Leftover Lentil-Stuffed Portobello Mushroom (VEG) (470 calories)
2. Lemon and Oregano Grilled Chicken (510 calories)

<u>Total Daily Calories: 1,500 - 1,610</u>

DAY 27

Breakfast:
1. Almond Butter and Banana Smoothie (VEG) (270 calories)
2. Poached Eggs with Asparagus Spears (250 calories)

Lunch:
1. Moroccan Chickpea Salad (VEG) (390 calories)
2. Baked Sardines with Tomatoes and Capers (480 calories)

Snack:
1. Fresh Papaya (VEG) (60 calories)
2. Hummus with Fresh Vegetables (VEG) (100 calories)

Dinner:
1. Leftover Eggplant Involtini (VEG) (440 calories)
2. Souvlaki with Greek Salad(540 calories)

<u>Total Daily Calories: 1,480 - 1,590</u>

DAY 28

Breakfast:
1. Berry Smoothie with Spinach (VEG) (270 calories)
2. Whole-Grain Pancakes with Fresh Fruit (280 calories)

Lunch:
1. Spanish Gazpacho Salad (VEG) (400 calories)
2. Grilled Tuna Salad (500 calories)

Snack:
1. Fresh Kiwi Slices (VEG) (60 calories)
2. Hummus with Sliced Cucumbers (VEG) (110 calories)

Dinner:
1. Greek Zoodle Bowl (VEG) (450 calories)
2. Mediterranean Turkey Stuffed Peppers (420 calories)

Dessert:
Moroccan Orange Cake (350 calories)

<u>Total Daily Calories: 1,720 – 2,050</u>

Appendix A: Building a Mediterranean~Friendly Pantry

Grains and Pastas
1. Whole grain bread (store long-term in the freezer)
2. Brown rice
3. Arborio or Carnaroli rice (for risotto)
4. Quinoa
5. Couscous
6. Orzo
7. Whole grain pasta (spaghetti, penne, fusilli, linguini, fettuccine, macaroni)
8. Farro
9. Freekesh
10. Polenta (cornmeal)
11. Bulgur wheat
12. Pearl barley
13. Millet
14. Israeli couscous (pearl couscous)
15. Amaranth
16. Buckwheat
17. Black rice (also called Forbidden Rice)
18. Wild rice
19. Spelt
20. Kamut
21. Oat groats or steel-cut oats
22. Corn tortillas (for a Mediterranean-Mexican fusion)
23. Pumpernickel or rye bread (store long-term in the freezer)
24. Multigrain crackers

Dry Legumes
1. Lentils (green, brown, red, black)
2. Chickpeas
3. Cannellini beans
4. Kidney beans
5. Black beans
6. Butter beans (lima beans)
7. Fava beans (dried)
8. Split peas (green and yellow)
9. Mung beans
10. Navy beans

Nuts and Seeds
1. Almonds
2. Walnuts
3. Pine nuts
4. Hazelnuts
5. Cashews
6. Pistachios
7. Chia seeds
8. Flaxseeds
9. Sunflower seeds
10. Pumpkin seeds
11. Sesame seeds

Herbs and Spices
1. Basil (dried)
2. Thyme (dried)
3. Rosemary (dried)
4. Oregano (dried)
5. Mint (dried)
6. Dill (dried)
7. Sage (dried)
8. Bay leaves
9. Coriander seeds
10. Cumin seeds and ground cumin
11. Paprika (sweet, smoked, hot)
12. Saffron threads
13. Cinnamon sticks and ground cinnamon
14. Nutmeg (whole and ground)
15. Black peppercorns
16. Red pepper flakes
17. Turmeric (ground)
18. Cardamom (green, black)
19. Allspice berries and ground
20. Anise seeds
21. Sumac
22. Cloves (whole and ground)
23. Fennel seeds
24. Juniper berries
25. Garlic powder
26. Onion powder

Oils and Fats
1. Extra-virgin olive oil
2. Cold-pressed avocado oil
3. Sesame oil
4. Walnut oil
5. Coconut oil (less traditional but versatile)

Vinegars and Acidic Elements
1. Balsamic vinegar
2. Red wine vinegar
3. White wine vinegar

Sweeteners
1. Honey
2. Maple syrup
3. Dates (dried)
4. Dried apricots
5. Raisins
6. Dried figs
7. Dried cranberries
8. Currants

Canned and Jarred Goods

Make sure there is no added salt or added preservative, home-made should be preferred to store-bought whenever possible

1. Canned tomatoes (whole, diced, crushed)
2. Tomato paste
3. Capers
4. Anchovies or anchovy paste
5. Pickled vegetables (cornichons, pickled onions)
6. Artichoke hearts
7. Preserved lemons
8. Sun-dried tomatoes
9. Canned or jarred olives (green, black, Kalamata)
10. Roasted red peppers
11. Tuna in olive oil
12. Sardines in olive oil
13. Vegetable or chicken broth
14. Canned chickpeas
15. Canned lentils

Miscellaneous

1. Tahini
2. Za'atar
3. Harissa paste
4. Pesto (jarred, shelf-stable)
5. Agave nectar
6. Cocoa or cacao powder
7. Pomegranate molasses
8. Grape leaves (jarred)
9. Garam masala
10. Semolina flour

Beverages

1. Herbal teas (chamomile, peppermint, sage)
2. Coffee (beans or ground)
3. Loose leaf green tea

Appendix B: Mediterranean Diet Refrigerator Regulars

Fresh Vegetables

1. Tomatoes
2. Bell peppers (multiple colors)
3. Cucumbers
4. Zucchinis
5. Eggplants
6. Carrots
7. Spinach
8. Arugula
9. Kale
10. Collard greens
11. Swiss chard
12. Radishes
13. Brussels sprouts
14. Green beans
15. Cauliflower
16. Broccoli
17. Cabbage
18. Asparagus
19. Beets
20. Artichokes
21. Sweet potatoes
22. Onions (red, yellow, white)
23. Garlic bulbs
24. Leeks
25. Celery
26. Fennel
27. Romaine lettuce
28. Green leaf lettuce
29. Iceberg lettuce
30. Shallots

Fresh Fruits

1. Lemons
2. Oranges
3. Apples
4. Bananas
5. Berries (strawberries, blueberries, raspberries)
6. Avocados
7. Pears
8. Peaches
9. Plums
10. Pineapple
11. Grapes
12. Watermelon
13. Cantaloupe
14. Figs
15. Kiwi
16. Pomegranates
17. Mangoes
18. Apricots
19. Cherries
20. Grapefruit

Dairy and Dairy Alternatives

1. Greek yogurt
2. Plain yogurt
3. Feta cheese
4. Parmesan cheese
5. Mozzarella cheese
6. Ricotta cheese
7. Kefir
8. Cottage cheese
9. Labneh (yogurt cheese)

10. Plant-based milks (almond, oat, soy)
11. Goat cheese
12. Halloumi
13. Mascarpone (for special occasions)

Fresh Herbs
1. Basil
2. Parsley
3. Cilantro
4. Dill
5. Mint
6. Rosemary
7. Thyme
8. Oregano
9. Sage
10. Chives
11. Tarragon
12. Marjoram

Seafood (for consumption within a few days)
1. Salmon
2. Tuna steaks
3. Sardines
4. Mackerel
5. Shrimp
6. Squid
7. Octopus
8. Shellfish (clams, mussels, scallops)

Meat and Poultry (for consumption within a few days or to be frozen)
1. Chicken breasts
2. Chicken thighs
3. Lean cuts of lamb
4. Lean beef cuts

Deli Meats (occasional and in moderation)
1. Italian Cooked Ham
2. Smoked salmon

Miscellaneous
1. Eggs
2. Tofu or tempeh (for plant-based protein)
3. Hummus
4. Tahini paste
5. Olives (green and Kalamata)
6. Capers
7. Anchovies
8. Fresh salsa
9. Pesto sauce
10. Fresh pasta (ravioli, fettuccine)
11. Pre-made (preferably not store-bought) salad dressings (vinaigrette, tahini-based)
12. Pickles (cucumbers, beets, onions)

Appendix C: Seasonal Fruits and Vegetables Guide

A seasonal fruit and vegetable guide can help you make the most of fresh produce throughout the year, which is an essential part of the Mediterranean diet. Here's a general guide organized by season. Please note that availability might differ based on your geographical location.

Spring
Fruits
1. Strawberries
2. Cherries
3. Apricots
4. Rhubarb
5. Grapefruit
6. Lemons
7. Early variety peaches

Vegetables
1. Asparagus
2. Artichokes
3. Spring onions
4. Radishes
5. Green peas
6. Fava beans
7. Spinach
8. Morel mushrooms
9. Watercress
10. Arugula

Summer
Fruits
1. Watermelon
2. Cantaloupe
3. Blueberries
4. Raspberries
5. Blackberries
6. Mangoes
7. Peaches
8. Plums
9. Apricots
10. Cherries
11. Nectarines

Vegetables
1. Zucchini
2. Summer squash
3. Bell peppers
4. Cucumbers
5. Corn

6. Tomatoes
7. Green beans
8. Eggplant
9. Beets
10. Okra
11. Swiss chard

Autumn
Fruits
1. Apples
2. Pears
3. Figs
4. Pomegranates
5. Cranberries
6. Grapes
7. Persimmons

Vegetables
1. Brussels sprouts
2. Butternut squash
3. Acorn squash
4. Pumpkins
5. Sweet potatoes
6. Cauliflower
7. Leeks
8. Shallots
9. Broccoli
10. Spinach
11. Turnips

Winter
Fruits
1. Oranges
2. Grapefruits
3. Clementines
4. Tangerines
5. Kiwi
6. Pomegranates
7. Dates

Vegetables
1. Cabbage
2. Kale
3. Collard greens
4. Winter squash
5. Parsnips
6. Carrots
7. Rutabaga
8. Endive
9. Chicory
10. Brussels sprouts
11. Broccoli rabe

Conclusion

Thank you so much for journeying through the pages of this book with me! I hope you've enjoyed exploring the Mediterranean lifestyle as much as I've relished writing about it. Remember, adopting a healthier way of living is not a sprint but a marathon. It's about making small, sustainable changes that add up to a vibrant, happier you. Enjoy the journey, relish every bite, and don't forget to pause and savor the simple joys of life.

If this book has positively impacted your life, I'd be honored if you could share your experience with others.
Please consider leaving a review on Amazon. Your insights could be the beacon that guides someone else towards a healthier, more fulfilling life.

Thank you for being a part of this incredible journey to wellness and happiness!

Made in the USA
Las Vegas, NV
29 December 2023

83686024R00079